Other books by Kenneth S. Stern

LOUD HAWK
The United States versus the American Indian Movement
(1994)

HOLOCAUST DENIAL
(1993)

Kenneth S. Stern

A FORCE UPON THE PLAIN

THE AMERICAN MILITIA MOVEMENT
AND THE POLITICS OF HATE

Simon & Schuster

NEW YORK   LONDON   TORONTO

SYDNEY   TOKYO   SINGAPORE

SIMON & SCHUSTER
Rockefeller Center
1230 Avenue of the Americas
New York, NY 10020

SIMON & SCHUSTER and colophon
are registered trademarks of Simon & Schuster Inc.

Designed by Jeanette Olender
Manufactured in the United States of America

10 9 8 7 6 5 4 3 2 1

Library of Congress Cataloging-in-Publication Data is available.

ISBN 0-684-81916-3

to Margie, Daniel, and Emily

THAT MAN IS LITTLE TO BE ENVIED WHOSE
PATRIOTISM WOULD NOT GAIN FORCE UPON
THE PLAIN OF MARATHON, OR WHOSE PIETY
WOULD NOT GROW WARMER AMONG THE
RUINS OF IONA.

SAMUEL JOHNSON (1709–1784), *Journey to the Western Lands* (1775)

Foreword

At 9:02 A.M. on April 19, 1995, when many parents had just dropped their children at the second-floor day care center of the Alfred P. Murrah Federal Building in Oklahoma City, a truck bomb went off, shredding the front of the building, collapsing its nine stories like playing cards, and leaving behind bloody rubble, body parts, a thirty-foot-wide crater, and at least 167 dead. It was the worst terrorist attack and the most egregious mass murder in American history. It was also a warning shot by those who would make civil war in America.

Among the first confirmed victims were twelve children from that day care center. Some were so badly burned that they could not immediately be identified; not even their sex could be ascertained. The day care center had been above the curb where the truck bomb was parked. Rescuers immediately sensed the dimensions of the tragedy when they saw toys blown onto the street.

Over the next hours and days it would be these children who inspired both the most irrational hope and the most terrible revulsion. Newspapers around the country displayed a picture of a rescue worker lovingly holding a tiny, limp victim. That baby died the same morning. Others were missing. Despite the devastation, Oklahoma City's assistant fire chief, Jon Hansen, said he was hopeful that some of the missing children would be found alive. "You know how kids are," he said. "Kids survive wherever people can't."

The bomb had targeted the federal government, but other neighborhood buildings were damaged too. Glass shattered and debris flew in every direction. The explosion was so powerful that people in offices two blocks away were blown out of their chairs. Inside the Murrah Building, people in the Social Security office—some who had come to plan their retirement—were projected through cinder-block walls. Many of the victims were literally blown apart, leaving bloody fingers, arms, and legs intermingled with the rubble. People thirty miles away felt the blast.

As the day wore on, political leaders expressed America's shock and rage. Oklahoma governor Frank Keating said, "Obviously, no amateur did this. Whoever did this was an animal." President Bill Clinton said the government would find the "evil cowards" responsible. "These people are killers," he said, "and must be treated like killers." U.S. Attorney General Janet Reno announced, "The death penalty is available, and we will seek it."

By nightfall hundreds were still unaccounted for. Rain began to fall, making the rescue effort more difficult because the rubble was unsteady. At 9:30 P.M., three more people were pulled from the wreckage. In the basement that evening workers heard the frantic cry of a woman. They had difficulty reaching her: Too many bodies were blocking the way. Another woman, named Dana Bradley, was more easily freed. But her leg had to be amputated. "She was lying underneath a beam," said Dr. Andy Sullivan. "The attempt to remove the concrete beams would have caused the rest of the building to collapse."

Families across America were frantic, coping with uncertainty and fear, not knowing if loved ones in the Murrah Building were dead, alive, or injured. Had their son, daughter, sister, brother, mother, father, wife, husband, friend been lucky enough to have been delayed in traffic, called in sick, sent out on assignment, or in a "safer" part of the building at 9:02 A.M.? Such thoughts occurred to Jackie Bairm, who used to work in that building with her sister, Vickie. When she heard the news she rushed to the site to wait. "Her office wasn't there anymore," she said. "The walls were so thin we used to hear each other talking through them. Now it's just a bunch of rocks. Lord, my heart hurts."

Anthony Cooper's wife, Dana, had run the day care center. It had needed more milk that morning, and he had volunteered to get it. When he returned from the errand, before 9:02, he said good-bye to his wife and their two-year-old son, Christopher. For the last time. "She was my friend," Cooper said. "And my little boy. I miss talking to my little boy."

The pain of the families included dashed hopes and dead dreams. Twenty-six-year-old Carrie Lenz had had an ultrasound the evening of April 18, 1995. She was expecting a boy. The night before the blast she and her husband, Michael, decided that their son would be named Michael J. Lenz III. For the Lenz family, Michael J. Lenz III was listed among the dead, too.

Rescuers had to move debris without risking further injury to those who might have been trapped alive—or, given the unsteadiness of the rubble, to each other. Working feverishly, many tried to do the impossible: put aside the implications of the carnage. Terry Jones, a medical technician, said, "I just took part in a surgery where a little boy had part of his brain hanging out his head. You tell me. How can someone have so little respect for human life?"

How could parents cope with the news that a bomb blast had destroyed a building with their children inside? Jim and Claudia Denny had had two children at the day care center. After a frantic search they found Rebecca, aged two, at the Southwest Medical Center. She had lacerations and a broken arm, but was in stable condition. There was no sign of her three-year-old brother, Brandon. Brandon's twenty-three-year-old brother, Tim, had heard that an unidentified toddler was in surgery at Presbyterian Hospital. He rushed over. He did not think it was Brandon. Jim Denny couldn't tell, either. "I couldn't see anything in his face at all," Denny said. "It was all puffed up, all bloody with scratches and stitches and black eyes." The boy's head wounds were so severe that doctors had to remove part of his brain. "But his legs," Denny said, "his little legs. His legs were so clean." Denny noticed a birthmark—Brandon's birthmark—on the boy's small thigh. "Hard to believe," he said, "a dad can't identify his own boy."

As Brandon lay unconscious in intensive care, convulsing, bandaged, deeply cut, Tim held his small hand. "Hey, Brandon," he said. "It's Tim. How you doing, buddy? You be good, O.K., buddy? You be good."

✗ ✗ ✗

Most of us went home that night and hugged our children. I have two young children. On that day in April, Daniel was three and Emily one. I was determined to shield them from the horrifying television images. That resolution faded as quickly as the media's assumption that Middle Eastern terrorists were responsible.

Nine days before the blast I had issued a lengthy report on the militia movement for the American Jewish Committee. (AJC is America's oldest organization dedicated to fighting bigotry. I am the Committee's expert on anti-Semitism, extremism, and hate groups. I've been doing this type of work since the late 1970s, when I was an attorney representing victims of racism in trial and appellate courts, including the United States Supreme Court.) In early April 1995 I had written that people connected with militias were poised to attack government officials, possibly on April 19, 1995, the second anniversary of the fiery end of the Branch Davidian compound in Waco. As soon as Timothy McVeigh was arrested for the bombing and the militia connection made, I was asked to appear on an endless stream of television news shows. Daniel demanded to watch. Seeing me on television, he asked about what I was discussing. I told him that some bad people had hurt a building. He asked if people were killed. I said yes. He asked, "Why did the bad men hurt the building?" How do you explain this to a three-year-old? I thought a minute, groping for something that would both make sense to him and not frighten him. I said, "Because they hated too much."

That hatred was not, and is not, limited to the few people who bombed the Murrah Building. Millions of Americans share it; thousands arm themselves in militias to express it; and there are an undetermined number who would act upon it. The question is, Why are Americans joining private armies to fight the American government, while defining their actions as "patriotism"? And how did those charged with the bombing—American veterans, yet—come to share some of the militias' core beliefs?

$$\chi \quad \chi \quad \chi$$

Although I didn't know it at the time, A *Force upon the Plain* began on a cool evening in early May 1994, over a pasta dinner in a quiet restaurant in the old-town section of Helena, Montana. I was on a tour of Montana, speaking about ideologies of hate. In Great Falls, in Kalispell, on Indian reservations, and in places in between, people had approached me with the question, "Have you heard about the militia?" I hadn't. These Montanans didn't know how to describe the militia. They only knew that lots of armed people were holding meetings. But they were concerned.

I ate dinner that night in Helena with my longtime friend Kathy McKay, and with Marlene Hines and Christine Kaufmann of the Montana Human Rights Network, a group that opposes Montana's far right. "So, what's with this militia?" I asked.

"This is something new in hate group activity," Marlene said. "A white supremacist by the name of Trochmann formed a 'militia' in February, and has been holding meetings around the state, drawing people through issues such as gun control and the Brady Bill." Meetings of two hundred, three hundred, five hundred, even eight hundred in small towns were not uncommon. Some local politicians, including sheriffs, were supporting the militia.

By late May 1994, Marlene and her co-workers had issued a report on the militia movement in Montana, documenting the white supremacist connections of its leadership, its dangerous rhetoric, and its amassing of firearms. On behalf of the American Jewish Committee I reprinted dozens of copies and sent them to television, radio, and print journalists around the country. Not one story resulted.

By December 1994, the militia movement had spread across the northwest, and to other parts of America. The Anti-Defamation League of B'nai B'rith had issued a report calling militias "armed and dangerous." Morris Dees of the Southern Poverty Law Center had written to Attorney General Janet Reno, warning of these groups. Still nothing happened.

I was growing increasingly frustrated by the end of 1994. America is fortunate to have a small, but energetic, number of national, regional, and local groups, as well as independent researchers, monitoring the far right. Despite their differences in ideology—some were centrist, others liberal—in less than a year they had all come to the same conclusion: These new private armies posed an imminent danger. They told government. They told the media. The three largest watchdog groups—the American Jewish Committee, the Anti-Defamation League, and the Southern Poverty Law Center—sounded this alert on the national stage. Law enforcement and the media were still silent and seemingly blind.

In January 1995, the Northwest Coalition Against Malicious Harassment, a Seattle-based organization founded in 1987 to fight neo-Nazis and white supremacists in the Pacific Northwest, called an emergency two-day meeting of researchers and activists who were monitoring the militia movement. It was the meeting's consensus that this was the fastest-growing grassroots mass movement any of us had seen; that these groups' violent antigovernment rhetoric, combined with their heavy armaments, was a prescription for disaster; and that most of the militias around the country were linked directly or indirectly with the white supremacist movement, who were seeking to "mainstream" their agenda. The media and the government—state and federal—were, however, still not taking these private armies seriously.

I returned to New York from Seattle worried. Given how fast the movement had grown in less than a year, there was no reason to expect it to slow; it was feeding off people's anger over issues such as Waco, the Randy Weaver siege at Ruby Ridge, and the Brady Bill, in part stoked by right-wing propagandists using faxes, shortwave radio, and the Internet. I determined to bring the problem to the nation's attention as quickly as possible.

In early March 1995, Thomas Diaz, a member of Congressman Charles Schumer's staff, expressed great interest in this issue, and together with my colleague Richard Foltin (AJC's legislative director and counsel), we devised a strategy. I would write an analysis of the militia movement, documenting the danger to government officials and the national scope of the problem. Diaz and Schumer would use the report to push for congressional hearings, and I would bring some of the grassroots researchers to Washington for a press conference and to meet representatives of the states' attorneys general. The report, entitled *Militias: A Growing Danger*, was released on April 10, 1995, along with a six-hundred-page appendix of media clips, Internet postings, and militia literature. It began:

> We issue this report . . . with a sense of urgency. [The militia movement] is quickly spreading and has all the ingredients to lead to disaster: an ideological caldron of disaffection, hate, conspiracy and violence brewing a fast-growing grassroots movement with documented ties to hate groups. Some

people connected with this movement advocate killing government officials. They may attempt such an act.

After documenting specific threats against government employees—including threats against children of government workers—the report continued:

> The first person murdered by a militia member may be a county clerk, a postal worker, a deputy sheriff, a tax collector, an FBI agent or U.S. Marshal, a firefighter, a forest service employee, a FEMA worker, an elected representative—in fact any representative of government or anyone perceived as opposing the militia and, therefore, seen as doing "the work of government."

While noting that militia groups had no central command structure, the report stressed their shared paranoiac, violent ideology and their belief that the American government was part of an imminent plot to take away their freedom:

> Why? Because the government laid siege to the Branch Davidians at Waco. Because the government attacked Randy Weaver in Idaho. Because the United Nations is expanding its military role. Because of the Brady Bill. ("Gun control is for only one thing," militia members say, "people control.") Some speak of government plans to shepherd dissidents into 43 concentration camps (mysterious numbers on the back of road signs, some say, are for this purpose, or for providing information to invading troops). Some claim that the government plans to murder more than three-quarters of the American people. Or that unmarked black helicopters are poised to attack them and sometimes threaten people by focusing lasers in their eyes; that Hong Kong policemen and Gurkha troops are training in the Montana wilderness in order to "take guns away from Americans" on orders of the Clinton administration; that UN equipment is being transported on huge trains and that Russian and German trucks are being shipped to attack Americans; that "international traffic symbols are used in America as a tool for foreign armies so they will be able to easily move through the country"; that there is a plot to give the North Cascades range in Washington state to "the United Nations and the CIA"; that urban street gangs, like the Bloods and Crips, are being trained as "shock troops" for the New World Order; that "[M]ilitary troops are lining up [to invade] on the Canadian border"; that "the federal government has implanted computer chips in government employees to monitor citizens"; that "those who want to take over the world are changing the weather"; that House Speaker Newt Gingrich is part of a

"global conspiracy" to create a one-government New World Order; that on a specific date the government is going to raid militias around the country.

In other words, the report explained, the belief system of the militias was a shared paranoia. If an individual went into a psychiatrist's office saying that he believed in black helicopters, that evil forces were changing the weather to harass him, that foreign troops were coming to take him away to a concentration camp, the doctor would diagnose the patient as clinically paranoid and prescribe treatment. The report warned that Americans could not ignore this same disease in the body politic: It was contagious, and those infected were well-armed. The report concluded:

> On the grass-roots level across the country, the militia movement is harassing its opponents, threatening law enforcement officials, stockpiling weapons, and spreading paranoiac rumors on the Internet. It is time that state and federal officials understand not only the danger of this movement, but also from a more parochial vantage point, that government employees around the country are going about their tasks while there are people planning just when to target them in their cross-hairs.

The report's covering memo warned of possible militia activity on April 19, 1995, the second anniversary of the fiery end of the Branch Davidian compound in Waco; as the memo said, this was the key ideological event for these groups.

Nine days later, as the horrifying events of April 19, 1995, unfolded, I had the disquieting feeling that my predictions concerning the militia movement were being fulfilled. I issued a press release citing the possible militia connection. Then I faxed a note with a few pages of my report's appendix—documenting Oklahoma-area militia members with military expertise—to Attorney General Janet Reno. In the next two days, as experts were talking about Middle East and other possible scenarios, I wondered why what was so clear to me was escaping others.

For the clues were clear. First, for any other group to have been responsible for a terrorist act on the anniversary of Waco would have been a one-in-365 chance. Second, there was the choice of target. The World Trade Center and the other objectives of foreign groups each fell into one of two categories: They were either great symbols (the World Trade Center, the United Nations) or things that would remind Americans of their vulnerability for a long time (imagine commuting from New Jersey to New York without the Hudson River tunnels or the George Washington Bridge). The Oklahoma City bomb destroyed a government building, a target that specifically fit the antigovernment ideology of the militia groups.

Finally, while some commentators claimed that car bombs were the trademark of Middle Eastern terrorists, I recalled an American book called *The Turner Diaries*, a key document for white supremacists and neo-Nazis. This 1978 novel, about a bloody terrorist war against the U.S. government and American minorities, was the blueprint for the 1980s American terrorist group the Order, which robbed banks, counterfeited money, and killed talk-show host Alan Berg. On page 38 members of the fictional "Order" inflict "immense damage" to a federal building. The explosive? A "mix [of] heating oil with . . . ammonium nitrate fertilizer" —just what government officials said was used to destroy the Murrah Building. I also remembered that on April 19, 1995, Richard Snell, a real member of the Order, was scheduled to be (and was) executed for two racially motivated murders.

Since April 19, 1995, and the revelation that those accused of the bombing—Timothy McVeigh and Terry Nichols—had connections to and shared the ideology of the militia movement, Americans have not needed reports with large appendices to tell them that there are people who call themselves patriots yet would commit terrorist acts. But we still need to understand why. What has drawn between ten thousand and forty thousand Americans to these private armies ready to make war with the American government? Why do hundreds of thousands of Americans —some say millions—sympathize with them? Has anything like this happened in America before? Can it happen again?

Kenneth S. Stern
New York City
October 1995

PART ONE **Weaver and Waco**

1 Ruby Ridge

I'M READY TO GET MY GUN AND MY CLIPS AND
TAKE OFF MY SAFETY AND PULL MY TRIGGER WITH
MY FINGER. I DON'T CARE ANYMORE. THIS IS THE
BEGINNING OF A REVOLUTION, A WAR.

JOHN BANGERTER, a skinhead supporter of Randy Weaver

andy Weaver, a former Green Beret in his mid-thirties, moved to
Idaho from Iowa in the early 1980s. He was attracted by more than the
area's natural beauty. One enticement was Idaho law. It would be easier
to home-school children in Idaho than in Iowa. Away from government
schools, the Weaver children would not be exposed to ideas that Weaver
and his wife, Vicki, did not like. "Everybody knows the government is
not right," Vicki said. "We don't have the freedom to believe what we
want. We moved here to remove our children from the trash being taught
in public schools and to practice our beliefs . . . to keep Yahweh's laws."

Another reason for the move was the "Northwest Territorial Imperative," the hope of neo-Nazis and white supremacists to make the mostly
white Pacific Northwest exclusively white. Some people had elaborate
plans for separating America by race. For example, the December 1984
NAAWP [National Association for the Advancement of White People]

News, published by neo-Nazi and former Ku Klux Klan leader David Duke, sported a map of what he called the National Premise. Whites would keep most of America. American Indians would be forced to move, again, to Navahona (Oklahoma); Asian Americans to East Mongolia (Hawaii); blacks to New Africa (most of Florida and a strip along the eastern Gulf Coast); Mexicans to Alta California (a strip contiguous to the Mexican border); Jews to West Israel (Long Island and Manhattan); Cubans to New Cuba (Miami and Dade County); French Canadians to Francia (a strip along northern New England); Puerto Ricans, Southern Italians, Greeks, immigrants from eastern and southern Mediterranean areas, and other "unassimilable minorities" to Minoria (New York metro area minus Manhattan and Long Island). "If all this sounds impractical," Duke's paper asserted, "we ask our readers to consider the alternatives. If the races are not separated soon, the Majority will have to fight for survival or go under. Already we have lost many of our largest cities. . . . Let blacks control their own area, let whites control theirs. As long as this country is majority white—and I hope to God that that is so for a long time—then this country should be run for the values of the white majority."

White supremacists Richard Butler and Robert Miles had a vision slightly different from Duke's. A new Aryan state would be created, comprising the land now known as Oregon, Washington, Idaho, Montana, and Wyoming. Butler moved from California to Hayden Lake, Idaho, in the 1970s, and built his compound, the Aryan Nations. It would conform to his vision. A sign on the sentry box would say "Whites Only." The office walls would sport pictures of Adolf Hitler, swastikas, and other memorabilia of the Nazis. Small busts of Nazi leaders—including, of course, that of Hitler—would be kept inside a glass cabinet. Past a door that read "Ministry of Truth" would be a wall of publications including "Our Nordic Race," "Did Six Million Really Die?," and "The Cain-Satanic Seed Line." In the chapel would be another portrait of Hitler. This one would have a caption: "When I Come Back, No More Mr. Nice Guy."

Butler, his compound built, sermonized about Jews: how they planned to take over the world, how they were "euthanizing the spirit of the white man into a state of vegetation." "To defend ourselves," he said, "we will have to eliminate Jewry." Every year the Aryan Nations hosted youth gatherings on the weekend closest to April 20, Adolf Hitler's birthday. Carl Franklin, a pastor at Aryan Nations, said, "Adolf Hitler was simply a son of God."

The Aryan Nations gave birth to an offshoot known as the Order, a terrorist group based on *The Turner Diaries*. In the mid-1980s the Order robbed banks, counterfeited, and murdered its "enemies," including the Jewish Denver talk-show host Alan Berg.

Randy Weaver was no stranger to the Aryan Nations compound; some say he even lived there for a while, until he was kicked out for drinking beer. Whether or not that is true, Weaver certainly attended Aryan Nations meetings. And he practiced its Christian Identity religion, which held that "Aryans" were the true Jews, that the people others called Jews were the offspring of the devil, and that blacks and other minorities— sometimes called mud people—were a different species.

Weaver built his home about sixty miles from Hayden Lake, at remote Ruby Ridge, in Boundary County, Idaho. Boundary County had 8,332 people. It fit the model of an Aryan Nation in the making. Its minority population comprised twenty-six Asian Americans and three blacks. Weaver was known to his neighbors as a white supremacist—or, as some would say, a white separationist. They knew him as someone who referred to the government as ZOG, meaning Zionist Occupational Government. He told them that the races should live separately, and that Jews were responsible for seeking a "new world order."

In 1988 Weaver ran for sheriff of Boundary County, saying he would only enforce laws people liked. He gave out a business card; one side said "Vote Weaver for Sheriff," the other "Get out of jail—free." Only about 400 people voted in the primary, a two-person race. Weaver drew 102 votes.

After losing the election Randy Weaver could have used one of his own "Get out of jail—free" cards. In 1989 the U.S. Bureau of Alcohol, Tobacco and Firearms (ATF) set up a sting operation targeting northern Idaho white supremacists, who were allegedly running an underground gun business. Weaver was indicted in December 1990 after selling two illegally sawed-off shotguns to an informant in October 1989.

On January 17, 1991, Randy and Vicki Weaver were on their snowmobile, heading to Bonners Ferry, Idaho, to buy supplies. They saw a truck with its hood up parked on a one-lane Forest Service bridge. A man with long hair was by the truck, apparently distressed. Weaver, his snowmobile blocked, asked if he could help. The longhaired man was an ATF agent. He pointed his gun at Weaver. Weaver was arrested by ATF agents who came out of the woods, and by Boundary County sheriff Bruce Whittaker, the man to whom he had lost the election.

U.S. Magistrate Stephen Ayers released Weaver without requiring a cash bond. Judge Ayers felt that Weaver had strong roots in the community—this although Weaver owed back taxes on his property and had warned ATF agents, "You'll never fool me again." As the agents feared, Weaver decided to hide out in his mountain cabin with his wife and three children rather than appear in court to answer the charges.

Weaver's mountain home was not much more than a shack. Measuring twenty by twenty-five feet, it had been built of plywood and mill ends, more commonly used for firewood. It had no electricity, except that supplied by a generator. It had no plumbing; the family drank water from a spring, or melted snow. The closest store, in Naples, Idaho, was seven miles away.

Weaver failed to appear for his February 1991 trial date and thus became an anomaly—a fugitive whose whereabouts were well known. Friends and neighbors—reportedly, a network of as many as fifty people—brought him food, supplies, and mail. The U.S. Marshals Service, charged with arresting people who fail to appear for their federal court dates, was "very prudent about going in there and storming the house, knowing he has a number of kids," according to U.S. Marshal Michael Johnson. Weaver had "threatened to shoot anyone who attempts to take him into custody," another marshal noted. So the service sent Weaver letters through the mail, and messages through his Coeur d'Alene attorney, Everett Hofmeister. "Whether we live or whether we die," the Weavers responded, "we will not obey your lawless government."

A year passed. The Weavers had a fourth child, a girl named Elishaba. The standoff continued until March 8, 1992, when Bill Morlin, a reporter for the *Spokane Spokesman-Review*, wrote a front-page article asking why Weaver had been allowed to avoid arrest for so long.

"He's not the only one living up there," said Ron Evans, chief deputy at the U.S. Marshals Service Boise office. "We have four children and a wife up there who have not been charged with any crimes." The three older children—Sam, thirteen, Sara, sixteen, and Rachel, ten—had all been spotted during government overflights, wearing holsters and carrying guns. These same overflights must have confirmed what the agents could see from the ground: The cabin was, in the words of Marshal Johnson, "the closest thing to having a castle with a moat. [It] is in the remotest place that's possible to find in the state of Idaho." At the east side was a nearly vertical drop of several hundred feet. The west side was accessible only by an abandoned, steep, and overgrown logging road. Evans told Morlin: "We do intend, at some point in the future, to bring Randy Weaver before the court." Weaver's friends told Morlin: "He's fully self-contained up there on his mountain. [He] says he don't want nobody on his mountain." An ATF agent told Morlin: "Hey, I've got kids and I see the point the Marshals Service is trying to make. I wouldn't want to be the one to go in there and find myself shooting at a 10-year-old who I know would be shooting at me."

Following Morlin's story, James Coates, a *Chicago Tribune* reporter, went to Idaho and talked with Weaver's supporters. Interviewed on radio, Coates said he was told "that Weaver said that if his family had to die at the hands of what he called ZOG, or the Zionist Occupation Government, it's better that that should happen than that they would be taken prisoner by these dark forces."

Two more months passed. Friends persuaded Weaver to tell the press his side of the story. He had, after all, cut off the shotgun barrels because an FBI informant posing as a gun trader had told him to. In an interview with the North Idaho News Network, Weaver said the standoff would end only in one of two ways—either the federal government would admit it was wrong, or he and his family would be dead. "If they admitted this whole thing was a setup," Weaver said, "I'd come down off this mountain and blast my mouth off four times as loud, and they won't allow that. Right now, the only thing they can take away from us is our life. Even if we die, we win. We'll die believing in Yahweh."

Why wouldn't he chance a trial, tell a jury his side of the story? "All they have against us is government-paid informants who can get on the stand and say anything they want," Weaver explained. "I feel I have no choice but to stay here if I want to keep my family together." The newspaper account described Weaver's cabin as a "fortress." And not only were the Weavers armed, so was Kevin Harris, a twenty-four-year-old family friend who had moved in with them nine years earlier.

The area press only wanted one thing—to know when the federal authorities planned to arrest Weaver. Local authorities urged action. Sheriff Bruce Whittaker worried that people all over America would hear that if you wanted to break the law with impunity, the thing to do was buy a gun and acreage in Idaho. "I have to wonder what the feds would do if this was a case involving Black Panthers in Philadelphia instead of white supremacists in Idaho," he said.

✗ ✗ ✗

Colleagues and friends described U.S. Marshal William F. Degan as a "hard-nosed, teeth-grinding, criminal-busting good guy." Forty-two years old, he said good-bye to his wife and children, then flew from his home base in Boston to a remote mountaintop in Idaho on Thursday, August 20, 1992. He was "selected to go up and retrieve vital intelligence on how we would extract [Weaver]," Marshal Thomas Nixon said. "It was about to come to a head." Degan had a reputation as one of the Marshals Service's best, a latter-day Wyatt Earp.

On Friday, August 21, William F. Degan and five fellow marshals were dressed in camouflage, surveilling Weaver's cabin in two three-man units. They had started their shift at about 2:30 A.M. Their day was almost over when a car drove into the valley. Weaver may have heard it. The marshals say Weaver and Harris and Sam—now fourteen— came out of the cabin with dogs, who were barking and yelping and who dashed down the hill.

The agents tried to hide. "I just looked around the tree," said Marshal Arthur Roderick, "and I saw the dog coming at us about 150 or 200 meters away, and Harris was behind him with a rifle." Roderick shot the dog, he said, to prevent it from leading Weaver and Harris to the hidden agents.

The agents retreated down the slope while trying to protect each other. "We were trying to get further cover," Roderick said, "because we knew the kid was there." All of a sudden Roderick saw a man off to the side, ahead of him, who he thought was Weaver. He was "screaming like a fool." Roderick feared that the marshals might have been outflanked. "Stop!" he yelled. "Federal marshal!" Marshals William Degan and Larry Cooper hollered too.

Then shots rang out. "I dove back into the woods," Roderick said, "and there were more shots." He realized that Degan had been hit. "I could see rounds all around us," he said. "Larry was taking shots too. He was trying to get Billy back." Degan had been shot through the heart. Roderick had a graze wound to his chest. Neither had been wearing a bullet-proof vest. Their job that morning had been to get a better sense of how they might approach the cabin. They had not expected a confrontation.

Three of the surviving deputies were able to escape. Two were pinned down for nine hours, some of the time in darkness, rain, and sleet. Finally, during the night, an Idaho state police tactical team rescued them and removed Degan's body. The FBI's elite Hostage Rescue Team was called in. Soon, Ruby Ridge, Idaho, would see more than a hundred FBI agents, twenty-six Idaho national guardsmen, and scores of U.S. marshals, state police, and deputies from nearby sheriff's departments, in addition to helicopters and armored vehicles. The Weaver case had become an armed standoff. Late the next day, Saturday, shots were exchanged again.

$$X \quad X \quad X$$

Law enforcement set up a barricade on the road to the Weaver cabin. Two dozen protesters stood on the other side, jeering at the officers, claiming that Weaver was being persecuted for his beliefs. "Tell the Truth," one placard read. "Freedom of Religion," said another. "Your Home Could Be Next," asserted a third. In the days to come there would be more protesters and more signs. "Government Lies, a Patriot Dies," "We're Fed Up with the Feds," "Christians Against Tyranny," "Leave the Family Alone, Go Home," "Let's Stop This Abuse of Our Freedom." Weaver's friends had little sympathy for the government. "The man ain't hurt no one," Bill Grider said. Grider, one of the people who had kept the Weavers supplied, said that the marshal's shooting was "a government setup, that's what it is."

In town, most of the people supported Weaver. "It's all a lot of [exple-tive]," said Eugene Mendenhall, "over a quarter-inch they say he cut off a shotgun barrel." Journalist Bill Morlin says that quarter-inch "was a rumor that got picked up. In fact the gun was five to six inches short." But that fact wouldn't have mattered. "Hell," said a neighbor who refused to give a reporter his name, "three-quarters of the people around here have sawed-off shotguns for grouse-hunting." His real problem with gov-ernment, Weaver's neighbors seemed to think, was that "Randy just didn't like black people," and that he had an odd religion. "Randy's a neighborly person," said Elva Grover. "He has his own religion, but that's all right. He respects mine too." Chuck Sandelin, a Baptist preacher, said, "Randy Weaver just wanted to be left alone, but the government went after his property, after his firearms, and now they're paying for it. That man, Randy Weaver, is a patriot, not a criminal."

What did the neighbors think about Weaver endangering his wife and children, whom he could have sent to safety? "They are a family," said Dawn Vinton. "They want to be there with him."

✗ ✗ ✗

On Monday, August 24, 1992, the FBI announced that Sam Weaver had also died in the initial shootout. Authorities, checking the property, had discovered his body in, and removed it from, a small outbuilding known in the Weaver family as the birthing shed. This revelation, along with the seeming invasion of a small army of heavily armed federal law enforce-ment officers, incensed many residents. The roadblock now drew more people, with angrier signs. "FBI Burn in Hell" and "30.06 Go Thru Your Vest Easy Fed Dogs," and "Zionist Murder" and "Your Home Is Next." A sign proclaiming "Baby Killers!" was held by ten-year-old Clint Mathews, whose father, Order leader Robert Mathews, had died in a shootout with federal officials eight years earlier. Friends and neighbors literally screamed at the authorities. "We're going to get even," one said, "they ain't getting away with this." "God," said another, "will strike them dead." Some yelled "Traitor!" at the officers. Others threatened: "We'll get you!"

Meanwhile, law enforcement, stationed about a hundred feet from the cabin, reported that the area was "riddled" with booby traps. One deputy told a newspaper reporter, "Now that one of their kids is dead, they'll never turn themselves in."

Soon the Aryan Nations inserted itself into the standoff. "He was set up because he refused to snitch on us," said Carl Franklin. "The govern-ment's been wanting him to be an informant ever since they indicted him. They wanted to make a deal with him." An Aryan Nations contin-gent heckled officers at the roadblock. "Baby killer, baby killer," they chanted. One handed out copies of a letter dated June 12, 1990, from Vicki Weaver to the Aryan Nations, asking for the group's help because Randy had been threatened by federal agents unless he "joined their team." (The Weavers claimed that Randy had sawed off the shotguns in 1989 only when an informant had asked him to, and that the authorities used the threat of charges to pressure him to testify against the Aryan Nations.) "I and the children are ready to stand for the truth and our freedom," Vicki had written. "We cannot make deals with the enemy. This is a war against the white sons of Isaac. Yahweh our Yahshua is our Savior and King. . . . Let the Edomites bring on the war. . . . Let Yah-yahshua's will be done. If it is our time, we'll go home."

Among the protesters at the roadblock was the Trochmann family, from Montana. John—who would soon become one of the militias' most important leaders—and Carolyn Trochmann had met the Weavers at an Aryan Nations family day. The two families had become friends. Carolyn said she had supplied the Weavers with food for a year. She even helped deliver Elishaba. Her son, Caleb, was Sara Weaver's boyfriend. Carolyn stood at the barricade with her children, telling reporters that she had visited the Weavers a month before, that everyone except the infant was armed. "We read from the Bible, laughed, played games," she said. "They were living one day at a time, and were not the least bit afraid to die. . . . I'm proud of Randy," Carolyn Trochmann said, "and I hope he doesn't surrender. . . . He just wanted to be left alone. . . . Most of us are willing to die to protect that. . . . He's willing to die for that."

Was he really willing to die? His family too? "Here we don't roll over," Carolyn Trochmann explained. "Biblically, it's wrong whenever we allow the government to take another law from God." Carolyn Trochmann's strong views impressed Timothy Egan of The New York Times. "Mrs. Trochmann expressed little sympathy for the deputy marshal who was killed," he wrote. "She said the agents 'provoked' the killing by trespassing on Mr. Weaver's property."

✗ ✗ ✗

People in Boundary County lived a contradiction. One of the places farthest away, both geographically and spiritually, from Washington, D.C., was also 80 percent government land. People viewed their largest neighbor as an impersonal and unfriendly absentee landlord, promulgating bothersome land-use rules seemingly at whim. These rules, in turn, affected what local residents could do with their own land, and produced an antifederal animus that worked to Weaver's benefit, even without the extra annoyance of the federal invasion. The "invasion" even postponed the opening of the high school so that the approximately two hundred law officers could use its gym for a barracks.

Many people in Boundary County had strong opinions about the unfolding drama. When local contractors volunteered to bring gravel to the muddy road law enforcement was using to get nearer the Weaver cabin, some bellowed threats at them. "It is totally erroneous," said Bob Miller, managing editor of the *Bonners Ferry Herald*, "to think that the people of Idaho are all a bunch of racists. While people do not condone Weaver's beliefs, there is quite a bit of support for his stand against the Federal Government. People think he was set up."

Other voices were critical of Weaver. "This is not a case of civil rights or harassment," read a statement by the Kootenai County Task Force on Human Relations. "If our system is to survive, we must respect the laws and the judicial system." Whether or not Weaver had been entrapped, the task force felt that he should have appeared in court and made his defense, rather than retreating to his cabin and challenging law enforcement to come in and get him. The one thing people agreed on was this: Weaver was not likely to give up.

Reporters from around the country descended on Ruby Ridge; they found the best quotes were to be gotten at the increasingly bizarre scene at the roadblock. On one side was law enforcement, on the other demonstrators. Mixed together were Aryan Nations adherents, wives and children of dead or imprisoned members of the Order, skinheads, and people from the area who wanted to express their support for Weaver. "Are there any damn rights left here in this country?" a woman asked. "Hell no," a man answered, "there ain't no rights left in this country." Bill Grider explained: "Randy realizes that the world is trying to get one brown race. Pigs breed with pigs, cows breed with cows, horses breed with horses. Whites should breed with whites, blacks should breed with blacks, and keep the ancestry and descendant lines together."

Some of Weaver's supporters did more than shout. Five skinheads were arrested for carrying concealed weapons—long rifles and bayonets—on a road leading toward an overlook near the government's base camp, where helicopters and other equipment were gathered. In addition to the weapons the skinheads were carrying, reportedly to bring to Weaver, was a "white power" banner. John Bangerter, a skinhead who had come from his home in Las Vegas to support Weaver, said: "I'm ready to get my gun and my clips and take off my safety and pull my trigger with my finger. I don't care anymore. This is the beginning of a revolution, a war."

✗ ✗ ✗

The federal strategy was to wait the Weavers out. "We can keep people fresh and provide them with rest," Steve Boyle of the Marshals Service said, "and the Weavers can't." Another consideration was that the children were regarded as "hostages" of their father. Waiting, furthermore, avoided a tactical problem: "You can't get within several hundred yards of the house without [risking] being exposed to gunfire," Boyle said. How much firepower did the FBI think Weaver had? "We are prepared to face an arsenal," said Eugene Glenn of the FBI. "But the fact is we don't have the intelligence to define the resources that he may have."

The FBI wanted desperately to talk with Weaver, but he did not respond to their bullhorn or pick up the phone a robot had deposited near the cabin. It took six days for Weaver to yell something back to the FBI. It wasn't much, but at least a dialogue was starting. What no one on either side of the standoff could know was that this was a prologue to the formation of the American militia movement.

2 Rambo

I WILL VOTE FOR BO GRITZ FOR PRESIDENT.

A VOTE FOR CLINTON OR BUSH IS A VOTE FOR

SATAN.

CAROL CRAWFORD

Late in the afternoon of Wednesday, August 26, 1992, retired lieuten-ant colonel James "Bo" Gritz—the former Green Beret upon whom the character "Rambo" was supposedly based—came to Ruby Ridge and asked to speak with the FBI. "I know Randy from 1969," he said. "I was a major, and he was a Spec. 4. I think he would talk to me. I want to see justice on both sides. Randy is highly skilled, but he is pushed into a corner. Maybe Randy has changed since I last saw him, but I am not saying what Randy is accused of doing is right. He may tell me he never did like me and that I should go away, but I want to try. I know Randy, and I know his 'Identity' religion."

Gritz was more than a retired military man; he was the 1992 presiden-tial candidate for the racist and anti-Semitic Populist Party. He first came to prominence in these circles when he was featured in the March 28, 1988, issue of *Spotlight*, the newspaper of the anti-Semitic Liberty Lobby.

Gritz was smiling, having accepted the Populist Party's vice-presidential nomination. He was pictured shaking hands with the presidential candidate, David Duke. Gritz had accepted the nomination at the behest of his self-described "good friend" Willis Carto, head of the Liberty Lobby.

Gritz's political views meshed neatly with those of Duke and Carto. "Do you see the sign, scent, stain and mark of the beast on America today?" Gritz asked in his *Center for Action Newsletter.* "Are there any outward signs that reveal who the enemy is?" He answered his own question: The "number of the Antichrist system is 666, a six within a six within a six. Six sides, six angles, six points." He said this immediately after mentioning King Solomon and a "six pointed star"—that is, the Magen David, the six-pointed star of Judaism. Bo Gritz also said that a "study of 72 regional FED [Federal Reserve] directors found 70 were white and 69 were male. What the study didn't show was the true owners of the federal reserve. Eight Jewish families virtually control the entire FED—only three are American Jews."

After losing the 1988 election, Gritz moved even deeper into the far right. He embraced Pete Peters, the key spokesman of the Christian Identity religion. At a 1991 Bible camp Gritz said:

> The enemy you face today is a satanic overthrow where he would change the United States of America, a nation under God, into USA, Incorporated, with King George [President Bush] as chairman of the board. And a Zionist group that would rule over us as long as satan [*sic*] might be upon this earth, that is your enemy.
>
> Do you think you're lucky to be an Identity Christian today? . . . I believe that the Identity Christian movement will continue to grow in this nation until it is able to stand self-sufficient in spite of the government. . . . I am telling you that He [God] has given us all that we need. He's given us the likes of Pete Peters, he's given us the likes of the Identity Christian Movement.

For two days in August 1992, Gritz pleaded to be allowed to speak with Weaver. Whether to agree with his request must have been a difficult decision for the FBI. Relatives of the Weavers and of Kevin Harris were incensed to see "Bo Gritz for President" signs taking advantage of a life-and-death situation. (The signs were then taken down.) And Gritz had spent the early afternoon of August 27 serving "citizens arrest" warrants on federal and state officials at the roadblock. The papers "charged" FBI director William Sessions; U.S. Marshals Service director Henry Hudson; Eugene Glenn, the FBI special agent in charge on the scene; and Idaho governor Cecil Andrus with responsibility for the deaths of Sam Weaver and William Degan.

Finally, however, at 7:00 that evening, Glenn allowed Gritz to become part of the negotiating team. The deciding factor was Weaver's request to see Gritz. The next day, Friday, August 28, Gritz was allowed past the roadblock, up to the cabin on Ruby Ridge. Hours later he returned. According to reporters his expression was extremely sad. He said that FBI agent Glenn would talk with the reporters later. Then he walked away and, with about 150 supporters, began praying.

Three and a half hours later Glenn spoke to the press. He told them that Kevin Harris, Randy Weaver, and the three surviving children were all right, although Harris and Weaver had been wounded. "Unfortunately," Glenn said, "Vicki is dead. This surprised me." She had been shot dead, and Harris and Weaver wounded, during the Saturday shooting.

According to Glenn, "Bo has been instrumental in the dialogue." Gritz was to be the main negotiator over the next days. He would stand outside the cabin, conversing with his old friend. He relayed an offer by Gerry Spence, a noted Cheyenne, Wyoming, defense attorney, to come to the cabin and speak with Weaver. He also inquired about Harris's health: Apparently, the man's condition was worsening. By August 29 he had a collapsed lung, which was filling with fluid. He was also coughing up blood. Harris said he would surrender if all charges against Weaver were dropped. That, of course, was out of the question.

Gritz also explained Weaver's version of events to the press. Weaver had told Gritz that on August 21, the family dogs heard something—they thought a deer—and Sam, Harris, and Weaver, armed with rifles, a shotgun, and a pistol, went to investigate. Weaver said he had come across a camouflaged man walking down the logging road. He said he tried to tell Sam and Harris that they should get back to the cabin. According to Weaver, one of the camouflaged men shot one of his dogs. Then Sam shot Degan. They ran back toward the cabin. Sam was hit, first in the arm, then in the back. He fell dead. His last words were, "I'm coming, Dad." Weaver and Harris raced back to the cabin. Later, with Vicki's help, they retrieved Sam, cleaned and wrapped his body, and put it in the birthing shed. (Vicki also stayed there when she was menstruating.)

The following day, Gritz said, Weaver returned to the outbuilding "to say good-bye to his son." As he was going to open the door, a shot rang out, and Weaver was hit in the arm. He rushed to the cabin, as did Harris, who was also outside. Vicki was standing there, holding the door open, the baby in her arms. Weaver heard another shot. Vicki was hit in the head. The bullet, it turned out, cut a path through her face, her tongue, her jawbone, and her carotid artery, killing her instantly. Bullet and bone fragments also hit Harris in the arm and chest.

Gritz agreed to pray with Weaver for a resolution of the standoff. He said Weaver wanted "a day or so" to decide whether to surrender. With communications improving, the FBI allowed Jackie Brown, a family friend, inside the cabin to comfort the children and bring them milk, peaches, juice, grapes, and a baby bottle. The next day Brown was permitted in again, to help clean the tiny cabin. All the while, of course, Vicki's body—by then she was a week dead—lay inside, wrapped in plastic, under the kitchen table.

Brown left the cabin that day with a four-page letter. Written by Sara, the eldest Weaver daughter, it gave the family's version of the shoot-outs. In it Harris admitted that he had shot Degan, after he had seen Sam hit in the back. Sam, the account said, had been killed after yelling at the officers for shooting his dog, Striker. The letter ended with expressions of faith in the Christian Identity religion and of willingness to die.

On Sunday, August 30, Harris surrendered. Bo Gritz and his "associate," a former Arizona police officer named Jack McLamb—who would later become an important figure recruiting police officers into the militia movement—helped Harris onto a stretcher and walked with him from the cabin to the government encampment. McLamb held Harris's hand throughout the helicopter ride to Spokane, where Harris was admitted to Sacred Heart Medical Center in serious condition with multiple bullet wounds, an infection in his shoulder, and a collapsed lung. One of his earliest visitors was U.S. Magistrate Cynthia Imbrogno, who held a special first appearance in the emergency room. Harris was charged with the first-degree murder of William Degan and with assault on federal officers. Then he underwent surgery.

After Harris surrendered, Vicki Weaver's body was retrieved by Gritz and Brown and taken to the government encampment. Gritz and McLamb then concentrated on Weaver. They met with a group of skinheads at the Deep Creek Inn, a restaurant not far from the roadblock on Ruby Road. Knowing how much Weaver respected the racist skinheads, Gritz and McLamb wanted them to sign a letter that they, the negotiators, would write. The skinheads refused, insisting that they would write their own letter, which Gritz and McLamb feared would only embolden Weaver to continue the standoff. "We drafted a letter," McLamb said, "one we thought would help bring Randy out and gave it to them and told them to think about it overnight. We were going to bed and would see them in the morning."

Only two skinheads showed up for breakfast the next day, August 31.

They agreed to forge the signatures of some of their comrades, since two names on the letter would not impress Weaver. It said that they believed Weaver's fight should be "in a courtroom, not up on top of that mountain."

When McLamb and Gritz trekked up to the cabin with the letter, Weaver had the door bolted, which surprised them. It had been left open the day before. Randy said that they had decided to stay in the cabin for another ten days. "We were all wired for sound," McLamb said, "and I could hear the guys back at [the base camp] groan. I looked at Bo and he was holding his head."

They shoved the letter under the door and talked to Weaver from outside. Finally, they were allowed in. "In the end it came down to Sara," Gritz said. "She had this fear that the government would not keep its part of the bargain. She wept and wept. But we said the battle was in the courts now."

On August 31, the eleven-day standoff ended. Weaver talked with Gritz in the cabin about Yahweh and the Zionist Occupational Government. He then changed the baby's diaper. The girls gave Gritz and Jack McLamb their weapons (Rachel had a .38-caliber snub-nosed revolver, Sara a nine-millimeter pistol). Then Weaver walked out holding the baby, while McLamb held the elder daughters' hands. Weaver surrendered. "He cried his wife's name, he cried his son's name, and then we just marched down the road like we said we were going to do," Gritz said. No doubt, Gritz was pleased at his accomplishment of bringing Weaver out alive. As he walked out of the woods, past the group of skinheads who were cheering, Gritz gave them a stiff-arm Nazi salute.

Randy Weaver was flown to Boise, where he was treated for a bullet wound in his armpit, then taken to jail. Inside the cabin authorities found rifles, shotguns, handguns, and thousands of rounds of ammunition, some of which was the armor-piercing variety that can penetrate a bulletproof vest. There was also a white sign with black letters near the doorway. Over the phrase "New World Order," a red circle and diagonal slash were superimposed.

X   X   X

While Gritz was negotiating Weaver's surrender, his supporters had been holding a rally in downtown Seattle. "The time is now," they said. "Let's take America back." "I have twenty-nine grandchildren," said Gene Goosman of West Seattle, "and when I see what Congress and 'King George' are doing to this country—giving it wholesale to the United Nations and World Bank—I think this may be our last chance." The *Seattle Times* reported why these people supported Gritz for president:

They want the U.S. out of the United Nations, foreign aid eliminated, a prohibition on foreign ownership of American soil or companies, a stronger national defense, a weaker Supreme Court, elimination of the Internal Revenue Service, the Federal Reserve System and the Department of Education. And they want a Christian America. Officially, Gritz rejects President Bush's foreign policy, U.S. military intervention outside our border, and the GATT treaty.

Two weeks after the Weaver surrender, supporters in Lewiston, Idaho, showed a videotape of Gritz articulating his platform. He explained that the Sixteenth Amendment (authorizing a federal income tax) might not have been ratified correctly. "There is no statute of limitations on fraud," he said. "Federal income tax will be eliminated." He also opposed the "New World Order."

Later in September, Gritz brought his presidential campaign to the Indianapolis Baptist Temple. "Constitutional law is the only way we can continue under our birthright," he said. "We are not living under those rights now." He suggested that people burn the United Nations flag. The U.N., he said, was "a godless organization. Alger Hiss and fifteen other communists founded it in 1945 in San Francisco."

By October, Gritz's supporters were hawking videotapes and transcripts of his press conference in the Weaver standoff. At the Preparedness Expo '92 in Seattle (a convention featuring survivalist wares and extremist speakers and literature, for which flyers had been distributed at the Ruby Ridge roadblock), Weaver and Gritz were on everyone's minds. Five hundred people came to a lecture by Jack McLamb. John Heil, "like in Heil Hitler," said he liked "the statements of McLamb, about how the government is protecting itself from the people." Carol Crawford said, "I will vote for Bo Gritz for president. A vote for Clinton or Bush is a vote for Satan."

Gritz said of the Weaver siege: "The lesson for America is this could happen to anybody. We've got to change the bureaucracy." He also had, or heard about, another idea, which he mentioned during his 1992 presidential campaign: People should form militias.

3 Weaver Fever

ALL INDIVIDUALS AND GROUPS OPERATE
INDEPENDENTLY OF EACH OTHER, AND NEVER
REPORT TO A CENTRAL HEADQUARTERS OR
SINGLE LEADER FOR DIRECTION OR
INSTRUCTION. . . . PARTICIPANTS IN A PROGRAM
OF LEADERLESS RESISTANCE THROUGH
PHANTOM CELL OR INDIVIDUAL ACTION MUST
KNOW EXACTLY WHAT THEY ARE DOING, AND
EXACTLY HOW TO DO IT.

LOUIS BEAM, Aryan Nations

While the confrontation between Weaver and law enforcement was under way, Identity leader Pete Peters was holding his "Scriptures for America 1992 Bible Camp." "Since we had 500 people in attendance from forty states," Peters later wrote, "we immediately set up a phone bank and began contacting the U.S. Attorney General's Office, with callers from forty different states, in an attempt to make the Feds think this had gained national attention."

Two months after the Weaver siege ended, Peters called a meeting in Estes Park, Colorado, of more than 150 leaders of the far right from around the country. The report issued after the three-day meeting predictably accused the government of "genocide" against the Weaver family. But more significant was the convergence of what Peters termed "men . . . who in the past would normally not be caught together under the same roof"—neo-Nazis, Christian Identity adherents, anti-abortion activists, tax protesters, Ku Klux Klan members, and others who either saw each other as ideological and organizational adversaries, or would have worried about the effect on their "mainstream" credentials from participation in such a gathering. Attendees included Richard Butler, head of the Aryan Nations; Louis Beam, another Aryan Nations leader; anti-Semite Red Beckman; Larry Pratt of Gun Owners of America; and Montana far-right activist Chris Temple. Temple had been an organizer for Bo Gritz's presidential campaign, and had written for *Jubilee*, a racist, anti-Semitic publication of the Christian Identity Movement. Temple was also on the steering committee of a newly formed Weaver support group, United Citizens for Justice.

What emerged from this meeting was a "Battle Plan for Future Conflicts," said the Portland-based Coalition for Human Dignity, one of America's premier "think tanks" studying the far right, which received information from inside the meeting. Larry Pratt, for example, reportedly downplayed the lobbying efforts of the National Rifle Association against gun control, and suggested instead a "national struggle for survival" with "armed militia units."

The "Special Report" issued following the meeting also reprinted the entire text of an article by Louis Beam entitled "Leaderless Resistance." "Leaderless Resistance" meant something akin to what both the Communist Party and the Nazis used to call cell structure—a legal, aboveground political group (protected in the United States by the First Amendment) and an underground to carry out illegal activities with minimum risk of exposing the entire organization to prosecution. Beam used the term "Phantom Cell" to describe his idea. "All individuals and groups," he wrote, "operate independently of each other, and never report to a central headquarters or single leader for direction or instruction. . . . Participants in a program of Leaderless Resistance through Phantom Cell or individual action must know exactly what they are doing, AND EXACTLY HOW TO DO IT." The purpose of Leaderless Resistance, wrote Beam, "is to defeat state tyranny. . . . Like the fog which forms when conditions are right and disappears when they are not, so must the resistance to tyranny be."

Some observers suggested that the October 1992 meeting in Estes Park launched two important, and interrelated, initiatives. One was to revitalize the type of paramilitary organization the far right had spawned in the 1980s, such as the Order. The other was to use these groups to promote "Leaderless Resistance." It may be an overstatement to say that this Colorado gathering was the birthplace of the American militia movement. After all, Eva Vail Lamb, a neighbor of Aryan Nations leader Richard Butler, had already started the Idaho Organized Militia in May of 1992, and Bo Gritz, on the campaign trail as the 1992 Populist Party candidate for president, was suggesting that his supporters form militias. (Gritz continued these calls after the 1992 election, when he began conducting survivalist—some say paramilitary—training he dubbed SPIKE, for "Specially Prepared Individuals for Key Events.") Regardless, by 1994 Beam's principles for white supremacist response to the Randy Weaver siege would become the model structure for many militia groups. "The fundamental rule guiding the organization of the free militia," said the "Field Manual" of Wisconsin's Free Militia, "is generalized principles and planning but decentralized tactics and action." This meant, the "Field Manual" asserted, that "the whole Militia must be committed to the same cause . . . but specific tactics should be left up to the individual elements so that compromise of a part does not compromise the whole."

The Estes Park meeting—held in reaction to the Weaver siege, and concluded before the Weaver trial—may have laid some of the groundwork for the militias' formation, not only in suggesting structure, but also in solidifying connections between longtime white supremacists and Identity followers, on the one hand, and others, such as Larry Pratt of Gun Owners of America. Yet its importance should not be overrated. Meetings happen every day. In order to have an impact they must plug in to a social fabric that is ready to receive the meeting's message. When the Estes Park meeting occurred, the Weaver saga had not yet been completed in the courts. The trial's conclusion would be only one of the three independent events that made a large-scale, decentralized militia movement possible.

✗ ✗ ✗

Weaver's supporters did not abandon him after his surrender. John Trochmann, who had first met the Weavers at the Aryan Nations compound and whose family had been among the protesters at the Ruby Ridge roadblock, formed the support group United Citizens for Justice in September 1992, right after Weaver's arrest. "We witnessed the tyranny of government," Trochmann said. "It was a devastating event for me."

The Weaver case was tailor-made for the Cheyenne lawyer Gerry Spence. (It should be recalled that he had offered his help to Weaver during the standoff.) Aside from his folksy western style, Spence had all the factual advantages: Degan couldn't testify about who had shot him; all the other witnesses to his death were federal agents, who had an animus against Weaver and Harris because of Degan's death; there was no videotape or other conclusive evidence of who shot whom in the woods. In fact, there was no conclusive evidence of who had fired first; even the agents contradicted each other in their testimony. To rebut a claim of self-defense, a prosecutor would need to establish that someone on the Weavers' side fired first.

A skillful lawyer such as Spence could also recast Weaver, despite his odious views, into a figure deserving sympathy, and remake his case into a trial of our rights as Americans to think as we want without government interference. Here was someone who had retreated to the woods to escape the system; but the system would not let him escape, even if all he wanted was a cabin on a hilltop with no running water and an outhouse. Weaver was someone who lost a dog named Striker, a son named Sam, and a wife named Vicki, who was holding their infant daughter while a government bullet shattered her skull.

Spence, living up to the defense attorney's creed—"contest everything, concede nothing, and when in trouble allege fraud"—put the government on trial. He called Weaver's a "case in which the government was obviously guilty of having committed murders and were attempting to cover those murders up by a murder prosecution against innocent people."

Spence hammered home his best point—one that troubles many people to this day, and that allowed Weaver's supporters to ratchet up their hatred of government and move their conspiracy theories and paranoia to a higher plane: After Degan had been killed, the FBI's standard rules of engagement—which allowed agents to shoot to kill when they believed their lives or someone else's were in imminent danger—were modified for Weaver and Harris. Now agents were allowed, simply, to kill. "Kevin Harris was running when he was shot," Spence said. "Randy Weaver had his back to the shooter when he was shot. The mother was standing in the door with her baby when she was shot. None of them presented any injury or any danger to anybody when they were shot."

The prosecution also fell into a trap. It argued, with some justification, that Weaver and his wife had essentially prophesied a confrontation with government, then created it. But in the controlled theater of the courtroom, Spence was able to turn that line of argument to his advantage: He said prosecutors had to "demonize" Weaver "so that they could cover up the murder of a boy shot in the back and a woman shot in the head."

Spence accomplished what every good trial lawyer tries to do—induce the jury to put itself in the defendant's place, rather than the victim's. Jury foreman Jerry Harris Weaver (no relation to either defendant) said later, "We kind of put ourselves on trial. If we were on trial, would we want to be convicted on this kind of evidence?" Spence rested without offering a single witness. As Judge Edward Lodge later said, three-fourths of the fifty-six prosecution witnesses helped the defense.

Spence successfully argued that the agents entrapped Weaver. He apparently sawed the weapons off at the request of the informant, and the delay between the crime and the arrest—coinciding with a failed effort to get Weaver to "snitch" on the Aryan Nations—also undercut the credibility of the government's case. The entrapment defense, of course, could have been presented had Weaver decided to appear in court in the first place, rather than hide on Ruby Ridge.

Charged with Degan's murder, conspiracy, and with firearms violations, Harris was acquitted. He walked out of the courtroom. Weaver was convicted only on minor charges, relating to his failure to appear in court.

On October 19, 1993, Weaver was sentenced to eighteen months in jail. Having already served over a year, he was released shortly before Christmas 1993. He returned to Iowa to be with his daughters.

✗ ✗ ✗

The total cost of the Weaver case was 5.4 million taxpayer dollars: $1 million for the surveillance and siege; $858,000 for trial security; $271,000 for the court-appointed attorneys; and $100,100 for jury expenses—and this included neither the salaries of the prosecution and judge, nor other incidental expenses. Add to that a $3.1 million civil settlement attorney Spence later won for Weaver and his surviving daughters, settling a $200 million claim arising from the deaths of Vicki and Sam.

The federal government, however, paid a higher nonmonetary price. Judge Edward Lodge said the FBI's actions during the trial "served to obstruct the administration of justice": "The actions of the Government, acting through the FBI, evidence a callous disregard for the rights of the defendants and the interests of justice." The judge fined the U.S. Attorney's office $1,920 for delays in turning over information to which the defense was legally entitled. For example, the judge had ordered the FBI to produce certain documents while an agent was testifying. The FBI mailed the papers—fourth class.

The Bureau had also tampered with evidence. After it had removed items from the scene, it replaced them, then took photographs, suggesting that they represented the original scene. A member of the Marshals Service also accused the FBI of actually hindering the prosecution, since it apparently had a different trial strategy than that decided upon by the prosecutors. E. Michael Kahoe, a senior FBI agent, was eventually suspended allegedly for destroying documents, as were other senior agents who, during an investigation into the siege, covered up their conduct. Randall Day, the Boundary County prosecutor, even considered filing murder charges against federal agents in the death of Vicki Weaver. "It's always a possibility," Day said.

To this day, the reasoning for the loosening of the rules of engagement is hotly contested. Perhaps dispassionate judgment was overcome by the death of Marshal William Degan, or maybe there was another reason. Conspiratorialists and Weaver supporters are not alone in questioning the government's actions. Most careful observers of the case, however, agree with FBI director Louis J. Freeh's conclusion that the killing of Vicki Weaver was accidental. FBI sharpshooter Lon T. Horiuchi testified that he was aiming for Harris, who was running, and fired slightly ahead so that he and the bullet would meet. The bullet missed Harris, hitting Vicki, who was holding the door open. Whatever the exact sequence — recollections were no doubt confused by the chaotic nature of the scene: Horiuchi thought Weaver was trying to shoot a helicopter overhead. Regardless, it must have been especially disturbing to white supremacists that Vicki, a white woman, was killed not merely by a government official, but by an Asian-American one.

✗ ✗ ✗

The events at Ruby Ridge, and in the federal courtroom in Boise, became distorted in many ways, aiding those who would soon begin forming militias. The white supremacists, of course, figured out how to use the case as an organizing tool, framing its discussion around a martyred child and mother. The mainstream press also distorted the events to make political points. The *Seattle Times* editorialized that "Agents racing in with guns blazing must not be the accepted way of dealing with fringe elements who spout antigovernment venom and stash arms." *The New York Times* called the whole law enforcement endeavor at Ruby Ridge a "reckless enterprise . . . It is not the job of Federal law enforcement agencies to behave in a way that seems designed to confirm their [the radical right's] paranoia — especially when there is no proof they have violated any laws."

Ruby Ridge was a series of mistakes and tragedies. *The New York Times*, from its safe distance, might blast the FBI for the sting operation that pulled in Randy Weaver. But what would the editorial board's reaction have been if its members had lived in Coeur d'Alene, Rathdrum, or Spirit Lake, Idaho, and nearby white supremacists (linked with a network that had resulted in murders, bank robberies, and counterfeiting only a few years before) were reported to be trading in illegal weapons? The *Times* might have applauded the FBI for arresting lower-level people with the same basic law enforcement strategy used to target others trading in illegal goods. The lower-level people would be encouraged to make a case against the more important criminals. White supremacists who "merely" advocate killing others on the basis of their religion or skin color should not be targeted for arrest. But if they are trading in illegal weapons, they should not be able to use the First Amendment as a shield either. Weaver's sawed-off shotguns — despite the claims of his supporters — had no legal purpose. They were gangster weapons. According to the informant to whom Weaver sold them, Weaver hoped the guns would be used by black street gangs "so they could kill each other."

Weaver should have appeared in court. And once he did not, the marshals were duty bound to bring him in. That the reconnaissance mission resulted in three deaths was an understandable, and tragic, mistake. The changing of the rules for opening fire was a fundamental error. No doubt the grief and pain law enforcement officers suffer when a comrade dies must be overwhelming. That is all the more reason for oversight to reduce the possibility that pain and anger will translate into regrettable actions.

The FBI is also to be faulted for playing fast and loose in trying to secure a conviction of Weaver after his surrender, and for dishonesty in later investigations. Unfortunately, the FBI tends to bend the rules, especially when a law enforcement officer has been killed or injured by someone whose views the Bureau deplores. When Russell Means and Dennis Banks were prosecuted in the 1970s for the American Indian Movement takeover of Wounded Knee (during which a federal law enforcement officer was wounded), the case ended in a dismissal because of government misconduct. "The waters of justice have been polluted," said the presiding judge, Fred Nichols.

The irony of the Weaver trial is that both Weaver and the FBI would have been well advised to play by the rules: Weaver to face trial, the FBI to treat this case as it would a garden-variety bank robbery. The FBI's errors, magnified artfully by Spence, gave ammunition to Weaver's supporters, white supremacists, and those who, shortly thereafter, would found the American militia movement.

With the Weaver case over in the fall of 1993, John Trochmann used a mailing list and contacts from United Citizens for Justice to start a new enterprise. As his UCJ colleague Chris Temple had heard at Pete Peters's meeting, the way to defend future Weavers and build the white supremacist movement was to form paramilitary groups. Trochmann, along with his nephew and brother, would form the Militia of Montana in February 1994. One of the first militias, it would also be one of the most active, spreading hate, conspiracy theory, and antigovernment venom. It would also become a clearinghouse for information on how to conduct war in America. In this, Trochmann and his friends would follow and build upon a long tradition.

4 Old Hatreds

THE COMMUNISTS NOW HAVE SUCH COMPLETE
CONTROL OVER THIS NATION'S NEWS MEDIA
AND THE POLITICAL PROCESSES THAT IT IS NO
LONGER POSSIBLE FOR THE AMERICAN PEOPLE
TO CHANGE THEIR GOVERNMENT'S POLICIES BY
NORMAL DEMOCRATIC PROCESSES. . . . RAID . . .
AMBUSH . . . SNIP[E] . . . SABOTAGE.

MINUTEMEN'S *Principles of Guerrilla Warfare*

The American militia movement, born in the 1990s, has deep roots
in American history. We have always had armed far-right groups with a
political agenda and a hateful ideology. The militias, although new in
many ways—they target government first, rather than minorities; they
communicate through the Internet rather than newsletters; they are a
loose network of groups, rather than an organization centrally controlled—build on that tradition. In fact, the idea at the core of the militia
movement—that government has been "taken over" by unseen interests
plotting to enslave ordinary Americans—is not original. It has its roots in
other American far-right formations over the last century and beyond. To
understand the rich ideological history upon which the militias feed, it is
important to have a general understanding of their antecedents, especially
of the ideas that drove American paramilitary groups of the 1960s and
1980s.

The most significant precursor of the militias was the Ku Klux Klan. Born in 1866, in Pulaski, Tennessee, it was formed by a group of defeated Confederate soldiers who wanted "to have fun, make mischief, and play pranks on the public." By 1868 the Klan had developed a political purpose. Its night-riding escapades terrorized blacks and northern whites who had moved south during Reconstruction. There were an estimated 550,000 Klan members in 1868. Their terrorism grew so intolerable that night riding was made a federal crime. In 1871 President Ulysses S. Grant ordered soldiers to South Carolina to stop the Klan's vigilantism.

Klan activity subsided after the military intervention. But the Klan was reborn after World War I. And it was no longer a uniquely "southern" organization. Between three million and four million Americans were Klan members during the 1920s. The KKK's intended victims were now not only blacks, but Jews and Catholics too.

The 1920s KKK boasted forty thousand ministers among its members. It had political muscle throughout the country. In Oregon, for example, its anti-Catholic agitation helped pass laws banning parochial schools. In 1924 the Klan promoted national legislation that put a firm cap on non-Anglo-Saxon-Protestant immigration. And despite its bigoted agenda, the Klan draped itself in the image of benevolence. A Georgia KKK group's 1916 corporate charter defined the organization as "a non-profit, charitable, benevolent eleemosynary [charitable] society for the promotion of True Americanism." Hatred of others, of course, has always been justified as love of self. Ask David Duke why he hates blacks, and he'll say he doesn't, he loves whites. Ask Nation of Islam leader Louis Farrakhan why he hates whites and he'll claim he doesn't, he just loves blacks. Ask a militiaman today why he hates government, and he'll tell you it's because he is a patriot who loves the Constitution.

By the end of the 1920s—after unions, veterans' groups, and others denounced the Klan, and after media exposés appeared—KKK membership shrank to 40,000. By the 1950s it had dwindled to 10,000. But by 1967, membership jumped to 55,000: The civil rights revolution had begun, and the Klan was organizing to fight it.

For years the KKK terrorized Freedom Riders and other civil rights workers. It burned and bombed houses and churches and synagogues. The Klan acted with relative impunity. Its torchlight ceremonies and cross-burnings, attended by men camouflaged in robes and hoods, gave it a powerful image. Under those hoods might be lawyers, policemen, judges—anyone. Through nighttime terror and daytime knowing winks, the Klan deeply affected government and the media in the South. For sympathy and political cover, it counted on white southerners who shared its hatred of blacks and integration.

The Klan's reign of terror began to collapse when three civil rights workers, two Jewish and one black, were murdered. James Chaney, Andrew Goodman, and Michael Schwerner had disappeared. A huge federal manhunt ensued, watched on television across the country. The young men were found buried in an earthen dam, having been executed by Klansmen. As in Oklahoma City three decades later, deaths were needed to bring a malicious ideology to light. The only difference was that after the Klan committed these murders, its movement slowed. The militias—which drew a larger segment of the American people by organizing around more mainstream issues such as gun control—grew in the aftermath of the Oklahoma City bombing.

✗ ✗ ✗

The 1990s militia member is not necessarily the same as the robed and hooded KKKer of the 1920s or the 1960s. But there are important similarities in both aspirations and association. The Klan developed as a political organization that sought to preserve the status quo through terror and an ideology of hate. Historians tend to focus on the armed confrontations, the bombings (such as that of a Birmingham church, in which four young girls died), the lynchings, and the KKK leaders' personalities. But the Klan's most significant impact may have been its intimidating role in day-to-day life. Whether in the 1860s or the 1960s, it counted on a shared perception that "outsiders" were trying to change "the way things were," leaving local folk with little control over their lives. By encouraging that shared perception of the white populace, and by scapegoating groups that seemed to threaten "the way things were," the Klan became an alternative social structure that gave many people a feeling of power.

Many of the people who join militias see themselves as Klan members did in the 1960s. They do not define themselves as belonging to hate groups, but as citizens trying to reclaim and preserve a way of life under attack. They count on their neighbors' shared concerns about gun control or the environment or abortion: about outside forces such as government and hidden power groups trying to change the way *they* live. And, like the Klan of the 1960s, they want to intimidate their perceived opponents in order to gain a feeling of political strength and perhaps real political power as well. But as much as their political tactics resemble Klan thuggery, the history of hate and conspiracy from which today's militias have grown is much broader.

Go to a militia meeting and pick up the literature. There are charts of "The Conspiracy to Rule the World," showing the House of Rothschild connected to the Illuminati, the Illuminati connected to London's Hellfire Club, the Hellfire Club connected to Oxford, Oxford to the Bilderbergers, the Bilderbergers to the Federal Reserve, the Federal Reserve to the United Nations. (With over seventy well known and obscure American and British groups represented, you can connect the lines and follow the supposed links between the Socialist Workers Party, the Rand Corporation, the "House of Rockefeller," the Mafia, and the New School for Social Research.) You may also find literature from the Liberty Lobby, the Populist Party, the Christian Patriots, the Posse Comitatus, Christian Identity groups, Bo Gritz, the John Birch Society, and the Ku Klux Klan. This rich compost of conspiracy theory and hate has fermented on the fringes of America for decades. The ideas found in all these right-wing groups have not faded away. They have been reborn as part of the militia movement. This time around, the ideas are more dangerous, for their proponents are heavily armed.

✗ ✗ ✗

Less than a month after the Oklahoma City bombing, a long treatise was posted on the Internet, entitled "Concerning the Oklahoma Bombing: Solving the 'Who Done It' Mystery!!!" Written by Pastor Peter J. Peters, it asked, "Who Has a Record for Killing Innocent Men, Women and Children?" Peters listed Janet Reno, U.S. marshals, FBI, ATF, "governments," "certain ethnic groups," the Israeli Mossad, President Clinton, and others. "Most often," he wrote, "when there is a major crime committed on the scale of the Oklahoma City bombing, there are many involved from the insider to the getaway car driver, to the one who misdirects the posse by saying he went thatta way when in reality, he went the other way. Could this be the role of the media?"

Peters believed so. And who, according to Peters, controlled the media for the benefit of the New World Order? "Up until late," Peters wrote, "the Antichrist forces have had a monopoly on the media." What proof did he cite? "The second Protocol of a document identified by some at the turn of the century as a basic blueprint for the creation of a one world government. The document is known as the *Protocols of the Elders of Zion*."

The strain of conspiracy theory that Peters and many in the militia movement believe can be traced to automaker Henry Ford. In 1920 Ford was given a copy of the *Protocols of the Elders of Zion*. The *Protocols* were a Czarist forgery based on a nineteenth-century novel about politics and Napoleon. Napoleon was removed, and Jews were substituted as a group whose "elders" met secretly to control the world. The *Protocols* served as fuel for European pogroms. Ford believed the forgery, and his *Dearborn Independent* newspaper started a mainstream campaign against the "international Jew." The articles, reprinted in book form, sold 500,000 copies in America in the 1920s. (Today you can buy *The International Jew*, as well as the *Protocols*, from far-right groups and some booksellers associated with the Nation of Islam and extreme Afrocentrism.)

Ford's newspaper described a conspiracy of Jews trying to control America since the days of Columbus. The *Independent* also blamed Jews for America's contemporary problems. The idea that Jews constituted a hidden hand controlling government was also popularized by others who used Ford's material and imagery, such as radio personality Father Charles Coughlin and the Reverend Gerald L. K. Smith, a minister who founded the Christian Nationalist Crusade and later the Committee of One Million. Although Ford retracted *The International Jew* in 1927, Coughlin, Smith, and others continued to use anti-Semitic conspiracy theories to decipher the world. Their anti-Semitism, and consequently their opposition to the effort to stop Hitler, became politically untenable after America entered World War II. But their ideas remained part of the far-right American landscape long after the war. The militias' claim that America has been taken over by a One World Government is not original. Smith (who gave every member of Congress a copy of the *Protocols* in 1947) claimed not only that Franklin Roosevelt was a secret Jew (and actually named Rosenfeldt), but also that his death was faked. FDR was supposedly being hidden by Jews, who would eventually anoint him as "President of the World."

Smith, who was a leader in the anti-Semitic far right from the 1930s through the 1970s, had started out a fundamentalist Christian. By the 1940s he had become a figure in the religious movement known as Christian Identity, which was to play a major role in the lives of Randy Weaver, John Trochmann, Pete Peters, and, more broadly, in America's far-right landscape. Christian Identity also had a critical influence on some of today's militia groups and the ideas they espouse.

✗ ✗ ✗

Christian Identity began as British Israelism, which traced its roots to mid-nineteenth-century claims that white Christians were the "true Israelites," that Jews were offspring of Satan, and that blacks and other minorities were "pre-Adamic," meaning that they were of another subhuman species created before Adam and Eve. In *Blood in the Face*, his study of American far-right groups, James Ridgeway pointed to the obvious conclusion from this theological premise:

> In his wisdom, they say, God fashioned the subhuman nonwhites and sent them to live outside the Garden of Eden before the Fall. When Eve broke God's original commandment, she was implanted with two seeds. From Adam's seed sprang Abel and the white race. From the serpent Satan's seed

came the lazy, wicked Cain. Angered, God cast Adam, Eve, and the serpent out of the Garden of Eden and decreed eternal racial conflict. Cain killed Abel, then ran off into the jungle to join pre-Adamic nonwhites. It's almost too neatly done: Identity theology provides both a religious base for racism and anti-Semitism, and an ideological rationale for violence against minorities and their white allies.

Gerald Smith wrote that "the great covenant that God made with Abraham has been fulfilled not in the profane blasphemies of those who dishonestly call themselves 'God's Chosen People,' " but in white Christians. If the covenant with Jews is a fraud, then of course the idea of Israel as the "promised land" is bogus. America, home of white Christians who are the lost Israelites, becomes the "promised land."

The notion that America is a divinely inspired country belonging only to white Christians is an important foundational idea to many people on the extremes of the militia movement; even if they do not share the premise, they may share the "logical" conclusions. As we will see, Terry and James Nichols's attempts to declare themselves "sovereign citizens" and Timothy McVeigh's racist views were not self-generating, but part of this far-right tradition.

Smith died in 1976. The people who espoused his ideas in the 1930s and later define a large part of the far-right landscape we—and the militia movement—inherit. An associate of Smith's, Wesley Swift, ran the Church of Jesus Christ Christian, an Identity group that moved to Hayden Lake, Idaho, in the 1970s under the leadership of Richard Butler. In Idaho, the "church" would become better known by its other name, the Aryan Nations, and attract people such as Randy Weaver and John Trochmann. It also produced the Order.

Before the Order, however, there was another armed far-right paramilitary group that sought to terrorize America: the Minutemen. Their history and structure were also an important model for many of today's militias.

✗ ✗ ✗

The Minutemen were a 1960s private army that took the philosophy of the John Birch Society one step further: They fought communism through guerrilla warfare. The Minutemen attracted not only people on the fringes of the Birch Society, but also people associated with Christian Identity, such as Wesley Swift and the Reverend William Potter Gale. Gale is best remembered for statements such as "You got your nigger Jews, you got your Asiatic Jews and you got your white Jews. They're all Jews and they're all offspring of the Devil. . . . Turn a nigger inside out and you've got a Jew."

The Minutemen first set up "guerrilla units" with ten to twenty-five members, then advocated smaller, underground "resistance networks . . . between five and fifteen [strong]," so that the discovery of one "unit" would not compromise the whole. Their *Principles of Guerrilla Warfare* rested on the assumption that "the communists now have such complete control over this nation's news media and the political processes that it is no longer possible for the American people to change their government's policies by normal democratic processes." Plans told how to "raid . . . ambush . . . snip[e] . . . sabotage." Any doubt about the need for guerrilla warfare was, of course, the result of "enemy propaganda." "Each member of the underground movement must be rendered immune to the enemy's propaganda," said General Rule Number 4, "by continuous counter-propaganda." Rule 26 instructed, "Most commonly any captured enemy must be shot."

Other Minutemen publications, dedicated to "the survival of a Christian America [i]n the name of our Lord, Jesus Christ," had instructions and diagrams for making many of the tools promoted in today's militia-linked literature: garrotes, explosives, Molotov cocktails, Molotov-cocktail launchers, torpedoes, booby traps, plastic bombs, hand grenades, time bombs, doorknob bombs, road-trap bombs, walk-trap bombs, incendiary pencils, pressure-trigger bombs, pull-trigger bombs, sabotage cigars, mines to blow up roads, to blow up cars, to blow up trucks, to blow up bridges, to blow up railways and railroad trestles, to blow up tanks. Minutemen also developed chemical and biological weapons. "They're portable, inexpensive to manufacture, and easy to conceal," said chemist and Minuteman leader Robert DePugh. "One man with a test tube in his pocket could wipe out a whole army base."

Some of the Minutemen's guns were supplied by the U.S. government. Under a program begun in 1903 to promote American marksmanship in case of war, firearms and ammunition were loaned to clubs affiliated with the National Rifle Association (NRA). Minutemen were encouraged to join the NRA, not only to get access to the hardware but also to fight against gun registration. The Minutemen termed gun control legislation a Communist plot; when the Communists took over America, gun registration would tell them whom to disarm.

The Minutemen's newsletter, *On Target*, contained the same type of conspiracy theory as the newsletters of today's militias. In 1994, material from the Militia of Montana said that United Nations troops were poised to attack Americans. The Minutemen's November 1963 issue of *On Target* asserted:

> Most Americans do not realize that a number of United States Army Troops
> were turned over to the United Nations command to make practice seizures

of a number of American cities as far back as 1952. . . . When these facts are known, however, the possibility of our personal firearms being confiscated by the end of 1965 seems less fantastic. The actual procedure discussed . . . calls for the United States to be divided up into areas of approximately five states each. . . . Each of these areas is to be sealed off with troops and systematically searched until all possible arms (supposedly) are found and confiscated.

On November 18, 1968, a small rocket was fired across the street from Houston's downtown federal building. It exploded at an altitude of approximately one hundred feet, releasing a "payload" of Minutemen literature. Other similar rockets were fired in Kansas City and Washington, D.C. The Washington rocket, aimed at the White House, misfired.

The Minutemen, like many of today's militias, took pride in their ability to stockpile weapons. Over the years Minutemen were arrested with thousands of dollars in cash and with submachine guns, aerial bombs, dynamite, fuses, grenades, grenade launchers, booby traps, bazookas, automatic weapons, cannons, flamethrowers, rocket launchers, machine guns, land mines, 80mm mortars with shells, automatic pistols, antitank guns, Molotov cocktails, gas masks, and huge quantities—well over a million rounds—of ammunition. When firearms were found by police, so was hate literature, including the *Protocols of the Elders of Zion*.

Minutemen planned to kill "Communists and one-worlders." They admitted that they had a list of twenty-five to thirty people whom they "considered assassinating." One target was a reporter who covered the United Nations for the *St. Louis Post-Dispatch*. Another was Senator William Fulbright, as part of an effort to terrorize members of Congress who were not "voting American." (Three decades later, a militia leader would advocate arresting Congress as a body and trying its members for treason.) Minutemen considered introducing cyanide into the United Nations through its air-conditioning system. They also planned to rob banks and blow up police stations, power stations, and the Redmond, Washington, city hall.

After their leader, Robert DePugh, was convicted and jailed in September 1970, the group slowly disintegrated. But it remained a model to many who dreamed of far-right paramilitary resistance. DePugh, on the other hand, was released from jail in 1973, and tried to reestablish himself in the far right first through the Liberty Lobby, then through other organizations. He failed. In 1992, when he was sixty-eight, he was convicted of sexually exploiting a minor; the case involved pornographic photographs of young girls. He was also convicted of weapons charges: While searching for evidence of DePugh's pornographic activities, authorities found a rusted arsenal, including a mortar.

✗ ✗ ✗

Identity religion also played a large part in the most recent precursor of the militias: the Posse Comitatus, an armed right-wing group founded in Portland, Oregon, in 1969, that was especially active in the early to mid-1980s. "Yahweh our father is at work setting the stage for the final act against the Christ-murdering Jews and their father, Satan," said Posse "National Director of Counter-Insurgency" and Christian Identity member James Wickstrom in 1985. A publication called *Christian Posse Comitatus Newsletter*, while noting that "America is the Zion of Bible prophecy," explained that "Our nation is now completely under the control of the International Invisible government of the World Jewry. Our United States Constitution, our Bill of Rights and our Christian Law has [*sic*] been trampled beneath the mire and filth of the International Money Barons of high finance who now control the government of these United States."

Posse members believed—as do many of today's militia members—that all government above the county level is illegitimate. ("Posse Comitatus" is Latin for "Power of the County.") The sheriff is seen as the highest legitimate authority. "The Supreme Court," Posse literature said, "is NOT the highest court in the land. The sovereign is of course, the highest authority as to the interpretation of the law or as to questions concerning its enforcement. Posse Comitatus then is a collection of sovereign citizens lawfully assembled to exercise that sovereignty."

What was the Posse's view of law enforcement agents who might disagree with its notions? "Any person interfering with a lawfully empaneled Posse is an obstruction of the Common Law of this country and should be considered a domestic enemy of the United States . . . this includes IRS, FBI, CIA or other usurpers of common law. Such interference constitutes an act of war and is treason under authority of the Constitution itself."

Posse actions and beliefs sound much like those of today's militias. "Posse people don't want gun control," wrote Susan Sward of the Associated Press in 1976. "Some refuse to pay state or federal taxes. They think government is gobbling up their freedoms. And some don't like Jews or blacks. . . . [Henry] Beach, the Posse's founder [who, incidentally, was a member of the pro-Hitler "Silver Shirts" in the United States of the 1930s] has predicted the day will come when people get 'so sick and tired' of government officials that they'll stage a rebellion in the country."

In the 1970s and early 1980s Posse members sent death threats to a U.S.

senator and many local officials, spread rumors that Soviet tanks and MIGs were mobilizing on the Canadian side of the United States' northern border, attempted to arrest law enforcement personnel, spoke of the need to "lynch . . . uncooperative public officials if they refuse to follow" Posse legal interpretations, claimed that a United Nations Advisory Committee on Inter-Governmental Relations controlled federal elected officials, said that the Federal Emergency Management Agency "is really a Gestapo-type organization," and stockpiled weapons. "The Posse has the capability to arm an army," said James Wickstrom. A 1981 raid in Wisconsin produced a cache of explosives and a network of bunkers and tunnels.

Posse members were urged "to erect a scaffold. Build it with the trap door and the hangman's noose of rope so that it is in readiness if needed." What could the need be? A handbook explained what to do with government officials who commit "unconstitutional" acts: "He shall be removed by the Posse . . . and at high noon be hung by the neck, the body remaining until sundown as an example to those who would subvert the law."

Like today's militia literature, Posse publications tried to appropriate the imagery of the American Revolution. "The United States of America was founded as a protest against taxation," said a pamphlet claiming that the "Internal Revenue Code is completely in violation of the Constitution."

As the *Chicago Tribune* explained,

> The theoretical underpinnings of this argument are based on English common law and tortured interpretations of the U.S. Constitution and American legal history. Mastering the details of the theory requires considerable study but understanding its implications almost none: State and federal officers are usurpers; the only real money is silver or gold; the Federal Reserve Bank is unlawful; and bank debts are just pieces of paper. . . . The Posse says taxation is theft. A citizen has a constitutional right to arm himself and defend his property from thieves, such as Internal Revenue Service agents.

A Posse publication from the 1970s sported a map of the United States on the cover, and made wild conspiratorial claims of evil government intentions, just as much of today's militia literature does. The Posse version showed the country divided into twenty-two river basins. "This," said the bold caption, "is the internal capture of the U.S. The proposed Potomac River Basin Compact—a new government of America, operated by citizens from another country—by 1975! The Master Land Plan of America—already in place, whose hidden effect is CONCENTRATION

CAMPS behind BARRIERS." The accompanying text explained the supposed concentration camp plan under subsections with headings such as "Citizens from Another Country to Govern America"; "Compact-Constitution is Superior to U.S. Constitution"; "Commission Supreme over U.S. President, Armed Forces, Treasury, etc."; "All American Lands and Property Given to the Potomac Commission"; "Mayor of Washington, D.C., Wil [sic] be Supreme Commissioner of Potomac and America"; "America Renamed—and a Colony of Another Country"; "Bill of Rights Eliminated"; and "Commission has the Right to Kill." (Apparently as filler, the Posse publication also printed articles on other subjects, including "Scientists Say Negro Still in Ape Stage" and "Jewish Ritual Murder." Not surprisingly, David Duke, who was then national director of the Knights of the Ku Klux Klan, said, "We work with the Posses wherever we can. . . . We get their material and funnel it to our groups.")

But the Posse did more than pass out literature. Like many of today's militia groups, it practiced for war. One of the leaders of Christian Identity, the Reverend William Potter Gale, joined with James Wickstrom, leader of the Posse, to cosponsor a string of "counterinsurgency seminars" in the early 1980s. In Kansas, the attorney general's office reported that people were trained as "killer teams in hand-to-hand combat techniques, the administration of poisons, night combat patrol and murder by ambush." At least one bomb-making seminar was also held.

Gordon Kahl of North Dakota was a member of the Posse Comitatus. He was also a tax protester, wore a miniature hangman's noose on his lapel, and had been convicted of tax evasion in 1977. Sentenced to one year in jail and five years' probation, upon release from prison he ignored his probation—and his taxes.

The authorities did not move to arrest him right away. As in the Randy Weaver case a decade later, they had to balance the physical risks of an arrest against the danger to law and order that waiting posed: People would know that the authorities would back off if threatened. On February 13, 1983, federal authorities decided to arrest Kahl. They set up a roadblock on a hill. Kahl's car was blocked. Armed, he and his son and another passenger got out of their vehicle. Kahl and the authorities faced each other and waited. Then someone fired a shot. Soon Kahl's son, Yorie, had been shot in the stomach. (Tests later showed that his gun had been fired.) Gordon Kahl, holding a Mini-14, shot and killed Deputy U.S. Marshal Robert Cheshire. In a matter of minutes Deputy U.S. Marshal Kenneth Muir also lay dead, and two other officers were wounded. Kahl spoke to the wounded officers, then drove his son to a doctor. Then he disappeared.

On June 3, 1983, Kahl was found hiding in a house in the Ozarks. Discovered, he shot a county sheriff—once, in the head. He was then killed in a blaze of gunfire. The house burned, his body in it. Kahl became a martyr to the far right. Two hundred came to his funeral to hear him praised as a patriot—as someone who went to church while holding a gun. That he violated the law and killed federal agents was not important to those who saw in him a symbol—much as today's militia groups tend to distort the facts of the Randy Weaver and Waco sieges.

As we shall see with the 1990s militias, the Posse of the 1980s also had some success organizing farmers and others who were having either economic hard times or difficulty coping with a changing world. Jim McCarthy, an expert on cults, said at the time:

> The Posse goes out to people who are under attack, who see their entire way of life disappearing while they stand by helplessly. . . . A man who is about to lose his farm is going to feel rage, fury. He wants to do something. Posse gives him a course of action and its ideology, which is basically a fascist ideology, gives him the justification. . . . [T]he Posse . . . offers its adherents support, solidarity, the comfort of like-minded people, and the chance to do something about what they perceive is ruining their lives.

The people attracted to the Posse, McCarthy said, were those "looking for some answer, a way to get some measure of control over their lives. Then the Posse comes along and says, 'Here's what you can do.' And [the Christian Identity] church comes along and says, 'Here's why God wants you to do it.' The ideologies might appear to be complicated but they actually explain things in very simple terms: It's the Jews, it's the Communists, it's the government. Get rid of them."

✗ ✗ ✗

By the mid-1980s, the Posse was not the only armed right-wing group in America. Another, organized more clandestinely, was an offshoot of the Aryan Nations called the Order. It had its origins in the very same book to which Timothy McVeigh would turn, leading him to Oklahoma City.

The Order was a terrorist group based on the book *The Turner Diaries*. Written in 1978 by William Pierce, and obsessed over in the late 1980s by Timothy McVeigh, it asked, "What will you do when they come to take your guns?" The answer is one you might expect from Pierce, the leader of a neo-Nazi group called the National Alliance: wage war to overthrow the U.S. government, kill Jews and other minorities, and remake America into an all-white fascist society. Revolution was to be achieved by guerrilla warfare, including robberies, bombings, and other terrorist acts. One scene was eerily suggestive of the Oklahoma bombing:

> *October 13, 1991.* At 9:15 yesterday morning our bomb went off in the FBI's national headquarters building. Our worries about the relatively small size of the bomb were unfounded; the damage is immense.
>
> My day's work started a little before five o'clock yesterday, when I began helping Ed Sanders mix heating oil with the ammonium nitrate fertilizer in Unit 8's garage. We stood the 100-pound bags on end one by one and poked a small hole in the top with a screwdriver, just big enough to insert the end of a funnel. While I held the bag and the funnel, Ed poured in a gallon of oil. . . . It took us nearly three hours to do all 44 sacks. . . .
>
> Meanwhile, George and Henry were out stealing a truck. With only two-and-a-half tons of explosives we didn't need a big tractor-trailer rig, so we decided to grab a delivery truck. . . . George and I headed for the FBI building in the car, with Henry following in the truck. . . . As we drove by the building . . . we saw no one in sight. We signalled Henry and kept going for another seven or eight blocks, until we found a good spot to park. Then we began walking back slowly, keeping an eye on our watches.
>
> We were still two blocks away when the pavement shuddered violently under our feet. An instant later the blast hit us—a deafening 'ka-whoomp,' followed by an enormous roaring, crashing sound, accentuated by the high-pitched noise of shattering glass all around us.
>
> The plate glass windows in the store beside us and dozens of others that we could see along the street were blown to splinters. A glittering and deadly rain of glass shards continued to fall into the street from the upper stories of nearby buildings for a few seconds, as a jet-black column of smoke shot straight up into the sky ahead of us. . . .
>
> We ran the final two blocks. . . . The scene . . . was one of utter devastation. The whole . . . wing of the building . . . had collapsed. . . . A huge, gaping hole yawned in the courtyard pavement just beyond the rubble of collapsed masonry.

Robert Mathews—a longtime anti-Semite and white supremacist who had been associated over the years with the John Birch Society, the National Alliance, and the Aryan Nations—was the leader of the Order. It started slowly, with eight members. Mathews thought his organization could be funded legitimately. He bid on what he hoped would be a lucrative trail-clearing contract with the Forest Service. But he didn't anticipate his dislike for arduous labor, nor the practical problems snow created. Armed robbery seemed an easier way to make money. Three members of the group held up a Spokane pornography store in April 1983. They netted $369.

In July 1983, a meeting of leading neo-Nazis and white supremacists was held at the Aryan Nations compound in Hayden Lake, Idaho. The death of Gordon Kahl the month before "was the catalyst that made everyone come forth and change the organizations from thinkers to doers," said James D. Ellison, who attended the conclave. The Order became emboldened after that summer. It gave up petty robbery, thinking that it could better finance its operation by manufacturing fifty-dollar bills. But the Aryan Nations printing presses could not make a good enough counterfeit. On December 3, 1983, Order member Bruce Pierce was arrested in Union Gap, Washington, when he tried to pass a phony fifty. After posting bond he disappeared.

Robert Mathews figured out how to get realistic-looking money by an alternative method. That same month he went into a Seattle bank, passed a threatening note to a teller, and departed $25,900 richer. On March 16, 1984, Order members robbed an armored vehicle in Seattle of $43,345. On April 23, 1984, Order members robbed another armored truck in Seattle, getting $230,379. And on July 19, 1984, Order members robbed an armored truck in Ukiah, California. Their take this time was $3.8 million. According to the Southern Poverty Law Center, the money was "allegedly distributed to white supremacists across the country including Glenn Miller [leader of the White Patriot Party] in North Carolina, [White Aryan Resistance leader] Tom Metzger in California and William Pierce of the National Alliance in West Virginia." According to other sources, funds from an earlier haul were also given to Richard Butler's Aryan Nations. No doubt some of this money is still being used by these groups.

Financing their revolution was only part of the Order's agenda; the other part was carrying it out, specifically against "enemies." One whom they hated with a passion was Alan Berg, a cocky Jewish radio talk-show host in Denver who had given Order members airtime, only to criticize and ridicule them. After Berg finished his June 18, 1984, program, he drove home. Order members followed. They killed him in a barrage of machine-gun fire.

In 1984 Order members continued to pass counterfeit money, planned additional armored car and bank robberies, bombed a Boise synagogue, and killed one of their own members in whom they had lost trust. In October, they shot it out with FBI agents in Sandpoint, Idaho. By November, the FBI had a plan to infiltrate the group. In June the Secret Service had arrested Tom Martinez in Philadelphia. Martinez, who had been a member of the Klan and the National Alliance, was apprehended when he tried to use counterfeit bills given to him by Order member David Lane. Martinez agreed to become an informant. He flew to Portland, Oregon, on November 23, 1984, to meet Mathews and join the Order, which was then planning to kill the number two man on its list: attorney Morris Dees, head of the Southern Poverty Law Center.

On November 24, 1984, Martinez slipped away from the Portland motel in which he, Mathews, and another Order member, Gary Yarborough, had been staying. The FBI raided the motel room. A shoot-out ensued. Yarborough was taken into custody. Mathews escaped. Three days later, on November 27, 1984, members of the Order signed an official "Declaration of War" against the government of the United States. On December 8, 1994, Robert Mathews died in a shoot-out with the FBI on Whidbey Island in Puget Sound.

All Order activity did not end with the death of the group's leader. For example, David Tate killed a state trooper in Missouri on April 15, 1985. And in 1985 the government charged twenty-four members of the Order with sixty-seven counts of racketeering predicated on conspiracies to commit robbery, counterfeiting, and murder. Twenty-three were convicted — thirteen as a result of guilty pleas, ten at trial.

✗ ✗ ✗

There were other far-right paramilitary formations in the 1980s, too, some with direct links to today's militia groups and to the Murrah Building in Oklahoma City. In Texas, Florida, and North Carolina the Klan had established private armies. Some Klan groups even studied how to conduct guerrilla warfare, including, the Anti-Defamation League said, how to create "chaos in certain selected cities, through the disruption of water supplies, electricity and telephone lines to divert law enforcement authorities while assassinations were being carried out." The most significant of these Klan groups was the Texas Emergency Reserve, led by Louis Beam. It was important not only because of its bold actions, including a harassment campaign against Vietnamese fishermen, but also because Beam would become an instrumental theorist of the 1990s militia movement, authoring the key organizing principle of Leaderless Resistance. Coincidentally or otherwise, that principle was used by the bombers of the Murrah Building.

Suits brought by the Southern Poverty Law Center and passage of state anti-paramilitary-training statutes curtailed these 1980s paramilitary units. On April 24, 1987, a Fort Smith, Arkansas, grand jury indicted fourteen leaders of the white supremacist movement. Ten, including Richard Butler and Louis Beam (by then of the Aryan Nations), and Robert Miles (an Identity leader and former KKK member), were charged with "seditious conspiracy"—that is, plotting to overthrow the government of the United States by force. Five were also charged with a specific conspiracy to assassinate an Arkansas federal judge.

All of the defendants were acquitted, but not all walked out of the courtroom free. Richard Wayne Snell, previously convicted of killing a black state trooper and a pawnbroker whom he mistakenly thought was Jewish, had been sentenced to death.

James Ellison, who had attended the July 1983 Hayden Lake meeting, led an Arkansas anti-Semitic paramilitary group known as the Covenant, the Sword and the Arm of the Lord, which firebombed an Indiana synagogue, burned a Missouri church, and tried to bomb a pipeline that supplied Chicago with natural gas. Ellison testified against Snell and others in the sedition trial. He told prosecutors that he became involved with the Aryan Nations at the July 1983 meeting. He also said that in October of that year people associated with the Aryan Nations hatched a plan to park a large vehicle in front of the Oklahoma City federal building and bomb it with rockets detonated by a timing device. Ellison had even cased the building at Snell's suggestion.

The bombing was not carried out. Nor were some other planned CSA actions, such as the use of cyanide to poison an unspecified city's water supply. Ellison entered the federal witness protection program, while continuing to serve a prior sentence for racketeering.

In March of 1995, Ellison would be nearing the end of his parole, scheduled for April. Snell, on the other hand, would be anxiously awaiting his execution. Like Gordon Kahl and Robert Mathews, who had become martyrs in the view of the white supremacist movement, Snell could count on the movement's support.

The March 1995 issue of the Militia of Montana's publication, *Taking Aim*, beseeched its readers to write to Arkansas's governor, demanding that Snell be spared execution, which was set for April 19. "If this date does not ring a bell for you then maybe this will jog your memory," the newsletter read. "1. April 19, 1775; Lexington burned; 2. April 19, 1943; Warsaw burned; 3. April 19, 1992; The feds attempted to raid Randy Weaver, but had their plans thwarted when concerned citizens arrived on the scene with supplies for the Weaver family totally unaware of what was to take place; 4. April 19, 1993; The Branch Davidians burned; 5. April 19, 1995; Richard Snell will be executed—unless we act now!!!"

Richard Snell was executed on April 19, 1995. Shortly before he died he saw early television coverage of the bombing of the Alfred P. Murrah Federal Building. He told Governor Jim Guy Tucker: "Look over your shoulder. Justice is coming."

5 Militia Day

IF I KNEW THEN WHAT I KNOW NOW, 5,000 TO
10,000 OF US WOULD HAVE WALKED IN FRONT OF
THE [BRANCH DAVIDIANS] AND STOPPED [THE FBI
AND ATF] IF IT WOULD HAVE SAVED JUST ONE OF
THOSE CHILDREN.

KEN ADAMS of the Michigan militia

In the middle of the fifteen months between Randy Weaver's surrender and the conclusion of his trial, a remarkably similar event would take
place near Waco, Texas, in a remote flat area ironically named Mount
Carmel. It would involve firearms, unusual religious beliefs, dead federal
officials, dead children, and some of the same government officials. The
fifty-one-day standoff at the Branch Davidian compound would become
the second of the three events—along with the Weaver siege and the
passage of the Brady Bill—that catalyzed the growth of militia groups
across America.

The Branch Davidians, an offshoot of the Seventh-Day Adventists, had
been in Texas since 1935. They had a history of preaching doom. For example, Florence Houteff, the widow of founder Victor Houteff, had prophesied a "new era" to start on April 22, 1959. Nearly nine hundred people
came to Texas to wait for the end. When the end did not come, most left.

Vernon Howell joined the group in 1981. In 1990, having matured from a stuttering, insecure young man into a charismatic leader, he changed his name to David Koresh. Dean M. Kelley of the National Council of Churches explained Koresh's message:

[He] focused on the decoding of cryptic apocalyptic passages (such as the Seven Seals of the Book of Revelation) that he understood to refer to the present: the inbreaking of God's will into human history was about to occur, with a cosmic struggle between good and evil; the forces of evil would be concentrated in the present center of earthly power, the government of the United States.... The Battle of Armageddon must be waged with maximum effort by the faithful to draw down the heavenly host and bring in the City of God. To that end [Koresh] accumulated arms... possibly even beyond the generous norms of gun ownership in Texas or the needs of the gun trade.

Between March 5 and March 9, 1992—coincidentally, over the same weekend during which Bill Morlin's initial story on Randy Weaver's fugitive status appeared—local police conducted SWAT training near Mount Carmel. According to a report by the U.S. Treasury Department, "Koresh ... react[ed] by: 1) bringing back members from California and England; 2) making large purchases of weapons parts; 3) acquiring chemicals which can be used to make explosives; 4) purchasing night vision scopes and sensors; and 5) accumulating large supplies of ammunition."

Two months later, in May, the United Parcel Service shipped a box for delivery to the Branch Davidians. It fell apart, revealing inert hand grenades. The driver told the local sheriff, who told the Bureau of Alcohol, Tobacco and Firearms, which started an investigation, which found that over $40,000 of what Dean Kelley described as "guns, gun parts, gun kits, grenade hulls, black powder, chemicals, fuses and ammunition" had been shipped to the Davidians by UPS. The ATF also spoke with former members of the sect, gaining additional information that corroborated the persistent rumors of child abuse in the compound.

Armed with a search warrant for illegal firearms at Mount Carmel, and an arrest warrant for David Koresh, ATF agents planned a February 28, 1993, raid. Given the amount of weaponry the Davidians were presumed to possess, the plan called for "dynamic entry." But in small towns secrets are hard to keep. The ATF had alerted local ambulances to the possibility of injuries. The ambulance staff had, in turn, told the media that "something big" was planned. That morning reporters were in the area, waiting. One was lost and asked directions from a local postal carrier. The mailman, David Jones, was Koresh's brother-in-law. The element of surprise vanished. When told that a raid was impending, Koresh said, "Neither the ATF nor the National Guard will ever get me."

Despite learning from an informant that Koresh now knew of the raid, the ATF decided to continue, hoping that the raid could be carried out before the Davidians could prepare to resist. But the "dynamic entry" had other problems, too. Diversionary helicopters—planned to draw the Davidians' attention to one side of the compound while the "dynamic entry" began at another—were late. Radio contact with commanders had been lost, so the plans could not be altered.

Seventy armed commandos in ski masks ran toward the buildings. Koresh opened the door and said, "What do you want? There's women and children in here!" The response was "Police! Get down!" Koresh shut the door. A shoot-out ensued. Four ATF agents were killed, others wounded. Koresh and his father-in-law were wounded. A few of the Davidians were killed, too, including a woman who had, just moments before her death, been nursing her infant.

The FBI Hostage Rescue Team—the same unit that had been deployed at Ruby Ridge—was called in. For fifty-one days it tried to end the standoff. Twenty-one children and two older women left the compound during the first week. Some others would leave, too, as the days went by and life inside became increasingly difficult. Electricity was cut off. Tibetan chants, Christmas carols, the sound of rabbits being slaughtered were blasted at the Davidians to harass them and make sleep difficult. The FBI was trying psychological warfare to avoid real warfare. After fifty-one days, however, it was the Hostage Rescue Team that lost patience. They planned to approach the compound in armored vehicles, and use gas to force the residents out. Attorney General Reno approved.

On April 19, 1993, the FBI carried out its plan to end the standoff. The vehicles approached. "This is not an assault!" the FBI announced to the Davidians inside. "No one will enter the compound. Do not fire weapons!" Nonetheless, weapons were fired, and the tanks released their CS gas into the buildings.

Fire broke out in several places. The FBI called the fire department, but kept the trucks away, for fear of gunfire. A strong wind quickly transformed the compound into an inferno. More than eighty people died, including the children.

The government said the Davidians set the fire, and tapes from monitoring devices placed inside the compound backed up this claim:

"They're coming in. They're coming in," a woman yelled. "They're tearing the building down."

"Have you poured it yet?" a voice asked.

"They want the fuel," another said.

"You got the fuel already," a fourth voice said.

"I already poured it. I already poured it."

After the fire, authorities found 292 firearms—forty-eight of which were illegal machine guns—as well as live hand grenades.

✗ ✗ ✗

Indianapolis attorney Linda Thompson's fascination with Waco started before the deaths of David Koresh and his followers; during the standoff she even offered her lawyering skills to Koresh. Gary Hunt, now of the American Patriot Fax Network, was then at Waco, having been given David Koresh's power of attorney. He accepted Thompson's offer. "We decided," he said, "since we had the power of attorney, to just walk into the compound and see what the cops would do." Thompson, however, publicized the plan, alerting law enforcement. Hunt fired her and decided to forgo a trip into Mount Carmel.

Thompson then sent a fax on behalf of the "Unorganized Militia." "JOIN US!" it read. "The Unorganized Militia of the United States of America will assemble, with long arms, vehicles (including tracked and armored), aircraft, and any available gear for inspection for fitness and use in a well-regulated militia, at 9:00 a.m. on Saturday, April 3, 1993, on Northcrest Drive, off I-35." Hunt was "shocked" and sent out another fax, a "Call for Peace," discouraging anyone armed from coming near Waco.

When the siege ended, Waco took over Thompson's life—as it would, in a different way, Timothy McVeigh's. "Before I got involved in this Waco stuff," Thompson told writer Jim Redden, "I was just your average, everyday dumpy broad from the Midwest." Waco transformed her Indianapolis law office into the buzzing American Justice Federation—a nerve center for distributing propaganda on Waco, government, and the New World Order. She made and sold videos, appeared on "patriot" radio programs (including her own on shortwave) and was plugged in to the Internet through her bulletin board, called the Motherboard. Thompson's office had twenty phone lines, a full-time staff of six, and a collection of bumper stickers: "Ban Guns. Make the Streets Safe for a Government Takeover"; "Your Gun Permit: The Second Amendment"; "Remember Waco: You Are Next!"; "Support the Militia: If You Can't Join or Fight, Leave Food on the Porch"; "Fear the Government That Fears Your Guns"; "Join the Militia"; and "Dictators Love Gun Control."

Linda Thompson's videotapes about Waco—*Waco: The Big Lie* and *Waco II: The Big Lie Continues*—were clever pieces, if a bit amateurish. That homemade nature fit the message well. Here was the proof that the government did not want you to know, that ordinary Americans had uncovered.

Waco was, of course, a terrible tragedy, which the government wished had not happened. Thompson, however, believed the result was intended: The government wanted to attack ordinary citizens as part of a larger plan. To make her audience more receptive to her conspiratorial themes, Thompson highlighted the deaths of the youngsters. One videotape showed pictures of Branch Davidian children. In between photographs, a young boy put flowers on small graves. Music played in the background; the tune was that of "Puff, the Magic Dragon," but with "patriot" Carl Klang's different lyrics:

> In a church they called the Waco compound
> Back in April, '93
> Seventeen little children
> All so helpless and so small
> Died a senseless death of gas and flames
> How many names can you recall? . . .

Waco: The Big Lie was slightly more than a half-hour long. It became a cult film to the far right and was shown at countless militia meetings, as well as on the public access stations of many cable companies. *The Village Voice* described the tape as a "motivational wonder," and so it was. Using footage of the Waco incident, it described, for example, how the government tank that sprayed gas into a Branch Davidian building spewed flames instead, intentionally starting the fire that engulfed the compound. Not shown, of course, was the full footage. This revealed that what appeared to be, as Thompson asserted, flames coming out of a tank was actually reflective material that fell on the tank as it pulled away from the building.

The Department of Justice's report on Waco included a refutation of Thompson's claims. Determined to have the last word, she made *Waco II: The Big Lie Continues*. It, too, was a model of conspiratorial "logic" designed to grab audiences who, if they accepted the premises and did not question the sleight-of-hand, easily could have been convinced.

The sequel showed close-ups of a government memorandum that, in passing, referred to the religious nature of the compound. Thompson made it sound as if this were a secret admission that the federal government had embarked on a program, a random one perhaps, to attack churches with machine guns and helicopters.

Any trial lawyer—or mystery-novel reader, for that matter—watching the Thompson film would criticize her for the illogical leaps she made, all in a stone-cold voice of certainty overdubbing film clips that did not show themselves to be what she claimed they were. Thompson offered a conspiratorial explanation for almost everything that happened at Waco. She claimed, for example, that some news footage she included from the first day of the siege was intentionally edited: At a certain point, the camera stopped. Maybe the footage was edited; but Thompson's statement takes no account of a voice, clearly audible on the tape, saying "Get me another tape, then." Perhaps the camera was stopped while the news crew changed tapes? Such commonplace, innocent explanations for things escaped Thompson. If the government was so evil and powerful as to alter a news crew's raw footage, couldn't it at least produce a seamless edit?

To make its conspiratorial premise seem stronger, the sequel noted that three of the four ATF agents who died in the initial approach to the compound had been bodyguards for presidential candidate Bill Clinton. "Three [of the agents] had virtually identical wounds," Linda Thompson said, "a shot to the left temple that exited through the rear of the head, professional execution style. . . . It would appear that someone in the government wanted to be certain these men were real dead." Her voice was so certain, you could imagine audiences pondering the idea as the next conspiratorial premise rolled across the screen. Thompson left no time for her audience to wonder: If someone wanted to get rid of three ATF agents, wouldn't there have been easier ways than assaulting an armed compound?

As in most of the conspiracy theories that saturated the militia movement, real events were transformed into something closely akin to the religious views of David Koresh. Everything that happened was part of a battle of good versus evil, evil embodied in the United States government.

✗ ✗ ✗

Waco galvanized the militia movement. The white supremacists "were ready to seize it as an opportunity," wrote researcher Paul deArmond. "The tragic outcome, with its overtones of the abuse of state power, played perfectly into the hands of the fledgling terror network." The images that the white supremacists hoped to seize upon from the Weaver case were now broadcast across America. Whereas Weaver, in his mountaintop cabin in remote Idaho, was the focus of a few news stories posted from a roadblock in the woods, Waco was made for television journalism and for videos such as those Thompson would produce. The assault. The compound. The armored vehicles. Waco was much like the 1970s American Indian Movement takeover of Wounded Knee in its ability to offer gripping visual images, evoking the tension of not knowing the end. When that long-awaited end was an inferno that killed children, Americans witnessed the gruesome scene on television and on front pages across the nation. The episode not only emboldened those who formed the militia movement a few months later but also allowed militia organizers to refer to an event most Americans understood, remembered, and were repulsed by.

"Waco awakened the whole [movement]," said Tom Lane, a sixty-six-year-old Korean War veteran and member of a Florida militia. "That put the fear of God into us." Longtime anti-Semite Eustace Mullins wrote: "The Waco Church Holocaust, in which many worshipers, including innocent children, were burned alive while worshiping in their church [was] an atrocity which surpasses the worst accusations made against the Nazis in Germany." The Florida State Militia's handbook stated: "We have had enough—enough Waco-style assaults on Americans." A member of an Arizona militia said, "I understand why [the original Minutemen] were willing to stand and face portions of the greatest military force in the world. And I understand why David Koresh and the other brave defenders of Mount Carmel [stood] fearlessly defending their home and mine."

For many who would become associated with the militia movement, the federal assault on the Branch Davidians became the ideological equivalent of Pearl Harbor—or at least, in the words of one commentator, the Boston Massacre, with the ATF in the role of the Redcoats. In fact, April 19 would become a day of religious significance to the militia movement. Some called April 19 Militia Day. On the one-year anniversary of the end of the Branch Davidian siege, Jon Roland started his Texas Constitutional Militia. He gave a "muster call" for militia members to head to Waco.

Others were preoccupied with Waco, too. According to an FBI affidavit, Terry and James Nichols were incensed over it. James Nichols reportedly "made comments stating that judges and President Clinton should be killed and that he blamed the FBI and [the Bureau of Alcohol, Tobacco and Firearms] for killing the Branch Davidians at Waco." Literature about Waco was found in the search of Terry Nichols's home.

Timothy McVeigh, who had reportedly visited the Branch Davidian compound during the siege, also become fixated on Waco. He talked about it incessantly. He went to a militia meeting in Florida because, he had heard, some of the surviving Branch Davidians would speak there. He put April 19 as both a date of birth and a date of issue on the phony driver's license he used to rent the truck that would take explosives to the Oklahoma City building, where some of the federal officials involved in Waco worked. After McVeigh was arrested, a search of his car revealed documents about Waco. One of his favorite videos was reportedly *Waco: The Big Lie.*

PART TWO **Montana and Michigan**

6 MOM

THE CONCERN OF THE PATRIOTS [IS] THE LOSS
OF THE CONSTITUTION OF THE UNITED STATES.
. . . WE DO NOT TARGET THE GOVERNMENT. WE
TARGET UNCONSTITUTIONAL PIGS THAT MAY BE
IN OUR GOVERNMENT.

ROBERT FLETCHER, Militia of Montana

Noxon, Montana—headquarters of the Militia of Montana, affectionately known as MOM—is home to 350 people, a store, a restaurant, and two bars. The Clark Fork, good fishing water, runs nearby. A one-lane bridge provides the only access to the town. Mountains rise in the distance. In early 1995 MOM spokesman Bob Fletcher boasted that, from Noxon, he could send information to a half-million supporters around the country in half an hour. From Noxon MOM claimed to send out two hundred "militia formation" packets per week to people across America.

John Trochmann, who would become Noxon's most famous resident, wore a full beard and had glaring eyes. He looked like a cross between a cowboy and a prophet. He led the antigovernment Militia of Montana from his property, which, ironically, was close to Government Mountain. The Trochmann compound, as the neighbors called it, was guarded around the clock. Trochmann claimed his militia members slept with shortwave radios. "We're prepared for war with the federal government," he said. "We also have several camps in the mountains where we can go."

Trochmann knew Randy Weaver from the Aryan Nations; his family helped supply Weaver while he was a fugitive, and came to his defense at the Ruby Ridge roadblock. When Weaver surrendered, Trochmann founded the United Citizens for Justice, a support group. But Trochmann said he would never end up trapped like Randy Weaver. Instead, he would have an escape plan; he wouldn't remain in his house, as Weaver had. He also knew better than to bury his "best" weapons, since he might need them immediately. "The .50-caliber guns," he explained to *Esquire* reporter Daniel Voll, "will down helicopters. And .50-caliber armor-piercing ammunition will stop an armored personnel carrier." Asked if he had weapons larger than .50 caliber, he answered, "If I say yes to that, we go to prison."

What would happen in a Weaver-type confrontation? "Next time, we'll throw up fifteen hundred militia on a moment's notice in a circle of protection," Trochmann said. "And if there's shooting it will be the shot heard 'round the world."

Trochmann's obsession with Randy Weaver was common in the culture of those who would join private armies to fight the American government. Many in the militia movement were drawn to images of the Weaver and Waco standoffs with an intensity that had no rational relation to the events. It was almost as if they wanted to fight those battles anew, personally, either as a test of their commitment to the cause, or as a validation of their strength. They wanted the government to acknowledge *them* as a worthy threat. Of such ambitions martyrs are made. Trochmann has serious martyr potential.

✗ ✗ ✗

John Trochmann and his MOM co-founders David Trochmann (his brother) and Randy Trochmann (his nephew) have extensive white supremacist histories. Just ask the people of Noxon.

Mona Vanek, a Noxonian who has written three histories of the town, was a longtime square-dance partner of John Trochmann's. She remembered that when he moved into the area in the mid-1980s, he would try to get acquaintances to adopt his views on government and people. John and David, she recalled, went to a taxpayer meeting convened because people were concerned about their property taxes. The Trochmanns advised residents to "refuse to pay. . . . Those government people taxed you at a meeting where you didn't get to vote. That's illegal government. . . . Common law, 'constitutional law,'" they said, holding up books, "says taxation without representation is illegal."

The meeting ended when Marlin Green stood and said, "Don't listen to these rabble-rousers. You'll just land yourselves in jail." He proposed, instead, that people "schedule a meeting with the county commissioners."

John Trochmann's racial views were well known too. When he said "shadow government" or "banking elite," people knew he meant "Jews." Trochmann believed that "sometime in the next century, America's white population will perish." His Noxon neighbors also knew that "north Idaho 'skinheads'" were not strangers to Trochmann. And they knew his religious beliefs from comments he would make while square dancing.

Some, Vanek wrote, engaged "Trochmann in debates over Old and New Testament theology, challenging his claims that only Caucasians who could blush were acceptable in the eyes of God. Derisive laughter met his idea that women should give up their right to vote or to own property." But these bizarre ideas had larger implications than Trochmann's square-dancing partners knew.

His beliefs involved not only people, but also government. Trochmann's was a "Christian Patriot's" view. The Constitution and the Bill of Rights were meant to empower white men; any government that wanted to uphold the rest of the Constitution, that is, the amendments that followed the first ten—establishing income taxes, forbidding racial discrimination, enfranchising women—violated the "organic" Constitution and the "common law," and was, accordingly, illegal and worthy of armed opposition.

The Trochmanns also "studied the Bible" with longtime Christian Identity adherents. And, confirming his white supremacist beliefs, Trochmann declared his "sovereignty" on January 26, 1992, as a "free white Christian man" who believed in the "organic Constitution of the United States." "I am not now, nor have I ever been," he swore, "a citizen of the United States or a resident of its subordinate territories, or a property appertaining thereto, in either a legal or factual sense." His proclamation, in affidavit form, was filed in the Sanders County Courthouse. Why did this confirm his racism? Because, according to the legal fiction by which people like Trochmann and Terry and James Nichols tried to relinquish their U.S. citizenship, black people (having received rights under the Fourteenth Amendment to the U.S. Constitution) and Jews (as non-Christians) could not be "sovereign" citizens.

Being "free white Christian men," the Trochmanns were welcome at the Aryan Nations compound, with which they developed a long relationship. According to the Anti-Defamation League, the Trochmanns had all been members of the Aryan Nations. John Trochmann spoke at the Aryan Nations Congress in 1990. His wife, Carolyn, told *Esquire* that they met Randy and Vicki Weaver at an Aryan Nations "family day." Asked about his association with this neo-Nazi group, Trochmann told the *Missoulian* in April 1995 that he had gone there only twice. In May 1995, Trochmann admitted to reporter Lawrence Cohler, "I went to the Aryan Nations compound four or five times. Once it was for a bagpipe festival. I love bagpipes." As if he hadn't noticed the "Whites Only" sign at the entrance, or the Nazi memorabilia.

John Trochmann's attempts to distance himself from the Aryan Nations brought an unusual response: a press release from Richard Butler, head of the Aryan Nations, denouncing Trochmann as an "anti-Christ." "It's time to reply," Butler explained to a reporter. Trochmann "came over here quite often. He made six or seven trips for Bible study. . . . Why lie about the number of times here?" Butler's statement asked rhetorically. "John, you even helped us write out a set of rules for our code of conduct on church property."

Floyd Cochran, a former Aryan Nations member, wrote an opinion column in the *Ravalli* (Montana) *Republic:*

> John Trochmann can deny it all he wants but the fact is, he has had a long-standing relationship with the Aryan Nations and its followers. I know because I was there. . . . I had the opportunity to meet with the Trochmann family and deal with them both on a personal, and professional level, sharing with the Trochmanns the same beliefs of white supremacy and the role of government based on the racist faith of Christian Identity. . . . John spoke at length on the merits of using the Bible and God, not the swastika and Hitler, to advance his brand of racism, bigotry, and Christian Identity. . . . The Trochmanns join their fellow Christian Identity believers in believing that the Jewish people have seized control of the government. . . . From teaching skinheads the Christian Identity values at their home in the summer of 1990 or holding "church service" at the Aryan compound . . . the Trochmanns are respected leaders in the organized racist movement in Montana and Idaho.

For public consumption, John Trochmann downplayed his racism; but when asked if there are any racists inside the Militia of Montana, he said yes. "Any organization that opposes the government will attract those elements," he said. "We just tell them to leave their religion at home." A telling statement: Trochmann saw racism as a function of religion.

Trochmann claimed, "I have a lot of good friends who are Jewish." Yet on the tables in Noxon, after a MOM meeting, were copies of *Contact*, a paper sporting articles such as "History's Longtime Deception—Vile, Secret Holocaust by Alien Satanic Khazarian Zionist Jews." Videos featuring anti-Semites were also for sale, hawked by a man proudly wearing a swastika belt buckle. "I don't have any animosities against the Jewish people," said Trochmann, who believed that "Jews, of all people, should be sympathetic to the notion we must be ready to fight against tyrants when they take over . . . I think they're being used," he said.

Trochmann's coded anti-Semitism was not lost on his audience. He showed them photographs of military equipment being transported inside the United States with either U.N. or Soviet markings. He and his cohorts talked of documents showing the United States being carved up into "ten manageable regions"; they spoke of mysterious black helicopters. "Who's behind all this?" a reporter attending the meeting asked an audience member. He was told: "The Warburgs and the Rothschilds. International finance. The Federal Reserve, and its chairman Alan Greenspan. 'The Anti-Christ Banksters.'"

✗ ✗ ✗

The Militia of Montana not only distributed diagrams of firearms, it disseminated sheets of diagrammed English. The Second Amendment was printed in pieces along squiggly lines parodying the style of an old middle school primer, announcing the verdict: "The command in the second amendment of the bill of rights . . . means that *the people* are the militia."

Why a militia? "Sarah Brady['s] Handgun Control, Inc.," MOM explained, "was founded . . . to lead in the legislation of the disarming of America. . . . Who would oppose Mrs. Brady in her task? The Militia."

What would the militia do?

> The security of a free state is not found in the citizens having guns in the closet. It is found in the citizenry being trained, prepared, organized, equipped and lead [sic] properly so that if the government uses its force against the citizens, the people can respond with a superior amount of arms, and appropriately defend their rights. . . . Remember Thomas Jefferson's words that the primary purpose of the second amendment was to ensure that Americans as a last resort would be able to defend themselves against a tyrannical government.

Beginning on February 15, 1994, the organizers of the Militia of Montana—John, David, and Randy Trochmann—used gun control as fuel to launch America's first active militia group. The Brady Bill had been enacted the summer before. Despite its limited effect—to require a waiting period before the purchase of a firearm—it was seen by many as an infringement on "the right to bear arms." So was the later federal ban on the manufacture of a small number of assault weapons. The Trochmanns used Montana's anti-gun-control sentiment to attract huge crowds to its meetings. One hundred and fifty came in Billings, two hundred in Great Falls, two hunderd fifty in Hamilton, over three hundred in Big Timber, eight hundred in Kalispell. There were truck drivers, housewives, lawyers, doctors, dentists, barbers, accountants, grocers, all listening to John Trochmann explain, "Gun control is for only one thing: people control."

The serpentine diagram of the Second Amendment—redefining the right to bear arms as a patriotic need to fight government—and literature about the dangers of the Brady Bill were free. For sale were videotapes and books that expressed a far more paranoiac vision of America. One video claimed that the government was hiring and training the Bloods and the Crips, urban street gangs, to take away people's firearms. Another suggested that America was in the process of being taken over by foreign troops. Tapes had titles such as *The Hidden Agenda, New World Order and Farm Confiscation,* and *Lucifer 2000.* (This last concerned the "Satanic World Order planned for the year 2000 . . . and Illuminati influences.") You could buy U.S. Army manuals on guerrilla warfare, booby traps, and survival. The less adventurous convert could buy a Militia of Montana baseball cap, proclaiming "Enough Is Enough."

✗ ✗ ✗

On March 10, 1994, eight hundred came to hear the Trochmanns in Kalispell. A month later, only 150 attended. Those who returned heard less and less about the Brady Bill and more and more about the New World Order, otherwise known as One World Government and the Global Conspiracy. MOM speakers were adept at making conspiracy theories sound logical, especially to home-state audiences for whom gun possession and rugged individualism were points of pride. It took a leap of faith, but if you bought the premise—say, that gun control was not really to control guns, but for "people control" by an evil government—everything fell into place.

Events were not to be analyzed; rather, they were to be scrutinized for "proof" that confirmed the theory. If government's secret aim was war with the American people, as MOM members suggested, then Ruby Ridge and Waco were evidence of that conspiracy. After all, in both cases the government shot people who only wanted to own guns and enjoy their own religion, like most folk in Montana. Soon, to those who returned to hear the Trochmanns and their cohort Bob Fletcher, nothing was as it seemed. In this parallel universe, everything had a different and specific meaning—as a sign of a government out to enslave ordinary Americans.

Take executive orders, for example. Executive orders are what they sound like: orders by the executive branch of the federal government that define various aspects of its administration. President Clinton, for example, promised early in his presidency to outlaw discrimination against homosexuals in the armed services, something that he could have done by executive order. For obvious reasons, some executive orders describe how the executive branch should operate during time of emergency.

A basic feature of our system of government is its provision of checks and balances. Presidential actions—including executive orders—can be challenged in court. Presidential programs require funding from Congress. Presidents can be voted out of office or impeached. Conspiracy theorists like the Trochmanns, conveniently forgetting this, ascribed almost magical powers to executive orders. A Militia of Montana publication entitled "Executive Orders for the New World Order" says

> Executive Orders are laws established by United States Presidents. . . . These laws are unconstitutional because the Constitution does not afford any person the right to creat [sic] laws by himself that negates [sic] the Constitution. . . .
>
> There are individuals in this world, within this county, and in our own government who would like to rule the world. . . . These power hungry individuals have corrupted our government and are working on sabotaging our freedom by destroying the Constitution of the United States, in order to establish the "New World Order" (a.k.a. "Global Community").
>
> To bring about this New World Order, and ultimately the single World Government, there are several things that must come about: . . . Because the Constitution is a document that safeguards the sovereignty of our nation it must be destroyed. Because of a genuine threat of the American militia, the American people must be disarmed . . . and thus become "sheeple."
>
> Executive Orders, and other treasonous acts, establish the basis for the Federal Emergency Management Association [sic] (FEMA). FEMA has the power to completely rule over the American people, any time the President should decide to declare Martial law.

If executive orders were bad, treaties were worse. Treaties, of course, are bargains with foreign nations in which each side gives up something to get something. Like any bargain or any law, they can be well- or ill-conceived. But to MOM, treaties are proof of a global conspiracy. For example, MOM spokesman Bob Fletcher said, "the recently approved GATT treaty [is] a treasonous piece of paper that will destroy the sovereignty of our country. . . . It is a merger under way for years involving the United Nations and the wealthy elite of the world . . . all coming together to put us under a singular, one-world government—a giant dictatorship."

Randy Trochmann said, "They've perverted the intent of the Constitution and come up with a bastardized form of illegitimate government. . . . There is a day of reckoning at hand. People," he said, "are just tired of all the bs coming out of Washington DC these days. We're helping people prepare unorganized militias to defend citizens against the foreign forces at work in this country and against the tyranny in our government."

David Trochmann said, "Three hundred families run the world and plan global conquest."

John Trochmann said, "The battle lines are drawn."

The Militia of Montana said, "The invasion is under way."

And those attending MOM meetings were encouraged to form their own militia groups to oppose the United States government, in cells with no more than eight to fourteen members.

7 Battle Preparation

IF THE GOVERNMENT USES ITS FORCE AGAINST
THE CITIZENS, THE PEOPLE CAN RESPOND WITH
A SUPERIOR AMOUNT OF ARMS.

Militia of Montana

Of all the militia groups that formed across the United States in 1994 and 1995, Trochmann's was not only the first significant organization, it was also the most active disseminator of militia propaganda around the country. Either through the mail or at a MOM meeting, just about anything you might want to know about conspiracy theory, or about the inherent evil of the U.S. government, or about setting up your own militia, or about weaponry, was available from the group in Noxon. MOM literature, for example, defined the role of the militia:

> To balance the military power of the nation with the might of the militia will put at odds any scheme by government officials to use the force of the government against the people. Therefore, when the codes and statutes are unjust for the majority of the people, the people will rightly revolt and the government will have to acquiesce without a shot being fired, because the

militia stands vigilant in carrying out the will of the people in defense of rights, liberty, and freedom.

The purpose of government is in the protection of the rights of the people, when it does not accomplish this, the militia is the crusader who steps forward, and upon it rests the mantle of the rights of the people.

MOM's manual suggested a structure for militia groups, with headings including "Unit Leadership," "Taking Up Arms," "Disobedience of Orders," "Funding," "Code of Conduct," and "Uniform." ("The Uniform of the Unit Shall consist of Blue Jeans and a Gray [medium shade] shirt.") The MOM manual also listed "basic equipment," including "1 Belt, Pistol," "1 Belt, Pants," "1 Sling, Silent," "2 Knife, Combat," "3 Opener, Can," "1 Utensil, Eating," "1 Mirror, Distress," "2 Soap, Ivory (UNSCENTED)," "1 Cap, Patrol, Ear Flaps," "1 Rifle, Colt AR-15," "600 Rounds .223 Ammunition," "1 Pistol, U.S. Govt. Issue Type," and "1 Balm, Lip."

MOM organized itself on a "cell structure," explained in its manual:

How to set up your cell system. This is based on a seven man cell format. Some like five or even three man cells. Starting out you build your first cell until it reaches a total of seven. One of you will be chosen the leader of this cell. . . . When one of the members of your cell recruits a new member, bringing your number to eight, three of your eight will break off to form a new cell. The other four, which includes the leader, will stay behind in the old cell. Both of these cells will now grow to seven again. The process of building and splitting will continue. Always have one of your members stay in contact with the cell from which the three originated from. This way there will always be contact.

After three tiers of cells have been built those in the fourth tier will not know who is in the originating tier. This will allow security from infiltration and subterfuge. If one cell messes up, the network as a whole will not fall.

For $75 you could buy MOM's Blue Book, touted as containing all the information on which MOM speakers rely during their public presentations. The Blue Book consisted partly of reprints from the Lyndon LaRouche organization. LaRouche is the former leftist conspiracy theorist and anti-Semite who became a rightist conspiracy theorist and anti-Semite; he believes, among other things, that the Queen of England is a drug pusher.

MOM's less expensive books included *Escape from Controlled Custody*, which would come in handy if you ended up in one of those concentration camps the militia said were being prepared. Other literature included anti-Semite Red Beckman's material on "jury nullification," intended to encourage jurors to disregard the facts and the law and vote their conscience; this was handy if you got into trouble because you thought of yourself, as many militia members do, as a sovereign white citizen with no obligation to obey laws or pay taxes. MOM could also sell you literature from Gene Goosman's Equal Justice for All, instructing you how to file multimillion-dollar, even multibillion-dollar "liens" and "criminal complaints" against public servants. Not only could you get the satisfaction of harassing government officials, you supposedly could use these "liens" to claim you were paying their "value" to the IRS when it filed charges against you for not paying taxes. From MOM you could also buy information on "allodial title," a feudal concept meaning ownership without obligation of vassalage or fealty. Political researcher Paul deArmond explains that "the theory is baroque enough that few agree on how it is correctly applied, but the basic notion is that land that is owned free and clear can somehow become a sovereign nation and thereby exempt the owner from income tax."

MOM also sold songs such as "Watch Out for Martial Law," "Wheresoever Eagles Gather" (aka "The Randy Weaver Ballad"), and "Seventeen Little Children." You could buy packets of printed matter, such as the "UN Packet" and the "Militia Packet," and reprints of MOM's newsletter, Taking Aim. Issues covered ranged from "Emergency Food Storage" to "Proper Weapons Caching" to "The Road to Slavery, Putting the Pieces Together." The latter was billed as showing "how FEMA, Police Departments, Military, UN, Churches, etc. are all working together for the same goal (even though some do not know it) — enslaving Americans." When out-of-state troops helped extinguish a forest fire, Taking Aim asked: "Mysterious deaths have been taking place since the troops appeared. Coincidence? We do not know."

Over fifty videotapes were for sale, many about Waco and Weaver, some featuring "patriots," such as Mark Koernke (a militia leader from Michigan), Jack McLamb, and Red Beckman. Other titles included A Call to Arms, Equipping for the New World Order, Battle Preparations Now. There were tapes on gun control, public lands, GATT, and other pressing issues. The Pestilence (AIDS) was a two-hour video about the "'Global 2000 Plan' to Exterminate Two Billion People by the year 2000." There was The Countdown Has Begun (BIOCHIP), described as "UN Police Force, One World Govt., chip implants, ALL BY THE YEAR 2000 — totally documented." You could also buy America in Crisis, a one-hour tape in which "newly elected Congresswoman, Helen Chenoweth, formerly a natural resource consultant explains how environmentalists are taking public and private property from American's [sic] and placing the property into the control of the N.W.O. [New World Order]. Over 50% of America is now in their control. An excellent presentation."

Audiotapes included *The Illuminati Today*, *The Committee of 300* (described as "the conspiratorial group that knows no national boundaries"), *Bio-Chip Mark of the Beast*, *Outer Space, Secret Projects & Laser Weapons*, and *The Philadelphia Expirement* [sic], described as "an explosive radio interview given concerning the ship that disappeared during a government expirement. The ship appears to have gone into a time warp. Also report on the US government expirementing in time travel for over 25 years."

Other books included *Big Sister Is Watching You* (about "Hillary's Hell-Cats" and "Gore's Whores" who are "lesbians, sex perverts, child molester advocates, Christian haters, and the most doctrinaire of Communists, whose goal is to end American sovereignty and bring about a global Marxist paradise"); *The Art of War; Citizen Soldier, Guerrilla Warfare, Sniper Training and Employment; Unconventional Warfare Devices and Techniques*; and *Booby Traps*. For $75 you could buy a 617-page collection of "training manuals" on everything from traps to combat to ambush to sabotage to "NBC" (nuclear, biological, chemical) warfare to "dirty tricks." Some of MOM's training manuals urged acts of terrorism, including kidnapping and attacks against federal buildings. One, entitled *MOD Training Manuals*, described "an action . . . involving the placement of a bomb or fire explosion of great destructive power, which is capable of effecting irreparable loss against the enemy. . . . Public offices, centers of government services, government warehouses are easy targets for sabotage." This manual also advocated raids on armories to gain "arms, ammo and explosives," and the killing of government officials.

"JUST IN," said a flyer inserted into the Militia of Montana catalogue. A "Chemical Protective Ensemble" in "O.D. Green" was on sale. Government cost, $320. MOM cost, $50, including shipping. "These nucler [sic], biological, chemical suits . . . are what everyone has been looking for."

If you wanted any of this vast assortment of militia material, MOM would be glad to sell it to you. But you couldn't use your Visa card, and don't bother bringing your American Express. In fact, you couldn't use a check—not because the Trochmanns didn't trust their customers, but because, as they explained, "We have opted out of the system and therefore we do not have any association with BANKS. We cannot cash your checks . . . we have no use for them. . . . Cash or M.O. only."

✗ ✗ ✗

Bob Fletcher resembled a traveling salesman—energetic, slightly disheveled, exhausting to watch. "You better damn well learn how to use a gun," Fletcher told a Colorado audience. "When the poop hits the fan, you will use those weapons." When he went on the road to organize militia groups, his message was clear: Armed combat, Americans against the government, was only a matter of time. A short time.

"How did our government reach the point where they are back-stabbing the American people?" Fletcher asked, then answered his own question: America was giving up its sovereignty to become part of a "one world government." How did he know? He pointed to the increasing stature of the United Nations. "Who the hell is the U.N.?" he asked. "The U.N.—that is the banner they will use to finally pull the plug on us." "We have to forget about right-wing, left-wing," he said. "We have good guys and bad guys, that's it."

The bad guys, according to Fletcher, were prepared to steal food and weapons from Americans, kill some, and lock others away in concentration camps. And that was just the start. The bad guys wanted to run the globe, and were already playing around with the world's weather to promote their conspiratorial agenda. For example, Fletcher told his audience that Colorado's sparse snowfall and Japan's earthquake might have been planned by these evil, powerful forces.

The ideology the Trochmanns and Fletcher sold, once they hooked people through gun control, was anti-Semitic conspiracy theory based on the *Protocols of the Elders of Zion* recast as antigovernmentism—the idea that "unseen hands" were pulling the strings of a government that had been secretly taken over in order to enslave Americans. This was not merely a theoretical position—it was inherently political and inevitably violent. The threat, not by armchair philosophers but by people who were assembling into armies, was always there. Government could not be reformed; it had to be overthrown, with dead public officials. "We don't want bloodshed," John Trochmann professed. "We want to use the ballot box and the jury box. We don't want to go to the cartridge box, but we will if we have to."

But the Militia of Montana did not spend its time sending out voter pamphlets and coordinating with the League of Women Voters. It distributed literature on how to make war. To the extent it thought about ballots, MOM had a narrow view of the voting process. "It doesn't make any difference what political party is in power," Bob Fletcher maintained. "The question people need to be asking their politicians is whether they are supporting bills that are unconstitutional and socialist in nature. If they are, then they need to get out of our country."

That, too, was not mere rhetoric, it was threat, and MOM was not the only militia group to poison the political atmosphere in Montana. The Boonville, Indiana–based North American Volunteer Militia had an active Montana branch, led by Calvin Greenup. On December 30, 1994,

Joe Holland, national director of the North American Volunteer Militia, sent a letter on militia stationery to Judge Jeff Langton at the Ravalli County Courthouse in Hamilton. It read:

> The reason this letter is being sent to you at this time is to make you aware of what to expect if you continue your aggressive activities against the people of Montana. . . . You have taken an Oath to uphold the Constitution of the United States. The Oath is your contract with the people. When you violate your Oath of office you become renegade to the Constitution and guilty of treason. I am sure you know what the penalty is for treason. . . . [Death.]
>
> We would prefer that you take a good hard look at what you and your agencies are doing and amend your ways immediately. We are prepared, however, to defend, with our life, our Rights to Life, Liberty, and the Pursuit of Happiness. We number in the thousands in your area and everywhere else. How many of your agents will be sent home in body bags before you hear the pleas of the people? Proceed at your own peril!

The North American Volunteer Militia group also sent similar threats to the Montana attorney general, the state Department of Fish, Wildlife and Parks, and the IRS. The people of Ravalli County fought back, however. Some posted signs in store windows, saying that they supported their elected officials. And three weeks after the North American Volunteer Militia's letters, a "proclamation" was printed in the *Ravalli Republic*. Signed by hundreds, it read: "We, the undersigned, express support for our local, state and nationally elected officials and public employees in their endeavors to do their respective duties. We abhor and speak out against threats of violence by any persons or organizations against these public servants. . . . We urge all thoughtful and responsible people to join us in communicating this message to our families, friends, neighbors, and all members of this community." That took courage. The elected officials were scared too.

City judge Martha Bethel presided over a traffic violation involving a Montana "freeman" linked to the militia. (The "freemen" are a Christian Patriot group.) She was presented with a twenty-eight-page ultimatum, stating that if she did not dismiss the traffic case, she would be subject to trial in the group's "common law" court. After Judge Bethel spoke out about this, the threats escalated. She was told that her home would be shot up, that she would be hanged. She received "hate mail from around the country," she said. "On two separate occasions, I've had to have my children live elsewhere a week at a time because of threats. I would like to spare my kids the terror of watching Mom kidnapped."

"Terrorism," said Judge Bethel, "is what it is. I hope someone takes this seriously, before blood is shed. If you let these people walk up one side and down the other, all you've done is empower them."

Law enforcement agents came to Judge Bethel's house and, after surveying the property, told her and her children—thirteen, eleven, and ten years old—in which rooms to hide to have the best chance of surviving a barrage.

✗ ✗ ✗

"The paranoia is so deep," said Ravalli County sheriff Jay Printz about the militia members, "I just hope it doesn't deteriorate into armed conflict." The paranoia about which Sheriff Printz spoke was self-perpetuating. If you believed the government was illegitimate, and you realized that the majority of Americans didn't agree with you, then you had to define yourself as among the privileged few who knew a "suppressed truth"—that the government had been taken over by secret evil forces. And since that "truth" was dangerous to the government, you were *compelled* to see the government coming after you. If you didn't believe you were a target of government repression, that meant that the government wasn't evil or powerful after all, a conclusion irreconcilable with your premise.

For an example of this frame of mind, consider a subset of Montana's militia members—the self-described "Constitutionalists." A constitutionalist is part of a movement also (and more commonly) known as the Christian Patriots, an umbrella term most white supremacists use to describe themselves today. Christian Patriot–Constitutionalist–"Super Patriot" thinking is closely akin to Christian Identity in that it sees white Americans as "chosen" and the original U.S. Constitution as divinely inspired. The Constitution, the Bill of Rights, and the "common law" are the only legitimate laws and are to be interpreted literally, along with the Bible. This is a good thing for white Christian men, who are called "organic" or "state" citizens, having gotten their rights from God through the Constitution and its first ten amendments.

Constitutionalist thinking had a strong place in the militia movement as a whole, and in Montana in particular. For example, at a MOM meeting in Snohomish, Washington, on February 11, 1995, Bob Fletcher advocated the creation of secret cells in militia groups, to be composed of "good friends." The meeting organizer was Snohomish resident Ben Sams, best known as a distributor of literature produced by the Association de Libertas, a Texas-based Christian Patriot group. The Association de Libertas, like other such groups, claimed that there was a fundamental legal distinction between white people, who were termed "state citizens," and minorities, who were "Fourteenth Amendment" citizens.

The "logic" went like this. White people, as "state citizens . . . [got]

nothing from the Thirteenth and Fourteenth Amendments." (The Thirteenth Amendment freed the slaves, and the Fourteenth required the states to provide due process and equal protection of the laws.) Since whites did not "need" either of these amendments, they could "have no rights and no duties" under them.

Minorities, who received citizenship under these amendments, were termed "Fourteenth Amendment" citizens, and *were* subject to "rights and duties." Whites, as state citizens, were "non-resident aliens" of the United States—having no obligation to pay income tax, for example. Minorities, as Fourteenth Amendment citizens, were subject to federal taxes.

It got better. The Thirteenth Amendment really didn't abolish slavery, the Association de Libertas claimed, only "involuntary servitude." "By electing to stay in the United States" after the passage of the Thirteenth Amendment, said Association spokesman Glen Ambort, "you can make a great case that slaves were now in voluntary servitude. . . . [U]ntil we free the black man [from] voluntary servitude," said Ambort, "we ourselves will not be free." How do we do this? Get rid of the Thirteenth and Fourteenth Amendments, of course. In other words, not only overturn the equal protection and due process guarantees of the Fourteenth Amendment, but reinstate slavery. The Association sold pseudo-legal kits, purportedly instructing how to "return" to state citizenship and thus "exempt" oneself from all federal laws, including those establishing taxes.

Montana had a chapter of the Association de Libertas. It was located in Ravalli County. In late 1993, Calvin Greenup, his son, Scott, and sixteen others claimed they had renounced their U.S. citizenship, just as John Trochmann and the Nichols brothers of Michigan had. The Greenups sent a letter to the *Ravalli Republic*, each announcing that:

> in the name of the Lord Jesus Christ, [I] solemnly Publish and Declare my American National Status and rights to emancipate absolute my "res" in trust from the foreign jurisdiction known as the municipal corporation of the District of Columbia, a Democracy. Any and all, past and present political ties implied by operation of law or otherwise in trust with said democracy are hereby dissolved. By this emancipation I return to an estate of primary sovereignty and freedom that preexists all government(s).

The various groups promoting these Christian Patriot legalisms gave the militia members extra ideological fuel in their battle against the "evil" federal government. These ideas not only made some feel special—it is heady to be a "sovereign citizen"—they made the battle lines clearer.

"Son of MOM" organizations spread around the Northwest. In Washington state, for example, there were the Unorganized Militia of Stevens County, Citizens for Liberty, Citizens for a Constitutional Washington (run by John Prukop, Bo Gritz's former press secretary), and the Olympic Sportsmen's Association, among others. The Lake Chelan County Militia was also led by people associated with Bo Gritz's 1992 presidential campaign. According to the Portland-based Coalition for Human Dignity, this group "mobilized to confront border patrol agents on maneuvers near the Canadian–U.S. border" during the summer of 1994.

Stevens County, Washington, had two militia groups. One, the Unorganized Militia of Stevens County, began in June 1994, following a John Trochmann speech at the Colville Grange. Seventy people showed up and they learned their lessons well. Mark Reynolds, who was also an important figure in Christian Identity, would become a leader of this group; he said things such as "Eventually we are going to hang people like Mr. Horiuchi [Lon Horiuchi is the FBI agent who shot Vicki Weaver]; . . . eventually people like Janet Reno will be . . . summarily executed. . . . The reason the Second Amendment was put into the United States Constitution . . . [was] so that when officials of the federal and state and local government get out of hand, you can shoot them." Reynolds also promoted Louis Beam's idea of "Leaderless Resistance."

The other Stevens County militia group was led by Jim E. Shaver, Sr., of the Posse Comitatus, a group ready to help local government in any way it wished. Or, as Stevens told the county commissioners, "What can we do to help you? Do we need baseball bats? Do we need billy clubs? Do we need .06's? Do we need fully automatics? Or do we need [inaudible on the official county tape] down here with napalm?"

According to Shaver, his Posse-cum-militia could "shut the Feds out of here completely. . . . The next time the Sheriff is approached by the IRS to enforce a lien," he said, "slap 'em in cuffs and arrest them."

It would not be long until the MOM-promoted militias found something to do. Whatcom County is in the northwest corner of Washington state, abutting the same border where militia members believed foreign forces were preparing to invade the United States. Dr. Donald Ellwanger practiced veterinary medicine there. Unusual signs were posted around his Animal Birth Control Clinic in early 1995. One said "STOP UNLAWFUL EVICTIONS," another "Land Patent Contract, Private Property. NO TRESPASS."

In a press statement Ellwanger explained that "about 10 years ago I discovered, after much study and searching of the law, that I was not required to file a form 1040 and pay income tax; it's strictly voluntary." The IRS disagreed. As of 1991 it calculated that Ellwanger and his wife, Judie, owed federal taxes totaling $130,226.86. It seized his clinic, then auctioned it.

On Christmas Day, 1994, Ellwanger released "Ellwanger's Call to Patriots." This document explained that:

> Ellwanger discovered that a "Foreign Private Corporation," international cartel known as the world bank/Federal Reserve Bank, who contract with the IRS to rob people like Dr. Ellwanger of the fruits of their labor and property [sic]. Such theft is forbidden by the Constitutions for the United States of America and for Washington State, and hence is unlawful and void, sedition, and economic warfare from a British banking cartel (Rothschilds Bank of London and Berlin). The bank owns 52% of the stock in the deceptively named "Federal Reserve System," which is also a Foreign Private Corporation and controls the IRS. The IRS is the Federal Reserve System's private collection agency. The remaining 48% of the Federal Reserve System stock is held by foreign and domestic subsidiaries of the Rothschilds Bank of London.

Like Calvin Greenup, John Trochmann, James Nichols, Terry Nichols, and many other "patriots," Ellwanger also disavowed his U.S. citizenship; he declared himself a citizen of the "Republic of Washington" and the "Kingdom of God." (He filed a "Notice of Affidavit of Change of Political Status From U.S. Federal Citizen to Citizen of Washington State and Surrender of Social Security Card and Use of Registration Number" in the local county auditor's office.) He also claimed exemption from taxes by a corresponding Christian Patriot fiction—that he had "allodial title" to his clinic. This claim left the IRS unimpressed.

Faced with eviction, Ellwanger turned to the Liaison Group, a Seattle-based Patriot organization run by Theressa Sundstrom. On January 3, 1995, she summoned the militias, issuing a notice on the American Patriot Fax Network. "There are fears this action may escalate into another Waco or Weaver," she explained. "Therefore, the militias of Montana, Idaho and Oregon have been alerted, as well as 'Bo' Gritz, who is advising them how to conduct themselves."

Militia members came, although they displayed no weapons. For three days they held off the Whatcom County sheriff. It wasn't until the third day that, reinforced, law enforcement agents removed Ellwanger's belongings from his clinic building.

"We had thirty Patriots up there on January third," said Sundstrom at a meeting at which the Militia of Montana participated, in Snohomish,

Washington. "We had forty patriots up there on January fourth and we had fifteen up there on January fifth. . . . It was a peaceful sit-in kind of stand-in demonstration. There were no weapons of any kind. . . . We did have the Bible, that is our weapon."

Those who watched the growth of groups promoted by the Militia of Montana worried about the weapons militia members had left at home, and about where the next inevitable confrontation would be.

8 Shooting the Help

[THEY] TOLD ME THEY WEREN'T GOING TO
BOTHER BUILDING A GALLOWS. THEY WERE JUST
GOING TO LET ME SWING FROM THE BRIDGE.

NICK MURNION, Garfield County, Montana, attorney

In February 1995, when the militia movement had been around barely a year, a shooting war almost broke out.

Calvin Greenup was a constitutionalist, as well as "Montana State Coordinator" for the North American Volunteer Militia. He considered himself exempt from paying taxes, so he did not pay them. The State of Montana had a different view—that Greenup owed $9,500 in income taxes and penalties.

Since Greenup didn't consider himself subject to the same laws as other Montanans, he had additional legal problems. He was sued for "improper closure of a landfill." And he battled with wildlife authorities over his elk. "He says they're livestock, just like cows," the *Spokane Spokesman-Review* reported. "Wildlife officials say they're wild animals that require a special license." This was more than a battle over definitions. Game farms were licensed and inspected in Montana, not only to ensure that the animals did not have infectious diseases, but also so that they would not be crossed genetically with red deer or other species. Saving the state's wild elk was apparently of little concern to Greenup, who saw state regulations as an intrusion on his personal "sovereignty."

Greenup failed to appear for a court date on charges of failing to pay taxes; instead, he retreated to the security of his 250-acre ranch. From that vantage point he saw his problems in global conspiratorial perspective: "Do the political officials want this state to blow or do they want to get it back and hear our pleas? In my opinion, looking at it militarily, it is obvious that this state is a test state to bring people under slavery under United Nations control—New World Order. We are fighting back, and we're not going to quit. We want our freedom and our country back. . . . There cannot be a cleansing without the shedding of blood.

"I've told the sheriff what I'll do," said Greenup. "I would turn my back and he could put a bullet in my head. But I wouldn't be hauled to jail alive. I've told him personally, you've got the first shot. Don't wound me. Kill me."

"I'm not inclined to go up to his home," Sheriff Jay Printz said. "I don't want to have to kill the man for something this minor, and I don't want any of our people hurt. . . . The fact that people have backed off since Weaver has really emboldened some of these fugitives," Printz acknowledged. "But I still intend to get my man. I just don't want to create a situation where I'm going to have to kill someone."

Calvin Greenup, of course, expected the government to come after him. In February 1995, an Idaho National Guard helicopter on a training mission flew over his property. Apparently thinking this one of the New World Order black helicopters that so obsess the militias, he contacted fellow militia members, twenty to thirty of whom rushed to his farm. "I told them to watch me," Greenup said. "If he [the helicopter pilot] makes a wrong move, we're going to dump him out of the sky. Yeah, we were going to shoot him down, but he never came back."

Two militia members rushed to the Darby town marshal's office. The marshal's wife had to call 911. Sheriff Printz said: "There was a lot of loud talk, because the marshal knew nothing about the helicopter, but they didn't believe him."

The National Guard helicopter was "practicing low level training" and was "on its way back from Boise to Missoula" when it happened to overfly Greenup's ranch, said Sheriff Printz. The helicopter in question was an AH64 Apache, painted a "real dark green, a flat khaki . . . with black markings," according to Idaho National Guard major James Ball.

"When I see a helicopter without markings, I refer to it as an enemy helicopter," said Greenup. "I was on the phone until after midnight talking to militia members all over the United States. They all support what I am trying to do and all stand ready to help."

Greenup's son was also a fugitive. On February 16, 1995, Scott Greenup was arrested after he allegedly assaulted a sheriff's deputy. He posted bond and was released, pending an appearance before District Judge Jeff Langton. Scott Greenup didn't show up in court. Instead "fellow Constitutionalist" Al Hamilton came with twenty-six-page notices addressed to Langton, Deputy County Attorney Mike Reardon, and Justice of the Peace Ed Sperry. The notices asserted that the charges against Scott Greenup were a "sham" and that Greenup was not subject to the court's jurisdiction. Additionally, the notices said that the "Constitutionalists" had established their own "common law venue Supreme Court." Langton, Reardon, and Sperry were ordered to respond within ten days. If they did not, the notices said, "arrest warrants" would be issued.

Langton instead issued a bench warrant for Greenup, setting his bond at $50,000. According to the Idaho Falls *Post Register*, "militia leaders threatened to take over the courthouse.... Randy Trochmann, cofounder of the Militia of Montana, [said], 'There is a day of reckoning at hand.'" According to *The New York Times*, "The fugitives ... issued 'a citizen's declaration of war' against state and Federal authorities. They have offered bounties on local officials, saying they should be hanged."

In the spring of 1995 Calvin Greenup picked up another criminal charge—criminal conspiracy, for planning to kidnap local officials, try them in his own "common law" court, and then, if they were found guilty, hang them. Tapping Greenup's phone, officials heard him ask other militia members for guns to use in arresting the officials. He also spoke of an escape plan that would involve breaking through a police roadblock with guns blazing.

"If he thinks he's going to get me," said Sheriff Printz, "he'd better get me good because I'm going to bite back. I don't hang easy."

✗ ✗ ✗

In March 1995, a Montana farmer-rancher named William Stanton was sentenced to ten years in jail. The sixty-four-year-old was found guilty of criminal syndicalism, a charge stemming from his role in a "freeman" group which, among other things, had established its own court system and advertised a bounty of $1 million for the "arrest" of county officials. "Before sentencing," an Associated Press story reported, "Stanton took 27 minutes to make a statement arguing the proceedings against him violated state law, the U.S. Constitution and Montana's 1889 Constitution. He frequently supported his position with references to the Bible's Book of Revelations." Musselshell County sheriff Paul Smith said that militia members were thought to be planning to kidnap the county judge who imposed the ten-year sentence on Stanton.

Ravalli County officials, described in the *Missoulian* as "admittedly shaken," passed an "emergency ordinance" barring explosives, guns, knives, and Mace from the courthouse and its immediate surroundings. "It's unfortunate that a small group of people who don't want to follow the rules can have such an effect on us," said Justice of the Peace Nancy Sabo. "But we also have a right to come to work without getting shot in the head."

Rodney Skurdal, a forty-three-year-old militia supporter and freeman from Garfield County, Montana, was part of a group that filed liens against various public officials, in response to the foreclosure of mortgages on some local farms. The Freeman group also offered a million-dollar "bounty" on a number of government employees. Skurdal filed a brief in Musselshell County in October 1994, explaining his views on why taxes need not be paid and why the laws that apply to others did not apply to freemen such as he. "How many of the People of Israel (Adam/white race)," he wrote, "have rejected the words of Almighty God, and rejected their 'faith' (surety) in Almighty God, to worship man made laws, 'color of law,' such as applying for a social security card/number, marriage licenses, driver's licenses, insurance, vehicle registration, welfare from the corporations, electrical inspections, permits to build your private home, income taxes, property taxes, inheritance taxes, etc., etc., etc. . . . Once you have applied for these benefits . . . you have voluntarily become their new 'slaves' to tax at their will, for you are no longer 'free,' i.e., a 'freeman.' "

Skurdal's explanation of his "exemption" from property taxes was based on a simple Christian Identity premise. "[If] we the white race are God's chosen people," he wrote, ". . . and our Lord God stated that 'the earth is mine,' why are we paying taxes on 'His Land'?"

On March 8, 1995, felony warrants were issued in Roundup, Montana, for Rodney Skurdal and another militia supporter, LeRoy Schweitzer. They were charged with "advocating crime, malicious damage to property and violence or other methods of terrorism to accomplish industrial or political ends." Sheriff Paul Smith said he knew where the men were hiding—in the Bull Mountains of central Montana—but was not prepared to arrest them, because he wanted to "see if this can't be de-escalated." Smith's entire department consisted of six officers—not enough, he pointed out, to "handle a standoff."

Skurdal and Schweitzer were not the only fugitives whom authorities were apprehensive about arresting. On February 10, 1995, Marc Andra, a "patriot" subject to a federal arrest warrant for intimidation and interference with federal officials, fled from a deputy and ran into the woods. The sheriff stopped the search, saying, "The main thing is, no one got hurt."

Gordon Sellner was another fugitive "patriot"; he had not paid taxes in twenty years and believed that the government was "choking the lifeblood out of us . . . our enemies are in our own country." Charged with shooting a deputy sheriff in the chest on June 27, 1992, with a .41 magnum bullet, he was a fugitive whose whereabouts were known: He was at home in Swan Valley. According to John Bohlman, Musselshell County attorney, "At MOM meetings and in public statements, Mr. Trochmann has made it clear that he and the Militia of Montana are protecting Gordon Sellner from arrest. . . . The use of force, deception, or intimidation to purposely prevent or obstruct anyone from performing an act that might aid in the apprehension of Mr. Sellner is a crime in Montana."

✗ ✗ ✗

The January 1995 edition of MOM's *Taking Aim* was entitled "Re-Establishing Our Constitutional Form of Government (Self-Government): THE SOLUTION AND THE PLAN." It gave step-by-step instructions for creating a "freeman" government, complete with notaries, constables, and a justice of the peace.

How would this new government finance itself? "These 'Freemen,'" MOM said, "discovered through years of researching our fore-fathers plan for self-government . . . a means for restitution." It worked like this:

> If you have been injured by an agent of the corporate government, such as the IRS, there is a remedy by filing a lien against the individual. [You fill out the forms, file them, then go to the bank and] deposit the liens in that account as an asset from which you will receive a line of credit in that amount. . . . As of this time the "Freemen" have deposited billions of dollars in liens. The banks are claiming that the accounts are closed. However, account status reports clearly have shown that the liens were entered. . . . "Freemen" have written checks on the accounts to credit card companies; paid off hundreds of thousands of dollars in farm mortgages, paid off IRS liens, etc. They have also purchased computer equipment from a local wholesale company.

Could these "liens" be turned around and used against "Freemen"? MOM responded: "Who is liable? . . . Let's look at the words unalienable and inalienable. . . . The Declaration of Independence . . . used the word 'unalienable.' . . . Unalienable [means] un (not in) * a * lien * able position. Inalienable [means] in * a * lien * able * position. . . . If you are a Fourteenth Amendment citizen then you have inalienable rights which can be liened. If you are a sovereign 'Freeman' then you have unalienable rights which cannot be liened."

Hardcore militia members were not the only ones to believe such tortured pseudo-legal and pseudo-religious doctrines. In early 1995 Mayor Tom Klock of Cascade, Montana, was under fire for depositing $20 million in phony money orders in the town's only bank, after declaring his town a "freeman enclave." The money orders had been printed by "freemen." Repeatedly asked the reason for his actions, Klock answered, "I done it in good faith. I had no reason to believe they [the money orders] were not good." They had been issued by freeman attorney Daniel Peterson, and notarized by Rodney Skurdal. Klock had also run an ad in the town's paper—the Cascade Courier—advocating that Cascade vote itself a "common law" government. He was subsequently suspended by the town council and charged with criminal syndicalism.

The next day, Friday, militia supporters reportedly met at the home of Rodney Skurdal. Afterward militia supporter Frank Ellena tried to file documents for Skurdal, whose property had been confiscated by the IRS for failure to pay taxes. The county clerk refused to accept the papers, because a court order prohibited the filing of freeman documents. The men had also visited each floor of the courthouse, and had gone near a judge's chambers. That caused alarm. The Musselshell sheriff's department was on alert that week, as they had information that freemen were planning to kidnap a judge or prosecutor, try him, convict him, and hang him—the whole sequence to be videotaped.

When Ellena left the courthouse and climbed into a pickup with fellow militia supporter Dale Jacobi, a deputy stopped them because the truck had no license plate. (Ellena, as a freeman, disdained the use of license plates. He felt that people gave up their "sovereignty" to the state by allowing it to license drivers or cars.) When the deputy stopped them, both men were speaking into "remote, hand held radio transmitter/receiver[s]." The deputy discovered that the driver had no license and both men had concealed weapons and no permits. Both were arrested. According to officials they had "numerous weapons" in the car, including "bullets that would pierce class II body armor commonly worn by law enforcement officers, approximately 30 plastic 'flex-cuffs' and a roll of duct tape, approximately $26,000 in cash and approximately $60,000 in gold and silver coins, a video camera and film and a 35mm Minolta camera with additional lenses, and sophisticated radio equipment."

The officers also found a hand-drawn map in Ellena's pocket. It showed the way to the homes of the sheriff and the county prosecutor in nearby Jordan, Montana.

At about six P.M., an hour and a half after the two men were arrested, deputies saw two vehicles in the courthouse parking lot. It appeared that people in both were speaking into "remote, hand held radio transmitter/receiver[s]." Soon three men from the parked cars—militia supporters Paul Stramer, Cajun James, and Amado Lopez—walked into the jail and demanded that they be given the property of Ellena and Jacobi. Sheriff Smith said one of the three pulled back his jacket, displaying a gun. They, too, were arrested.

Deputies then found John Trochmann and militia supporter Marc Basque sitting in a car in the courthouse parking lot. One of the two was "speaking into a hand-held radio transmitter/receiver." The men locked the car, refused to get out, and continued speaking on the radio. Seeing that Trochmann had a gun in his pants and Basque was unzipping his jacket, as if going for a gun, the officers shattered a window and arrested them. Basque had a handgun in a shoulder holster beneath his jacket.

A *Spokane Spokesman-Review* editorial quoted police as saying they believed the suspects intended " 'to possibly kidnap, try and hang' a District Court judge." The Associated Press quoted Sheriff Smith as saying he believed that Trochmann and the others came to Roundup "to take out the law enforcement and then get the government." Smith said the men were believed to have been planning to kidnap the judge who sentenced William Stanton.

On March 4, 1995, MOM's view of the arrest was distributed by its fax network and then posted on the Internet. The Liberty Lobby's *Spotlight* printed an account of the arrest under the headline "Militiamen Arrested in Montana: Is the Federal Government Making Its Long Anticipated Move Against Citizen Militias, or Has One Local Law Enforcement Agency Jumped the Gun?" It instructed readers how to contribute to the Trochmann Defense Fund.

Musselshell County prosecutor John Bohlman described what happened next:

> Within an hour after the arrest of John Trochmann, telephone calls began coming into the jail from all over Montana, and other states as well. In the week that followed, the jail received hundreds of telephone calls from all over the United States demanding that the arrested individuals be released and making threats against the Sheriff and his deputies. . . . My office telephone was ringing continuously and my secretary and I received approximately 40 threats on our lives and threats that included my secretary's family. One caller identified himself as being with the Militia of Montana and made threatening comments about my secretary's adopted Korean daughter. Because of the racial comments made by some of the callers, my secretary drove to another state during the night to hide her daughter. One

of the deputies sent his family out of town after he received a call that neither of the two arresting deputies could find a hole deep enough to hide in. Some callers said that armed men from militia organizations in various states would come to Roundup to see that justice was done to those of us responsible for the arrest of the "fine patriot John Trochmann."

In late March 1995, the felony charges against all the men were dropped without prejudice (meaning they could be refiled); misdemeanor charges remained against Jacobi and Ellena. Ken Toole, president of the Montana Human Rights Network, agreed that the reduction was proper, because there were proof problems with the felony charges, and to proceed with a prosecution that could not be sustained would only embolden the militia. The problem, Toole said, was that there was no statute in Montana outlawing "criminal intimidation" of public officials.

✗ ✗ ✗

Montana politicians fell into three categories: those who were trying to avoid the issue of the militias, those who were supporting the militias' antifederal animus, and those who saw the environment of conspiracy, paranoia, and threat poisoning the democratic process.

Aubyn Curtiss, a member of the Montana House, helped legitimize the militias. He introduced a bill that would have made federal agents subject to criminal charges of kidnap, trespass, or theft if they did not receive written permission from county sheriffs before making arrests or conducting searches and seizures. Testifying in favor of this bill was longtime Constitutionalist and tax protester Red Beckman—a man who had once written "Was . . . Hitler's Nazi Germany . . . not a judgment upon a people who believe Satan is their god?" Beckman testified that the IRS was a "terrorist organization." The bill passed both houses and would have become law but for Governor Marc Racicot's veto.

The *Spotlight* applauded Curtiss's reported plan to introduce a measure "to prohibit the presence of all foreign military forces in United Nations efforts and to cease support for the establishment of a new world order." And it praised another ballot initiative that might be proposed: to suspend the Montana Constitution and "secede from the United States."

Other politicians, however, felt the sting of the militias' threats and conspiracy theories. To them, MOM was not a group of overgrown boys playing soldier in the woods; it was a collection of well-armed bullies with a political agenda, who wanted to make public officials wonder whether the militia would come after them when any decision was to be made. Increasingly, the militia was to them—as the Klan had been to southern officials in the 1960s—a source of threat and terror.

Devon "Smut" Warren hadn't expected his position as Ravalli County commissioner to be so stressful. After all, he was a local fixture, a politician with a pet burro named Rudy. Every Christmas season Smut would dress up as Santa Claus, and Rudy would be decked out as an ersatz reindeer. It was tradition. Smut said he had been "getting calls that I haven't been living up to the Constitution." When two of Calvin Greenup's elk were confiscated by the state, and then died, Smut received death threats—for Rudy. "How would you like this," the callers asked, "after Calvin's elk got killed?" These repeated threats, Smut believed, were the direct cause of the heart attack his wife suffered.

Dave Mason was a Democratic candidate in Flathead, Montana, who supported land-use planning—meaning that rather than let this gorgeous part of the country grow by chance and greed, with an industrial plant next to a home, a garbage dump next to farmland, a McDonald's here, a used-car lot there, economic expansion should be planned. But many militia members saw such planning as part of a conspiracy. During the campaign, Mason received a phone call saying that he would "be a dead man" before election day. His wife got one as well. Tom Jentz, another advocate of land-use planning, was approached at a public meeting and told: "Get out of town while you still can . . . your life isn't worth anything." Colleen Allison, a Columbia Falls city council member, was told, "Stop all this and get out of politics. . . . We know where you live."

Steve Herbaly is the planning director of Flathead County, Montana. "Some people literally tell me I slip off to Denver to be debriefed by federal officials laying the groundwork for a United Nations takeover of the United States," he said. "We are trying to forge a policy for the future to safeguard components of life that make this place special—and it is heart-attack beautiful. But we're dealing with some folks who call us 'utopian socialist planners' and believe shooting the help is an option. And what I'm seeing now is an ominous silence from the general community about that. When the driving force of our analysis is whether an action will trigger an attack from the community, heck yes it's affecting democracy. I've had staff members ask if they can stay home for a few days after certain planning board votes."

"In Helena, Montana," wrote reporter Louis Sahagun, "opposition to changes in school district operations and land-use regulations is so strong that many supporters of such plans have stopped attending public meetings—or even writing letters to local newspapers—out of fear of harassment." Official Mike Reardon said, "Last week I was threatened with burning, hanging, being shot in the back and being backed over with a pickup truck." Nick Murnion, the Garfield County attorney, said freemen "told me they weren't going to bother building a gallows. They were just going to let me swing from the bridge."

"We were recently advised by law enforcement authorities," said Mike Murray, a Lewis and Clark County, Montana, commissioner, "that it's not wise to have our addresses listed in the phone book or to have personalized license plates on our cars. Sadly, people who want to be involved in government are being discouraged from participating, so we're losing the best and brightest we've got."

One response was legislation that would make it a felony for people who threaten public officials. State representative Deb Kottel, testifying in favor of this bill, said, "Yell at me, argue with me, don't vote for me, but don't threaten to kill my child or destroy my property because of the views I take." She had received late-night telephone calls threatening to kill her seven-year-old son.

"Enough's enough," said Judge Martha Bethel. "I lie awake at night wondering if they're going to come and get me." According to Flathead County clerk and recorder Sue Haverfield, "county workers have been instructed to dive under their desks with a telephone in hand if anyone storms the place." On April 18, 1995, the Ravalli County Courthouse had to be evacuated because of a bomb threat. As far as anyone could remember, that had never happened before. The courthouse now has a metal detector. One judge admitted to buying extra ammunition for his guns, and to using an intercom system before receiving visitors. Another judge carried Mace *and* a gun. Believing that home was too dangerous for her children, she sent them out of town.

In the year following the birth of the militia movement, a new political reality had been created in Montana, as real as the big sky and the snowcapped mountains. Many of its most dedicated public servants had gone from worrying about losing elections to wondering whether doing their jobs could cost them their lives.

9 Night Maneuvers

WE'RE NOT FOOLISHLY LOOKING FOR TROUBLE.
BUT TYRANTS SHOULD KNOW THAT THEY WILL BE
MET WITH FORCE.

NORMAN OLSON, Michigan Militia

By early April 1995, there were militia groups in at least thirty-six states. A few, such as the Militia of Montana, craved media attention. Many preferred to prepare for war quietly. The more visible groups believed exposure for their ideology and training materials could best serve the cause. The Michigan Militia—which drew some of those charged in the Oklahoma City bombing to its meetings—followed the Militia of Montana model.

Ray Southwell was a real estate agent, a father of three, and a "patriot." In the spring of 1994 he was also incensed. He had taken on his local school board for teaching what he called socialist values. He had lost. Southwell was aware of the fledgling militia movement. He consulted his pastor, the Reverend Norman Olson, and together they decided to create their own "God's Army" in Michigan. Founded in April 1994, two months after the Montana group, the Michigan Militia gave its first unit the impressive-sounding name "1st Brigade, 2nd Division, Northern Michigan Regional Militia."

Southwell and Olson's message sounded a lot like John Trochmann's. However, their racism was either less developed or better hidden than that of their Montana colleagues, although the Southern Poverty Law Center claimed that Southwell had connections to the Aryan Nations. Regardless of any such overt links with racists, however, Olson and Southwell claimed that Ruby Ridge and Waco were their wake-up calls. These were, for them, a clear indication that government was out of control and willing to attack ordinary citizens. Apocalypse was imminent. They preached that in 1996, the U.S. economy would collapse because the national debt would exceed revenues, and martial law would be declared. They thought the Brady Bill and the assault-weapons ban had left Americans defenseless, and that One World Government would take over. They claimed that foreign troops would spirit "patriots" away to concentration camps. "I'd guess that within the next two years," said Southwell in 1994, "you will see the Constitution suspended. Christian fundamentalists will be the first to go . . . this time. Just like the Jews were the first last time."

The Michigan Militia trained twice a month with weapons. The London *Daily Telegraph* described their encampment as a "highly defensive patch of ground. The fort has earthworks, and ridges overlooking steep, wooded valleys several miles from the nearest metalled road. A cavalry raid by helicopter would be the only obvious military option."

The Michigan Militia's goal was to "stand against tyranny, globalism, moral relativism, humanism and the New World Order threatening to undermine these United States of America." To do so, Olson wrote, "Many thousands are prepared to go to Washington in uniform, carry their guns, prepared to present the ultimatum to the President and to Congress. This may be the beginning of a Concord-like confrontation." Michigan Militia members took an oath to defend the Constitution "against all enemies, foreign and domestic." But they were not safeguarding the same document you and I know as the Constitution. They pledged allegiance to the Bill of Rights and to the United States Constitution—the original U.S. Constitution, the one without those bothersome amendments that followed the first ten. They also promised never to surrender or to talk about their militia if they became "prisoners of war."

"If this country doesn't change," Norman Olson said in August 1994, "armed conflict is inevitable." "Who is the enemy?" Olson asked rhetorically. "Anyone who threatens us." Such overblown rhetoric would seem silly if the group weren't so well armed.

By the fall of 1994 the Michigan Militia claimed to have units in sixty-three of the state's eighty-three counties, and 10,000 members. Even if this number was a gross exaggeration, Reverend Olson knew the militia was good for business. He also owned a gun shop and after training would say, "Don't forget, boys, that the gun shop's open, and there's ten percent off for militia members."

✗ ✗ ✗

In the year between the founding of the Michigan Militia and the Oklahoma City bombing, Ray Southwell, Norman Olson, and Ken Adams of the Michigan Militia became nationally known figures. They appeared on the Phil Donahue show. They were quoted extensively, and they gave good sound bites, edging right up to preaching armed revolution.

"Armed conflict may be inevitable if the country doesn't turn around," Norman Olson said. "We see a conspiracy here, a two-prong conspiracy, either to bring us into a fire fight to destroy us that way or to destroy us by legislation, to make us illegal."

"I'm afraid . . . at some point the government will cross the line," Southwell said, "and it will be neighbor coming to the aid of neighbor. Just like at Concord and Lexington. . . . There is one last hope to avoid armed confrontation, and that's if our state governments rise up and tell our federal government to back off. If the state does not rise up . . . the American people will." He said the militia was preparing to fight "tyrants." Who was a tyrant? "Anyone that would break that Constitution would be a tyrant." The Michigan Militia had a chaplain. He said, "We need to know collectively that we're right. And then, when our own army and navy decides to stand against the Constitution of the United States of America, we'll call in a higher court."

The Michigan Militia's rhetoric was seductive, using the images of American history to validate hatred of the American present. Here, the "organic" Constitution became a sacred document. Who was a tyrant? Anyone who would go against that Constitution. What power can elections, lawsuits, checks and balances, protest, petitions, and other democratic norms have when the problem is not an ill-advised or illegal act, but a sacrilegious one?

The conspiratorial message, combined with the religious overtones, had a powerful impact. Wayland Andrews, interviewed after a Michigan Militia meeting, said, "Well, to tell you the truth, I wasn't really ready to join today because I wanted to see what was going on, but I got kind of swept by it." Was there a danger of people being "swept by it"? Asked this before the Oklahoma City bombing—but after some of those who would be accused of that bombing attended a Michigan Militia meeting—Southwell discounted the possibility. "I keep asking the news media," he said, "show me one example in America where somebody in camouflage has done something that has frightened or harmed citizens. We keep hearing about paramilitary groups. Tell me where there's been a problem in America?"

✗ ✗ ✗

Militia members and others who shared their fear of One World Government planned to protest United Nations Day, October 24, 1994. The demonstrations were to be nationwide, and for many the invasion of Haiti made the protests urgent. As one rally organizer explained, "We invaded a sovereign nation without permission of our Congress. If the president only needs the permission of the U.N., what about our Constitution?" Demonstrations were planned at government buildings around the country; some also spoke about burning the United Nations flag as "part of a nationwide flag-burning."

Lisa Estlund Olson, the spokesperson for Lansing, Michigan's mayor, was "shocked" about the planned demonstration. After all, Lansing had had a U.N. event every year since 1979. "All of a sudden this year," she said, "we're getting calls from people saying we're massing Russian troops on the Upper Peninsula. These guys have just glommed on to this." And, in fact, members of the Michigan Militia—in camouflage—protested United Nations day in Lansing. While marching high school bands played, and the U.N. flag was raised, militia members shouted "No U.N.!" and "Take it down!" "If we saw the Russian flag up there instead of that beautiful pink powder-blue flag," said militia member Beverly Jackson, "then maybe our country would wake up." "The U.N.," said "Major" Kevin Shane of the Michigan Militia, "started out with a good idea, but now it stands for socialism. We pay seventy-five percent of the tab and get one vote. We support the rest of the world—they turn on us." The militia went home after the U.N. flag was hastily removed, leaving the U.S. flag without any symbolic opposition.

Ideas—such as the militias' claim of a political takeover by the U.N.—have consequences. Norman Olson and Ken Adams (the Northern Michigan Militia's communications chief) told people that military invasion was coming. They had pictures to "prove" it. Olson pointed to foreign military vehicles with inverted V's painted on their sides. These, he said, had been seen on Michigan highways. What was more, military helicopters were in the area.

Of course, there was an element of truth in what Olson and others asserted. "Since the end of the Cold War," said Lieutenant Patrick Swan, a U.S. Army spokesperson, "we are training Russian troops here and in Russia to promote better understanding between our countries and between the two militaries, with the hope that we will lessen the likelihood of war." And what about the V's? These dated from Operation Desert Storm, when they had helped identify "friendly" troops. "Some of those vehicles with that marking from Desert Storm are now back at Camp Grayling, and may have been seen on the highways. These are American vehicles," said Jerry Foehl of the Michigan Army National Guard. The helicopters belonged to the National Guard and were used by local law enforcement to spot marijuana plants.

Olson, of course, was not persuaded. "The government is encouraging citizens to turn on citizens. People are cheering on the government for saving us from marijuana; then we will find out it is pre-staging of the military. This is an abuse of power." Olson had further "proof." If these foreign troops were not here to invade, how could you explain the stickers on the back of road signs? "The speculation," said Southwell, "is that these are similar signs used by our troops in World War II to provide directions." Olson claimed that the colors of the stickers were the key, with blue indicating water nearby; brown, oil; green, a place to rest.

"I can assure you," said Bill Shreck of the Michigan Department of Transportation, "these are not for invading troops." Rather, the stickers indicate which company made the signs, and when.

✗ ✗ ✗

"The juggernaut that we refer to as the New World Order is in motion and it's a terrible creature," said janitor Mark Koernke, better known as "Mark from Michigan." In his late thirties, Koernke was one of the militia movement's best motivational speakers. He claimed to have been a military intelligence officer. According to the Center for Democratic Renewal, Koernke had a "criminal record for carrying a concealed weapon and [for] felonious assault"; this gave his words some weight when he advocated hanging public officials.

Unlike Olson and Southwell, who concentrated on Michigan, Mark saw the country as his to organize. He called his organization the Michigan Militia-at-Large. It was clandestine, while Olson's was public. According to *The Washington Post*, Koernke's was a "heavily armed group whose members have been ejected by the larger Michigan militia or who have rejected it themselves as too tame."

In February 1995, Koernke spoke for three and a half hours in a high school auditorium in Meadville, Pennsylvania. State Representative Teresa Brown (R–Meadville) introduced him, saying, "I want to know more about what is going on." According to Koernke, "what is going on" was the coming of one world government, which would arrive complete with black helicopters and concentration camps. And, he claimed, foreign troops were already on American soil.

In Bozeman, Montana, Koernke said, "If you are going to fight, fight to win. That means destroy the enemy that is before you." That enemy, as he described it, was formidable. He told his audiences that the government was so cunning it put bar codes into money so that agents could drive by people's houses with scanners and count their cash.

Koernke promoted his message through travel. He made two trips to Montana, one a week-long speaking tour with John Trochmann and Bob Fletcher. MOM marketed tapes of the tour. "We had a great time with Mark," the promotional flyer said. Seven and a half hours of Koernke-Trochmann-Fletcher videotape cost "only" $40.

Koernke, like Linda Thompson, also marketed his message on tapes and shared his ideas via shortwave radio. This little-noticed band, usually associated with international programming, has become a magnet for America's far right, and Koernke was one of its biggest stars. Through these media he told anyone who would listen about the evil government that had taken over the United States to serve its "one world" masters. For example, Koernke on "black helicopters":

> Back in the early part of 1990, approximately 3,000 rotary aircraft were withdrawn from our strategic reserve. These are not from the reserve or guard, these came from the mothball fleet. These units were transferred to FINCEN [Financial Crime Enforcement Network] and painted in flat black.... They bear no markings or identification to determine whether they are American or foreign national. The fact of the matter is they are now foreign national assets, no longer in the hands of the United States Air Force. We supply and support them with your tax dollars but we do not control them completely now.... Because of the detention camp mechanism that exists, they do not feel that it will be safe to transfer prisoners on the ground. That's why a large preponderance of the aircraft that they've received are heavy-lift aircraft capable of moving large numbers of people at once.

Koernke also spoke of Gurkha troops being enlisted to incarcerate Americans. He claimed that "FEMA is not a Federal Emergency Management Agency. FEMA is the secret government.... FEMA has approximately 3,600 employees and yet, of the 3,600 employees, only about 59 to 63 actually deal with emergency management such as storms, disasters, hurricanes or man-made catastrophes such as nuclear attack.... What do [the others] do?"

In Koernke's two-hour movie, *America in Peril*, he told audiences about the dangers of the "shadow" government and said: "We will slow them down. We probably will not stop them completely, and this will become an armed confrontation." He spoke while holding a rope and a Kalashnikov rifle; about the rope he said:

> Now I did some basic math the other day, not new world order math, and I found that using the old-style math you can get about four politicians for about 120 foot of rope. And, by the way, DuPont made this. It is very fitting that one of the new world order crowd should provide us with the resources to liberate our nation. Remember, whenever using it, always try and find a willow tree. The entertainment will last longer.

Koernke's video also claimed that the Environmental Protection Agency can track vehicles by remote control, that "biochips" were going to be inserted into the populace as a mark of the Antichrist, and that U.N. troops, street gangs, and Gurkha troops were poised to take away America's guns and lock up gun owners in concentration camps after they are processed through Oklahoma City. *America in Peril* ended, like Koernke's shortwave radio show, with these words: "God bless the republic, death to the new world order, we shall prevail."

Koernke's neighbors noticed many armed men in combat attire around his house in Dexter, Michigan. "We used to call it the army house," said one of those neighbors, Lynn Wilcox. Among the visiting men may have been Timothy McVeigh. Bob Johansen, a militia member from Florida, said McVeigh had been a bodyguard for Koernke. *The Washington Post* reported that Koernke had had a "purported ideological influence on bomb suspect Tim McVeigh." Michigan attorney Mark Osterman, a radio-show host, said he had Timothy McVeigh listed in his Rolodex as the contact for Koernke. And McVeigh reportedly traveled with Koernke and six others, in a van, from Michigan to a militia meeting in St. Lucie County, Florida. McVeigh, whose interest in the meeting was reportedly sparked by the participation of Branch Davidian survivors, was described by others there as one of Koernke's bodyguards.

✗ ✗ ✗

At 2:30 A.M. on September 8, 1994, a policeman in Fowlerville, Michigan, stopped a car. "What got his attention right away," said police chief Gary Krause, "was a loaded nine-millimeter clip on the back floor." Inside were three men, two of whom said that they were bodyguards for Mark Koernke. They were arrested with gas masks, two-way radios, night-vision binoculars, and loaded semi-automatic rifles with seven hundred rounds of ammunition. They were also dressed in camouflage and had blackened their faces. According to police sources, notes found suggested that they had been surveilling police communications. Some of the ammunition was armor-piercing.

The three men failed to appear at their court hearing the following week. Meanwhile, nearly fifty protesters, at least two dozen of them armed, marched in front of the courthouse. They trod on a United Nations flag and called police "punks in badges." Chief Krause said, "We've got such an insurgency here. . . . There's a very high potential of something disastrous happening." He quoted the protesters as saying that "the next time one of them was stopped they'd shoot the cop."

Michigan militia leaders defended the three who did not appear to face the charges: They said these men were on "night maneuvers."

PART THREE **Eye of the Funnel**

10 **Guns**

I FEEL IT IS MORE LIKELY THAT I WILL BE KILLED
BY AN AGENT OF THE GOVERNMENT THAN BY A
CROOK. IT'S GOTTEN THAT BAD.

DAVE FEUSTEL, a computer programmer in Indiana

Why were all these people attracted to the militias? "It's like a funnel moving through space," said Ken Toole of the Montana Human Rights Network. "At the front end, it's picking up lots and lots of people by hitting on issues that have wide appeal, like gun control and environmental restrictions, which enrage many people here out West. Then you go a little bit further into the funnel, and it's about ideology, about the oppressiveness of the federal government. Then, further in, you get into the belief systems. The conspiracy. The Illuminati. The Freemasons. Then, it's about the anti-Semitic conspiracy. Finally, at the narrowest end of the funnel, you've drawn in the hard core, where you get someone like Tim McVeigh popping out. . . . [T]he bigger the front end of the funnel is, the bigger the number that get to the core."

Gun control legislation not only helped pull people into the militias' funnel, it plunged those already in further down. "Some wanted to more or less go into becoming survivalists," said Florida militia member John Adams. "I guess you could say some people decided to go underground. They've had enough."

✗ ✗ ✗

"My definition of gun control," said Bo Gritz, "is hitting the target with every shot." That is a sentiment shared by many. Americans own 216 million guns.

The Brady Bill, passed in 1993, imposes a five-day waiting period on the sale of handguns. Thus people can't obtain a gun in the heat of anger, and during the delay a computerized background check is performed so that guns will not be sold to felons. The 1994 crime bill banned nineteen types of assault weapons and put a ten-bullet limit on gun clips.

Many Americans, especially city-dwellers, want gun control. Not a year, maybe not even a season, goes by in a major city without a news story of a kid accidentally shooting a sibling, a friend, a cousin. There are urban neighborhoods that turn into battle zones at night, where parents are afraid that their children will not make it home from school, where they have to think about the risk before walking past their own living room window. They position children's beds based on possible bullet trajectories. Police officers in urban settings worry they will be outgunned. Government officials hesitate before increasing the police force's firepower, because stray bullets become that much more dangerous.

Some minimal regulation of guns makes sense to the majority of Americans. As Senator Dianne Feinstein of California has said, "This is a society [in which] our dogs have licenses. We regulate baby toys, we regulate automobiles . . . you can't put a Formula One automobile on a freeway. And yet [the gun lobby's] position is there should be no regulations of guns which killed forty thousand people last year." She could have carried the analogy further. No one has an absolute right to drive an automobile, even though the Constitution protects a right to travel. Driving is a privilege. You must have reached a certain age and have passed written and practical tests, as well as an eye exam, to show that you know what you're doing with a machine that can kill people. Guns—which are designed to kill—are at least as much of a public safety hazard as cars. But a bumper sticker answers Senator Feinstein: "You can have my gun when you pry it out of my cold, dead hand."

It is easy to understand how many gun lovers feel when they are told by the NRA and others that the Brady Bill or the assault weapons ban are just steps on a slippery slope toward full-scale gun control. Go back to Senator Feinstein's metaphor and imagine that the Automobile Club of

America keeps telling you that new federal regulations on, say, auto emissions were just the first step toward taking your car away as part of a plan to reduce mobility.

Now, take a global perspective and this fear of the government taking away guns doesn't seem all that irrational. Other countries—democracies like Canada, Britain, Australia—have much stricter gun control laws than America. In fact, commentators in those countries think our liberal gun laws are insane, even after the enactment of the assault weapon ban and the Brady Bill. But to gun control opponents, the opposite is true. Gun ownership has become a benchmark of liberty. A California man expressed what a lot of people might, explaining what drew him to the militia: "I'm an avid sportsman," he said, "and the government wants to do away with my right to play. I've only registered three of my fifteen guns. The government will never get them. They'll have to take them out of my dead hand."

It is no coincidence that the militias began forming shortly after passage of the Brady Bill—the third event, after Weaver and Waco, that built the foundation for the movement. Concern about gun ownership drew thousands to meetings as no other issue could have. With audiences whipped into fury over the Brady Bill, it was easy to portray the issue as transcending the differences between urban and rural life and the issue of crime versus safety. Trochmann and others used guns as a symbol of freedom. Those who would regulate guns were cast as tyrants who were coming for people's guns *first*. The government had to disarm citizens in order to subjugate them. With the people disarmed, the theory went, tyrants could do anything they wanted, the people no longer having the hardware to resist. The United Nations could march in and take over America; loyal Americans could be sent to concentration camps.

In the militias' world, gun owners were recast not only as the logical first targets of those who would enslave America, but also as freedom's first and last line of defense. And, to be effective, people like Trochmann suggested they should be organized as a group, a well-armed militia.

Once it was established that gun ownership equaled liberty, the notion that government had any reasonable basis for restricting assault rifles was unbelievable. In fact Doug Fales, a California militia leader, asked, "How can you defend against the government if you have inferior arms to the military?" That idea—that the people had a right to arm themselves to defeat the U.S. Army—became the basic anti–gun control premise of the militias. Presumably that idea was capable of expansion. The government, after all, has nuclear weapons.

✗ ✗ ✗

The Second Amendment to the United States Constitution reads: "A well regulated Militia, being necessary to the security of a free State, the right of the people to keep and bear Arms, shall not be infringed." When the Bill of Rights was ratified, the idea of a "well-regulated militia" reflected, as the U.S. Supreme Court wrote in *United States v. Miller* in 1939, "the sentiment of the time [which] strongly disfavored standing armies; the common view was that adequate defense of country and laws could be secured through the Militia—civilians primarily, soldiers on occasion." At the time of the Second Amendment's adoption there was no regular army-issued firearm. The defense of America rested upon "citizen-soldiers," who would grab their gun from the fireplace mantel and muster when the security of the state was in jeopardy. The Second Amendment did not grant Americans an individual right to keep and bear arms: guns, bazookas, tanks, torpedoes, nuclear missiles. Nor did it suggest that people had the right to stockpile such weapons for the common defense; the security of the state would not be enhanced if we relied on the call-up of privately owned tanks, for example. Rather, the amendment meant what it said—that the individual right of arms ownership existed for the purpose of having a well-regulated militia that could preserve the security of the state. "Judicial consensus," wrote attorney Dennis Henigan, "[is that] the scope of the people's right to keep and bear arms is limited by the introductory phrase of the Amendment. . . . [T]he Supreme Court also has held that the modern embodiment of the 'well regulated militia' is the National Guard, which does not use privately owned guns at all."

Wayne LaPierre, head of the National Rifle Association, had a different view. Like many Americans who are unaware of the Second Amendment's history and the court decisions that have interpreted it, he claimed that the Second Amendment granted an individual right of gun ownership. And, like Trochmann and other militia leaders, he asserted that the amendment was the cornerstone of individual liberty.

In a six-page fund-raising letter dated April 13, 1995, LaPierre wrote that "the semi-auto ban gives jack-booted government thugs *more power to take away our Constitutional rights, break in our doors, seize our guns, destroy our property, even injure or kill us* [emphasis in original]. You can see . . . our freedoms slowly slipping away when jack-booted government thugs, wearing black, armed to the teeth, break down a door, open fire with an automatic weapon, and kill or maim law-abiding citizens."

LaPierre's letter continued: "In Clinton's administration, if you have a badge, you have the government's go-ahead to harass, intimidate, *even murder* law abiding citizens. . . . Randy Weaver at Ruby Ridge . . . Waco and the Branch Davidians . . . Not too long ago, it was unthinkable for Federal agents wearing Nazi bucket helmets and black storm trooper uniforms to attack law-abiding citizens. . . . Not today, not with Clinton."

LaPierre painted a picture of America sliding toward chaos. He said that gun owners were the vanguard of resistance. "America's gun owners," he wrote, "will only be the first to lose their freedoms. If we lose the right to keep and bear arms, then the right to free speech, free practice of religion, and every other freedom in the Bill of Rights are sure to follow."

LaPierre also published a "special report," entitled "The Final War Has Begun," in the June 1994 issue of *The American Rifleman*. It asserted: "A document secretly delivered to me reveals frightening evidence that the full-scale war to . . . eliminate private firearms ownership completely and forever . . . [is] well underway. . . . I firmly believe the NRA has no alternative but to recognize this attack and counter with every resource we can muster."

It is understandable that those who want to maintain private gun ownership would fund-raise with a worst-case scenario, but the NRA's scare tactics were as baseless as would be fund-raising among Holocaust survivors by claiming that the Nazis are about to take over. LaPierre's extreme rhetoric depersonalized and demonized federal law enforcement and, in Ken Toole's terminology, helped enlarge the open end of the funnel.

Those, like the NRA leaders, who claimed that the Second Amendment meant that Americans have an individual constitutional right to gun ownership distorted the law, and they did so in much the same manner as militia members who claimed their group's existence was recognized in the same constitutional provision. (This is one reason why they call themselves militias rather than vigilantes or gangs.) The focus on the Second Amendment to give legitimacy to their respective agendas explained, in part, the great overlap in the rhetoric of the NRA and that of the militia movement.

The militias and the NRA advanced an alternative interpretation of the Second Amendment to justify not only the right to individual gun ownership, but also the right to have guns to match or outmatch government. This view, which is unsupported by cases that have addressed the issue, is called the insurrectionist theory of the Second Amendment. To argue this point the militias quoted Thomas Jefferson as saying "the strongest reason for the people to retain the right to keep and bear arms is, as a last resort, to protect themselves against government tyranny." Jefferson's view, however, was not that expressed by the language of the Second Amendment, and in any event, was offered in the days of single-shot muskets. Could anyone imagine Jefferson today arguing that citizens had the right to own, say, ballistic missiles or antiaircraft guns, to match the firepower of government?

What militia leaders are relying upon in their "insurrectionist theory" is not the Second Amendment as much as the generalized principle, expressed by Mao and many others, that power comes from the barrel of a gun. Throughout history there have been tyrannical governments against which armed resistance was the only option. That militia members see the current U.S. government as such an evil entity explains, but does not justify, their efforts to contort the Second Amendment to mean that the Founders envisioned people like John Trochmann as a leader of a constitutionally ordained American resistance movement.

The Second Amendment, rather, was crafted in the context of a serious debate about the power of the states versus that of the federal government. The country was still new. The Articles of Confederation, which preserved a great degree of each state's sovereignty after the Revolution, had produced chaotic results. How should the states now bind together with common currency, foreign policy, mutual defense? How would the various aspects of sovereignty be shared between the central government and the states? Which should have the balance of power, including that which came with having the most guns? *This* was the battle between the federalists and the antifederalists. It was never between those who advocated government rights versus mob rights.

A few of those who helped shape the Constitution and the Bill of Rights advocated a nearly unrestricted individual right to bear arms; one proposal read, "Congress shall never disarm any citizen unless such as are or having been in Actual Rebellion." The fact that the Second Amendment did not contain such broad language ends the debate for all courts and most scholars, but not for militia members and many gun owners, who rely on two-hundred-year-old quotes taken out of context, and on shoddy historical analysis.

"What insurrectionist theory amounts to," Dennis Henigan wrote, "[is] the startling assertion of a generalized constitutional right of all citizens to engage in armed insurrection against their government. . . . [I]t represents a profoundly dangerous doctrine of unrestrained individual rights which, if adopted by the courts, would threaten the rule of law itself."

Other premises underlying the "insurrectionist theory" are false as well. For example, Professor Sanford Levinson, arguing for the theory, cited "the implication that might be drawn from the Second, Ninth and Tenth Amendments: that the citizenry itself can be viewed as an important third component [beyond the national government and the states] insofar as it stands ready to defend republican liberty against the deprecation of the other two structures, however futile that might be as a practical matter." In other words, he believed that the right to keep and bear arms provided a check on any tendency of government to go astray—or, in his words, there was "a privilege and immunity of the United States citizenship—of membership in the liberty-enhancing political order—to keep arms that could be taken up against tyranny wherever found, including, obviously, state government."

One practical problem with the idea that the Second Amendment allows people to have guns in order to point them at a government they do not like is that such an interpretation creates the ultimate political paradox. The right to have arms in order to threaten government necessarily implies a right to use them for that purpose. (Otherwise, how could it be a valid check on power?) The Constitution set out many ways to reform government, even to remake it entirely: Elections. Petition. The free press. Impeachment. Constitutional amendments. No government provides for the right of groups of armed, disgruntled citizens to revolt by blowing up and gunning down government officials. That is called sedition, assassination, and treason, and is punishable by law. Yet that was the role many militia members saw for themselves. They used some of the same rhetoric as the NRA in order to repaint their plans into something not merely legal but in the best constitutional tradition.

The plain language of the Second Amendment also defeats the militias' "insurrectionist" theory. The amendment protects the right of citizens to bear arms in order that militias can exist. Why? In order to protect "the security of a free State." But the militias saw the state as of dubious legitimacy, and themselves in a possible war with it. They were not owning guns to protect "the security of the State," but to make the state insecure through revolution. If their "insurrectionist" view of the Second Amendment were correct, they could succeed in a criminal trial—such as that arising from the Oklahoma City bombing—by arguing that they had a good-faith belief that the government was tyrannical, and they were only protecting the Constitution by armed insurrection. Obviously, such a defense would be groundless.* If the insurrectionist theory were correct, a person who threatened public officials with imminent "fighting words" could be punished under the First Amendment, but not for shooting these same officials under the Second.

And what about the term "well regulated"? Militia members say, "See, we have regulations." But the amendment's intent was that the militia be regulated by government, not by private citizens like John Trochmann and Norman Olson.

Militias also tried to wrap themselves, and their "right to bear arms," in the suggestion that the Second Amendment was meant to create private militias, and that all white men of a certain age automatically belonged to the militia movement. Journalist Jeff Goldberg, attending a militia meeting where anti-Semitic statements were made, was surprised to hear that he, too, was considered a member of the militia. The "insurrectionist

---

* In the 1980s the Knights of the Ku Klux Klan similarly argued that their armed operations targeting Vietnamese-American fishermen were protected by the Second Amendment. This defense was rejected.

theory" holds that all white males between eighteen and forty-five are members of "the militia," and Mr. Goldberg fit that definition. Why were all white males part of the militia? Because, in colonial times, militias were made up of white men. But today's militias thus confuse the idea of "membership in" with that of "definition of" the militia.

Some state laws have distinguished between the "organized" and "unorganized" militia. The former was the National Guard; the latter consisted of, again, males of an age suitable for armed service. Here is what the Militia of Montana attempted to make of this difference:

> There are two distinct and separate classes of militia of the State of Montana—the organized and the unorganized. The Governor is commander of both. The organized is defined by Montana law (Title 10) as the national guard and the Montana home guard. The unorganized consists of all those who do not belong to the organized and are able-bodied unless exempted by law. That's pretty simple. None of the members of the Militia of Montana are members of the organized militia of the state. Therefore, being able-bodied and not exempted by law, they are members of the unorganized militia of the state, as required by law.

What the law meant was that the governor might be able to call upon men of a specified age and order them about in time of emergency—a power that made sense back when Montana was a territory. No governor has called out John Trochmann or any other civilian to be part of an "unorganized militia." In fact, if the governor acted on the authority that MOM suggested he has, MOM would have a legitimate concern about erosion of freedoms. For example, if the governor headed both militias, and people of a particular age were, by definition, in the militia, and the militia was a paramilitary organization, the governor could say, "I command every able-bodied Montana male between eighteen and forty-five to stay one hundred yards away from John Trochmann. No male between these ages shall communicate with Trochmann, directly or indirectly. And if any man disobeys this order he shall be jailed and tried under the code of military conduct."

And what about the Constitution? Article I, Section 8, Clause 15 gives Congress the power "to provide for calling forth the Militia to execute the Laws of the Union, suppress Insurrections and repel invasions." Article I, Section 8, Clause 16 gives Congress the power "to provide for organizing, arming, and disciplining, the Militia, and for governing such Part of them as may be employed in the Service of the United States, reserving to the States respectively, the Appointment of the Officers, and the Authority of training the Militia according to the discipline prescribed by Congress."

As Henigan notes, and the NRA and militia members conveniently ignore, "the Framers understood the militia to be *an instrument of governmental authority*."

The idea that any self-appointed group of citizens can arm itself to oppose the government is an open invitation to chaos. One only need think of the Somalian warlords to realize what can happen when armed bandits take the law into their own hands.

✗ ✗ ✗

Militia members not only criticized any federal effort at gun control, they were infuriated by the idea that the government had any legitimate right to arm itself. MOM handed out what it said was a copy of a September 1993 purchase order from a sports shop in Libby, Montana. The Forest Service was the "consignee." Three items were listed: eighty boxes of "Federal 12 Gauge 2 3/4 oo Buckshot 45 Auto," 240 boxes of "Winchester 230 Gr. Ball Jacket," and three hundred boxes of "Federal Premium 230 Gr. Hydra-shok J.H.P. 45 Auto." The purchase of this ammunition led MOM to ask: "Have Forest Service employees become part of a national police force?"

The Militia of Montana also published a twenty-seven-page "Information and Networking Manual," which not only provided its analysis of the Second Amendment, but also presented a "History of the Militia," which it traced back to 54 B.C. and "Caesar's Invasion of Britain." According to MOM, the British leader "Cassivellaunus knew he wouldn't stand a chance against Caesar's 23,000 troops. It was time to call out the militia." Other examples of militias in MOM's history come from Afghanistan and Finland. Also mentioned were Greece, Rome, and Israel; they supposedly had militias, and when those were abolished, "Greece, Rome and Israel all passed into oblivion." Noting the presumably positive attributes of modern militias, MOM asserted that "in current Croatia, Bosnia Herzegovina, and Yugoslavia, we have seen that it has been by and through the militia that Croatia gained its independence." What an attractive model for America.

All these examples, besides their other flaws, involved fighting off foreigners. To the militia, there was no logical leap in defining American government in the same light. As a Militia of Montana manual asserted:

> If the army has control of the militia, then the militia will be obedient to the command of the army, which is in the command of the government. If the militia is independent and viable, then only laws which are right and just will come forth from the government, keeping the populace supportive and loyal to the government. To balance the military power of the nation,

the might of the militia, will put at odds any scheme by government officials to use the force of the government against the people. Therefore, when the codes and statutes are unjust for the majority of the people, the people will rightly revolt, and the government will have to acquiesce without a shot being fired, because the militia stands vigilant in carrying out the will of the people in defense of rights, liberty and freedom.

The choice MOM saw was clear: "Join the Army and Serve the U.N. or Join the Militia and serve America."

✗ ✗ ✗

A self-described "extreme individualist libertarian" on the Internet wrote two weeks before the Oklahoma bombing that the militias' "anger was provoked quite needlessly by the insane desire of the Establishment for 'gun control.' Back off and everything will go back to normal." He was right to the extent that the emotion that drew people to the militias was "anger," and that the issue of gun control was recast as one of freedom. Part of the mythology of the militias was the exaltation of the gun into an icon of liberty. History was rewritten to this end. According to a "Free Militia" field manual, the Revolutionary War wasn't about taxation without representation; it claimed that "American patriots took up arms against the British and began the revolution only when—and precisely because—the British attempted to disarm them." Wrong, says historian Rosemarie Zagarri. "The British fought the Americans," she says. "They didn't try to disarm them."

More disturbing than the wholesale revision of American history to honor the gun is the rewriting and use of the Nazi era as a propaganda tool. "We have a contingency plan," claimed Ron Fisher, leader of the Orlando-based "187th Regiment." "Had the Germans had militias . . . against the Nazis, a whole lot more would have survived—and the Nazis might not have gotten in power." A member of the Michigan militia said, "When Hitler took over power, they [sic] took all the people's guns away from them." A highly circulated anti-gun-control poster showed Adolf Hitler giving a Nazi salute; the caption says that all in favor of gun control should raise their hand. At an Indiana militia meeting a commander named John lectured about gun control: "After registration comes confiscation. And also, genocide comes soon after that. . . . It was gun control that brought Hitler to power."

Hitler, of course, did disarm his opponents once he gained power, but that is the only part of Nazi history that the militias seem to have right. The Nazi Party came to power in part because the Weimar Republic was too weak to curtail it and its Brownshirts, who threatened their political opponents. It's not hard to guess what a Montana public official might answer when asked whether the militia resembles the Nazi street agitators of the late 1920s and early 1930s or their underground opposition.

That the militias pointed to Nazi Germany as a justification for their existence was grotesque. Clinton was not Hitler; the FBI—despite its problems—was not the Gestapo; the government was not, is not taking members of "undesirable races" to factories of mass murder. Many Americans remain ignorant about the history of the Nazis and of the Holocaust. To many, Nazis were just "bad guys," and the militias seem happy to distort history in order to paint themselves as "good guys."

✗ ✗ ✗

Difficult as it may be to believe, with its rhetoric about "jackboots" and "Nazis" and "police state," the NRA was not the fringe of the gun lobby. That honor belonged to Gun Owners of America, which claimed to have 150,000 members. According to the Coalition for Human Dignity, Gun Owners of America actually had 100,000 members and was known as the "No Compromise Alternative to the NRA." "Movement activists such as . . . Gritz and McLamb," the Coalition reported, "advise people to trade in their NRA membership in favor of the GOA."

GOA's leader, Larry Pratt, has appeared in all the right places—on the anti-Semitic *Radio Free America*; in *Spotlight*; at Preparedness Expos along with people like Jack McLamb, Bo Gritz, and Mark Koernke; at Pete Peters's meeting after the Ruby Ridge siege where he reportedly called for the formation of armed militias. Pratt has written a book, *Armed People Victorious* (1990). Citing Guatemalan civil defense patrols as a model, he wrote: "The history of the United States for years before and after the founding of the Republic was the history of an armed people with functioning militias involved in civil defense (or police work, if you will). . . . While the United States has forgotten its successes in this area, other countries have rediscovered them. It is time that the United States return to reliance on an armed people. There is no acceptable alternative."

That the leader of an anti-gun-control group of 100,000 regularly associated with racists and anti-Semites was troubling enough. But he did more: He addressed their meetings. Pratt spoke at the 1993 "Jubilation Celebration," an annual conference of bigots organized in conjunction with the Christian Identity tabloid *Jubilee*, along with Pete Peters and other Identity leaders. He also spoke at the June 1994 convention of the Constitutionalists Networking Center, as did Klan members, skinheads, and other racists. The CNC is a white supremacist organization (headed by former Arizona governor Evan Mecham), and the agenda of that meeting was unmistakable. Its opening anthem was "Dixie." "Yeehaw!" said the Reverend John Lewis. "Those are the values your granddaddies died for." Pratt, obviously, wanted to rely on these folks to help thwart gun control, and by doing so he not only forced the NRA closer to the fringe, he helped push some of his audiences, and their racist agendas, further into the funnel of the militias. In fact it was no coincidence that, with the NRA and GOA promoting an antigovernment message, the militias were able to build their membership and spread their message through gun shows around the country—shows that people such as Timothy McVeigh and Terry Nichols would attend.

The gun remains a significant part of American culture, and an important political issue. Americans are passionately for or against guns. That debate should be conducted without powerful groups such as the NRA rewriting history and contorting the Constitution like a pretzel. From distortion comes the most dangerous delusion that empowers many in America's private armies: the idea that shooting American public officials is a patriotic duty.

11 This Land Is My Land

ALL IT WOULD HAVE TAKEN WAS FOR ONE OF
THOSE [FOREST] RANGERS TO HAVE DRAWN A
WEAPON. . . . FIFTY PEOPLE WITH SIDEARMS
WOULD HAVE DRILLED HIM.

DICK CARVER, Nye County, Arizona, commissioner

As the militias grew in 1994 and early 1995, they also attracted people frustrated over environmental regulations, especially in the West. Everyone may agree, abstractly, that clean water and air is a good idea. But when the government decides you cannot use your land in a certain way because it may impact something you can't see—some plant or animal you have never heard of, or someone three states and a thousand miles away—there is a sense of unfairness and intrusion.

As with gun control, the issues around land use were made for militias: Not only did they involve strongly felt concerns, but also the question of who was "in control" was meat and drink to conspiracy theorists. There was also a tradition to be built upon: In the 1970s and 1980s the Posse Comitatus had organized farmers who, like loggers, miners, and ranchers today, saw economic hardship or government regulation affecting their ability to make money. For example, in 1980 the Wisconsin Posse published "American Farmer: 20th Century Slave" to "explain" why banks were foreclosing on farms: Jews, incapable of farming, had to control the world's monetary system in order to control the global food supply.

The militia movement's environmentally targeted literature was more sophisticated than the Posse's. Rather than gripe directly about Jews, it focused on environmentalists and the federal government. MOM distributed an undated (circa 1994) article from *The Montanian* with the headline "Will People Give Way to Ecosystems? Proposed Actions Would Limit Property Rights and Population." The first paragraph, written by a reporter who, in another article, had called John Trochmann a "peacemaker," had a subjective bite:

> The federal government considers people to be a "biological resource" that must be managed to protect ecosystems; the government also wants to manage human reproduction to achieve its ecological goals, according to internal documents from the Environmental Protection Agency and the federal Bureau of Land Management. The documents show that these agencies also want to control private property in order to protect ecosystems.

The article described a proposed "Ecosystem Protection Act" that would look at areas as "ecosystems" rather than political boundaries. *The Montanian*'s reporter explained this "holistic" approach thus:

> The ecosystem concept is based on the belief that every natural thing in the world is related, and everything is of equal value. Under the ecosystem approach to land management, any activity can adversely affect components of a biological area and should be regulated to preserve all the member components. Logging, mining, farming and residential development in an area are activities that can negatively change a portion of the natural world. adverse [sic] affects [sic] of the activities should be reduced or prohibited in order to "protect people's health," according to the EPA. . . . One of the EPA's key tools to protect ecosystems would be to "develop human population policies that are consistent with sustainable economies and ecosystems."

It was overstatement to suggest that environmentalists have no more regard for people than, say, extreme animal rights activists who go beyond wanting to protect animals from abuse, and insist that no lab mice die, rather than use them to find cures for diseases that kill men, women, and children. Protection of the environment *is* an important national and local concern—a long-term one. Today's industrial activities may poison tomorrow's water, kill salmon, and destroy important links in the food chain—losses that will not only harm animals but also have potentially devastating economic and health effects. Ask the fisherman in the North-west, for whom government regulation might be a nuisance but dwin-dling salmon counts a disaster. Or ask former loggers from towns that have been dismantled—stores, schools, houses bulldozed—because big timber was no longer available for the mill saws.

There is also the question of the beauty of the land—especially na-tional land, which belongs to all Americans. Who cannot understand the grief of people like John Witters, who wrote of the planned logging of Spider Meadows in the Glacier Peak Wilderness: "I've seen Spider Mead-ows from Spider Gap, and I thought it was beautiful. . . . I hope I can get there before the logging starts. At least I'll have some pictures and memo-ries of what Spider Meadows used to look like. The Washington I knew as a child is disappearing. It is being cut down, filled in, paved over, fragmented and polluted."

It also makes sense to think in terms of ecosystems. Rivers run, birds migrate, mountain ranges affect climates—all with disdain for maps and for the boundaries marked by "Welcome" signs on the interstate. Environ-mentalists tend to think of long-term implications. American culture tends to focus on immediate impacts, not on those on our great-grandchildren. And while there must be a balance between the ex-tremes—only the ideologue would believe that Manhattan should have the farmland, livestock, and landscape it had in the early 1800s—there is a political factor pulling against environmentalists: Angry great-grandchildren do not vote.

On what scale are these competing emotional and economic consider-ations balanced? And how do you weigh the moral imperative behind the overstated *Montanian* assertion that environmentalists see "everything [as having] equal value"? While most environmentalists don't think that people and snail darters are indistinguishable, they are concerned with whether we have the right to kill off any species. But how many snail darters, for example, are worth the loss of how many jobs, with how much inevitable stress? Can anyone quantify this?

To underscore the complexity of this issue, consider the testimony before a congressional panel in 1995 about the Endangered Species Act. Representatives Helen Chenoweth (R–Idaho) and Wes Cooley (R–Ore-gon) railed against the act. Representative Frank Riggs (R–California) said that in order to protect the northern spotted owl, timber communities had been traumatized throughout the Northwest. J. D. Hayworth (R–Arizona) complained that safeguarding the loach minnow had forestalled road and bridge repair in Arizona. Tennessee Republican Ed Bryant complained that in order to preserve the Cumberland monkeyface pearly mussel, a dam could not be built.

But Representative Elizabeth Furst (D–Oregon) noted that, thanks to the Endangered Species Act, the Pacific Northwest could no longer ignore dying salmon runs. And Churt Weldon, a Pennsylvania Republican, told of six-year-old Jackie Buckley, who had been diagnosed with leukemia at age three and expected to die. She now had "a 99 percent chance of living a long, productive life—thanks to a cancer-fighting medicine derived from a rare wildflower," he said. Weldon also pointed to the Pacific yew tree, a source of taxol, used to treat cancer; to the purple foxglove, used for heart ailments; to the Australian mulberry and the Cameroon vine tree which play a role in the fight against AIDS. "We are just beginning to discover the medicinal value of our plant species," he said. "The Endangered Species Act plays an important role in protecting these resources from danger."

Just as with gun control or abortion, issues of the environment are difficult ones on which to compromise. Either you can or cannot use the water, mine the hill, cut the tree, graze the cattle. But if you live in the West, and regulations that affect your livelihood come from far-off urban Washington, the resentment becomes an easy magnet for the "us versus them" ideology of the militia movement.

✗ ✗ ✗

Catron County, New Mexico, is known for unusual legislation. In the summer of 1994 it passed a resolution encouraging every home to have a gun and ammunition—a purely symbolic action, since most households were already armed. Three years earlier it had enacted an ordinance that was more than symbolic: It had called for the arrest of any agent of the federal government violating the civil or property rights of county residents.

That strong antifederal stance drew attention to Catron County. On one side were ranchers like Richard Manning, who complained that as a result of federal regulations, including those protecting the spotted owl, "We have 700,000 acres of land, 2,500 people left and no economy." On the other side were people like Robin Silver of the Southwest Center for Biological Diversity, a Phoenix-based public interest conservation group which has gone to court opposing Catron County loggers and ranchers. "Their whole way of life had been subsidized by the rest of us," said Silver—meaning that while Americans own these lands in common, the people living nearby have been able to harvest publicly owned trees and graze cattle on publicly owned vegetation at minimal cost. "They have been permitted to denude public lands with little scrutiny," Silver said, "and now the chits are being called in."

Many people in Catron County saw themselves as literally under the gun of the federal government. So, following examples from other states, they formed a militia. Nancy Brown, aged seventy-two, said, "We're organizing to defend against all enemies, domestic and foreign. We feel we need to protect our property rights." Three hundred of the 2,500 people in Catron County came to the first militia meeting. "People are justifiably afraid that we're moving toward a point of confrontation in this country," said Howard Hutchinson. County Commissioner Hugh McKeen said, "We're trying to keep our livelihood and our homes here. The federal government wants us out of here in a moment. They want complete authority. . . . My ancestors had to fight Indians, and several of them died to settle this county. You're looking at the same people who settled this place. We're still here, and we're willing to fight."

Apparently the federal government was not. Even though permits had been canceled for ranchers who grazed livestock in numbers or at times deemed harmful to the land by the Bureau of Land Management, many such ranchers continued to graze their cattle, illegally, on federal property. One rancher insisted that his family had grazed cattle on public land since the Civil War, and that he would continue to use Forest Service land for his 150 head, although he had lost his permit for ignoring an order not to send his cattle into an area that had been burned and reseeded. The Forest Service and the Bureau of Land Management had the authority to impound such cattle—which were, after all, trespassing on and harming public land. "We can't protect the resource," said Ann Morgan, director of the BLM in Nevada, "because we are afraid our employees will be shot. It's not worth that."

Forest Service employees in Catron County received orders to travel in pairs. In the spring of 1995 their colleagues across the west were encouraged to do likewise, and to keep in contact with their offices by radio. Their families—even their children—have been threatened. The Washington State Department of Ecology thought it too dangerous for its employees to drive in cars with state logos. The insignias were erased.

In Nevada, Forest Service employees reported that they were being treated like lepers. No one would share a pew with them at church; their children were ostracized at school. In a video store and a family-style restaurant in the eastern Oregon town of Burns are signs reading: "This establishment doesn't serve federal employees." An area rancher whose grazing permit was not renewed told a federal employee that "he was going to tear [another employee's] head off and shit down his neck." He also said he would kill Forrest Cameron, the area refuge manager. Many local people supported this rancher.

Cameron's family was threatened; one caller said he would toss Cameron's twelve-year-old son down a well. Mrs. Cameron moved a hundred miles away with their four children. Mr. Cameron was asked what was currently the most important part of his job as a federal employee. "Well," he answered, "it's about learning to keep your head down."

✗ ✗ ✗

If you were concerned about gun ownership and went to a Militia of Montana meeting, you would have learned quasi-legal theories not only justifying your right to keep firearms, but also explaining why the law wanted you to point them at the evildoers threatening that right. Similar twisted history and legal theories were also used by ranchers, loggers, and miners attracted to the militia movement. These people had a more basic fear than gun owners: They believed their jobs and way of life were being threatened. They were dependent on public land for trees to cut, minerals to mine, and vegetation on which to graze their cattle. If someone from faraway Washington passed legislation that restricted their access to these resources, the regulation must be, by definition, unjust, and those who promoted it must be, by definition, the enemy.

Richard Manning was a rancher in Glenwood, New Mexico. "We have groups affecting the customs and culture of communities without suffering the results," he said. Manning and others adopted a legal theory that would allow them more control over the lands where they lived. "These lands were to be national in name only," he asserted, "and were to be managed locale by locale. But something has come into the midst of our lives called 'interested parties.' And whether their comments are good science or not, they don't know what promises the president of the United States made to our fathers about this land. It's as if people from Phoenix or Albuquerque were allowed to vote here. It destroys our way of life."

Michael Evans of Arizona Common Cause did not agree that the federal government was ignoring the ranchers' needs; he saw it the other way around. He said that by failing to regulate federal land, and by setting low rates that subsidized grazing, mining, and logging, the federal government had greatly helped those using the land. Now that the pendulum was swinging back toward environmental protection, "these groups are screaming for a bygone era to be back," Evans said. There were two thousand ranching families in Arizona. "That those few people," he asserted, "trying to maintain a way of life that in reality only existed for fifty to seventy-five years should be able to set the policy agenda for the other 3.5 million people in Arizona is absurd."

The debate was complex, and left little room for compromise. Environmentalists from the cities looked at public land and wanted to preserve it for future generations. Government, in their view, had failed as a steward of this land, handing over resources—owned collectively by Americans—for exploitation by companies and ranchers, in exchange for a few dollars. On the other hand, those who called themselves part of the "Wise Use" movement rejected environmental regulations as unwise, unfair, and un-American. Since they used the land for their livelihood, they said, they knew best how to preserve it and preservation was in their long-term economic interest.

The argument was heated. Should grazing be stopped, as environmentalists suggested, because cows destroyed natural vegetation, eroded land, and otherwise changed the habitat in ways that increased fire danger? Or should grazing be unregulated, as ranchers argued, because where it had been stopped mesquite, cottonwood, and other combustible plants flourished, increasing the fire danger?

Two hundred counties across America have debated, and seventy have enacted, laws challenging federal controls over forests and rangeland. These laws were based on legal fictions such as the assumption that federal control over public land violated the "equal footing" clause of the Constitution, making the "new" Western states inferior to the original thirteen. But to the local inhabitants, the ordinances were like a declaration of independence from the American government.

X X X

Nye County, Nevada, in the south-central part of the state, is twice as large as New Hampshire, but in the mid-1990s only 20,000 people lived there. Many of these were ranchers, who were dependent on public land. The government owned 93 percent of Nye County.

Dick Carver was a Nye County commissioner. He was also a leader in the Wise Use movement. And even though he railed against the federal government, he said that federal law was on his side. He kept a copy of the Constitution in his breast pocket.

In December 1993, the Nye County commission "declared" that federal land in Nevada really belonged to Nevada, and that Nevada counties "have a duty to manage these lands, to protect all private rights held on these lands, and to preserve local customs, culture, economy and environment." In that spirit, on July 4, 1994, Carver climbed aboard a county bulldozer, and attempted to cut a roadway through Toiyabe National Forest. At least fifty supporters, some armed, cheered on their commissioner as he started the engine. A ranger holding up a sign telling Carver to stop had to jump out of the way to avoid being hit. Carver's theory, backed up by the Los Angeles–based Individual Rights Foundation (a conservative legal group affiliated with the Center for the Study of Popular Culture), was that the land was never the federal government's to rule over anyway. Relying on that premise, Carver tried to bring charges against Forest Service employees for "wrongful exercise of official power," "obstructing a public official in the performance of his duties," and "impersonating a peace officer." The Nye County district attorney would not initiate a prosecution. He lost the next election.

Carver said of the incident, "All it would have taken was for one of those rangers to have drawn a weapon. . . . Fifty people with sidearms would have drilled him."

A month later the Nye County board wrote to Theodore J. Angle, area manager for the Bureau of Land Management. "Our Board decided," it asserted, "that since you have yet to provide proof that the BLM has ownership of the public lands, or that the BLM has constitutionally-granted jurisdiction, or that you have been delegated the proper authority over grazing allotments in Nye County, your decisions are of no consequence. Should anyone make any attempt to enforce your final decisions this Board will take action to see that charges are brought against those persons as individuals for acting outside their authority."

After that incident Carver became a hero, not only to the Wise Use movement, but to the militias as well. He went on a speaking tour of Washington state and elsewhere, encouraging people with what researcher Paul deArmond called a "red-faced, angry, podium-pounding harangue" about the "Third American Revolution." Sounding like a Posse Comitatus member, Carver claimed that the Articles of Confederation—the post–Revolutionary War arrangement between the states that was replaced by the Constitution—were still good law, that the Constitution was a "compact" that could be terminated, and that county government was the "supreme elected power in the United States." Carver reportedly also spoke at Christian Identity meetings.

The Snohomish Property Rights Alliance, having hosted the Militia of Montana only weeks before, welcomed Carver. People applauded when, using the same rhetoric that the militias wielded against the New World Order, Carver called the Endangered Species Act and other similar legislation "treaties with foreign nations" that reflected a conspiracy driven by "federal bureaucrats." "They think they are above God and they can do anything they want," Carver said. "And they are the ones who are taking away your property rights." Carver said that, through the Endangered Species Act, the federal government, in conspiracy with environmentalists, was first coming after people's water, then their land.

The Department of Justice filed two suits against counties that have adopted antifederal Wise Use ordinances. One, against Dick Carver's Nye County, Nevada, was designed to "send a message, loud and clear, that the United States does indeed own and manage federal lands," according to Lois J. Schiffer, assistant attorney general for environment and national resources. Schiffer said, "We expect the court to quickly affirm that the federal government has sovereignty and that federal employees must be allowed to do their jobs without interference." Associate attorney general John Schidt added that the suit would "put to rest the idea that any county has the right to enact laws to override the Constitution."

As for Carver, he said: "You're talking to the happiest county commissioner that ever walked on the face of this earth. We got what we worked hard for fifteen months and now we've got to get it through the court." Carver believed that the issue would get to the Supreme Court, where the Wise Use side would win, 9–0. But the Supreme Court is unlikely to give away all federal lands to local counties. Militia leaders no doubt hope that their friends in the Wise Use movement who, like Dick Carver, share their antifederal animus and county-supremacy theories, might then decide that the courts have been taken over by an unseen enemy of the people and conclude, as militia members do, that armed resistance is the only answer.

The National Federal Lands Conference, a group working toward that end, was also involved in a second Justice Department lawsuit. In that case, the government intervened in a suit against Boundary County, Idaho, challenging its adoption of what Tarso Ramos of the progressive grassroots organizing group the Western States Center termed "illegal county rule ordinances distributed by the National Federal Lands Conference." Ramos noted that the "NFLC is a vocal supporter of armed citizen militias. . . . Carver, the NFLC and various militia formations appear to have overlapping constituencies." In fact, the October 1994 newsletter of the National Federal Lands Conference had a lead story entitled "Why There Is a Need for the Militia in America." (The need was "to overthrow the men who pervert the Constitution.") The article's author thanked various militias, including the Militia of Montana, for their help, and noted that these groups would "be more than happy to assist you in starting your own militia."

✗ ✗ ✗

In the earlier part of this century, ranchers killed wolves because wolves ate livestock. Parts of the West have not seen a wolf in generations. In early 1995, a few dozen gray wolves were released in Yellowstone and elsewhere in the Rockies as part of a federal plan. The idea was to reintroduce them into the ecosphere. Many ranchers and farmers protested, concerned about their livestock.

One of the wolves released in the Frank Church Wilderness Area was found shot to death, on land belonging to a seventy-four-year-old Challis, Idaho, rancher named Gene Hussey. On March 8, 1995, armed officers of the U.S. Fish and Wildlife Service executed a search warrant on Hussey's ranch. They were searching for evidence about the wolf's killing, including bullets.

Sheriff Brett Barsalou of nearby Lemhi County disapproved. Barsalou —who in January 1995 had threatened to stop federal workers bringing in the wolves, for fear of violence—told reporters that "sending three armed agents to serve a warrant on a seventy-four-year-old man is inappropriate, heavy-handed, and dangerously close to excessive force." Two days later, on a bitterly cold, bright, and crisp Saturday, between two hundred and three hundred people attended a rally in Challis's town square. The townsfolk cheered Barsalou and Hussey, calling them heroes. State representative Lenore Barrett told the rally, "We are not Waco. We are not Ruby Ridge. We are exercising our constitutional rights. [The feds should] back off."

National politicians echoed the anger heard in tiny Challis. Representative Helen Chenoweth said she would ask Congress to pass legislation requiring federal law enforcement agents to secure written permission from county sheriffs before enforcing federal laws. Equally shocking was Senator Larry Craig of Idaho, who advocated disarming federal officers. "There has always been a healthy suspicion of the federal agent," said Craig. "Now there is developing a healthy fear, especially if the agent is armed." Craig, an opponent of gun control and an NRA board member, was asked if his view that citizens should be armed, and federal officers disarmed, was inconsistent. "The Second Amendment applies to private citizens," he explained. "We have always controlled and determined who packs a gun as a law enforcement officer. What I'm trying to express is a growing frustration in the West amongst the private citizens of the increasing presence of an armed federal entity in the states where you have these resource agencies [the Forest Service, the Bureau of Land Management, and Fish and Wildlife]. . . . What happens in the West when all of a sudden they see these folks in the Forest Service and BLM being armed and carrying arms, they grow frightened."

When public officials such as Chenoweth and Craig affirmed the militias' antifederal ideology and premises, organizing became easier for the militias—and life harder for federal workers. On March 22, 1995, the Forest Service sent this notice to its employees:

As you receive this letter, some of your coworkers are receiving "contact cards" for their convenience from the Law Enforcement and Investigations branch of the agency. These cards are being issued to field-going employees in areas where "local control" ordinances have been passed, or where the possibility exists that employees may be detained or arrested in the course of their official duties. "Local control" ordinances typically prohibit employees from performing their jobs or require them to get permission from local authorities first . . .

The contact cards tell employees who are "confronted, detained or placed in custody by State or local authorities" while engaged in their official duties to cooperate, not to resist, and to contact the Forest or Regional special agent.

✗ ✗ ✗

A T-shirt proclaims "End of the World 12 miles, Challis 15." Samuel Sherwood, head of the United States Militia Association, came there to organize militia members. Unlike the potato country of Blackfoot, Idaho, where Sherwood lived, Challis was a mining community. Half of Challis's adults worked either at the local molybdenum plant or at the Hecla gold mine. The town and all its jobs were directly affected by a lawsuit brought by the Sierra Club Legal Defense Fund and the Wilderness Society. Federal District Court Judge Dan Ezra of Hawaii agreed with the Sierra Club that a Forest Service plan had not protected salmon habitats under the Endangered Species Act. The habitat was a four-foot-wide stream, 900 miles upriver from the Pacific. Even the town's oldest residents had never seen a salmon there; the last salmon programmed to return to Challis had likely been gobbled up by the Columbia River's hydroelectric dams long ago. Nonetheless, Judge Ezra issued an injunction, which residents feared might close down all "resource activities" in five national forests in Idaho in March 1995. Four thousand jobs, with an estimated payroll of $83 million, would be lost if the forests were closed. "That's our total economy," said Randy Pearson, whose four hundred head of cattle grazed in the Challis National Forest. "If they close these ranches, we might as well move to the big city and go on welfare, because there's nothing else left."

A real tragedy, brought about by laws passed thousands of miles to the east and enforced by federal officials thousands of miles to the west, was an organizing dream for Sherwood. At a meeting in Challis he said, "All it's going to take is for this crazy judge in Hawaii to actually shut down the forests and there will be blood in the streets." What should the people of Challis do? Sherwood suggested everyone "get a semi-automatic assault rifle and a revolver and a uniform." He wanted them to join his militia in order to oppose "the green Gestapo."

Politicians spoke too, including Idaho secretary of state Pete Cenarussa. He explained that if all mining, ranching, and logging in the national forests were closed, then the "sovereignty of Idaho [must be restored] through the court system." But if that didn't work, "there is going to be a great uprising among the people here. It's a matter of survival and when these instincts are aroused, anything can happen." Lyn Hintze, a commissioner of Custer County, Idaho, claimed "three platoons of militia" would be prepared. He said the militia would insist the Forest Service prove the land was federal. If it couldn't, "we're going to take over." Sherwood said, "We want a bloodless revolution, [but if we have to] we'll give them a civil war to think about. We're ready to look the federal government in the eye." Secretary of State Cenarussa said that if the courts ruled against Idaho's sovereignty, the government might confer legal status on the militia.

The court finally decided to leave the forest open, asking the parties to work out a plan to protect the salmon. However, it was too late to protect the county from the idea that forming a private army to fight the federal government might be a reasonable thing to consider.

✗ ✗ ✗

How do you view the world if you live in a place like Challis, Idaho, or Nye County, Nevada? The resources upon which your livelihood depends are being depleted, so environmentalists and urban lawmakers will only work that much harder to preserve what remains. You and your employers have a common agenda: to fight regulations and the urban "yuppies" and "trust-funders" who are more concerned with preserving animals no one ever heard of than with your job. You might cheer a politician such as Idaho's Helen Chenoweth, who held an "endangered salmon bake" fund-raiser, but what good would that really do?

What can you do to feel that you are holding on to your heritage and livelihood, even saving your town? Washington, D.C., is far away. But the forest ranger, the BLM manager, perhaps an environmentalist or two are living in your area, and are easy targets. As an Oregon Wise Use activist said, "We have no way to fight back other than to make them pariahs in their community."

In the fall of 1994, fifty people gathered in tiny Joseph, Oregon, tarred and feathered two dummies, and strung them up on a beam on Main Street. The dummies represented Andy Kerr and Ric Bailey, two neighbors, who were environmentalists.

Ellen Gray of the Audubon Society testified at a public hearing in Everett, Washington, on November 14, 1994. After her presentation, she said, a "man . . . reached under his seat, pulled out a hangman's noose, shook it in my face, and said, 'This is a message for you.' Immediately afterwards another man . . . leaned toward me and he said, 'We have a militia of ten thousand, and if we can't beat you at the ballot box, we will beat you with a bullet.' "

Veteran Forest Service workers lament the days when they were thought of as friendly people associated with Smokey the Bear. Now they see themselves as targets. "I've had militia members . . . asking me if I believed in the Constitution and did I take an oath of office," says Tom Wagner, a district ranger in the Bitterroot National Forest. "I tell them my job is not to interpret the Constitution, but to enforce the law Congress passes. They're not satisfied with the answer."

In February 1995, at a meeting of a group called People for the West, the president of a farm association said that Forest Service agents with "bubble gum helmets" have no authority beyond that of an ordinary citizen to effect arrests. He suggested that if a Forest Service or Bureau of Land Management official tried to arrest someone, the proper response was to take his or her gun. And, he said, all federal officers should be removed from federal land.

"We've stopped doing road maintenance in one county because of concern about the safety of the lives of the crews," said Jim Nelson, who is supervisor of the Toiyabe National Forest. Forest Service workers have also planned to avoid helicopter flyovers of the land of certain militia members—even in the event of forest fires—so they won't be shot.

"It has become really hard to be a federal employee out here," according to John Freemuth of Boise State University. "They feel intimidated, isolated, demoralized. They wonder how they became the bad guys."

At a public meeting in Ely, Nevada, a rancher threatened a Bureau of Land Management official. "He stood up," says Michele Barrett of the BLM's Nevada office, "and told the agent that if he had only two bullets left, he would save one of them for him."

These are not simply the protests of peeved people, not just the ravings of a few fanatics. Representative George Miller, a California Democrat, has said that a "very serious pattern of violence and intimidation aimed at federal employees has emerged in several Western states that both endangers human life and public property and interferes with the enforcement of federal law." He called on five members of Congress, including Idaho's Craig and Chenoweth, to "end the casual demeaning of federal employees who risk their lives every day to defend public property and U.S. citizens."

Miller was correct. Craig and Chenoweth and some others were contributing to, and legitimizing, the demonizing and dehumanization of federal officials. This vilification went beyond not liking the particular FBI agents and marshals at Waco and Ruby Ridge; it encompassed not only them, and not only the Forest Service and BLM, but *all* federal employees. Such hatred was of a different dimension than that expressed in the 1960s by some in the antiwar movement, who referred to police as "pigs"; those protesters did not degrade forest rangers or other government employees in similar terms.

The militias and Wise Use proponents both lamented regulations and restrictions on "federal land," which they saw as their local land. By defining it as "federal land" policed by "federal officers," they portrayed federal workers as part of an occupying force, rather than as public servants who were helping preserve "public land." What they were doing, with the help of some public officials, was reinventing bigotry. Now the victim group, seen as a threat and not worthy of neighborly treatment, was not Jews or Catholics or blacks or Hispanics; they were federal employees.

In America in the mid-1990s it is taboo to express overt hatred of minorities. Disagreement with government, however, is a fine and important American tradition. What the Wise Use groups and militias accomplished was to redirect the old-fashioned hatred onto an "acceptable" target. America has progressed remarkably in the last thirty years. Today, if stores anywhere bore signs refusing service to blacks or Jews or Asian Americans, there would be outrage. When that type of hatred is made acceptable by being transferred to our public servants—such as those who used to work in the Murrah Building—a new strain of bigotry has the chance to thrive in the American mainstream. America's private armies are eager promoters of this new, inward-looking hatred.

12 **Arresting Congress**

AMERICA WAS BUILT ON WAR, AND I FEEL LIKE
THAT'S THE ONLY WAY WE'RE GOING TO BE ABLE
TO TAKE IT BACK. THE ENEMY IS ALL AROUND US,
BUT THE MAIN TARGET IS WASHINGTON.

FRED, a militia member

The idea that Americans should take up weapons and form private armies to oppose the government gained a following across the country in 1994. The Michigan and Montana militias were the most visible, but those in Florida, Texas, North Carolina, Idaho, and elsewhere grew fast, too. Some had direct connections with hate groups; others did not. But they all shared an antigovernment venom, a conspiratorial outlook, and a penchant for threat. In the six months between September 1994 and March 1995, the militia movement resembled a pressure cooker waiting to blow.

✗ ✗ ✗

Linda Thompson, having proclaimed herself the "Acting Adjutant General" of the Unorganized Militia of the United States in April 1994, was not content to harp on Waco and sell videotapes. She believed her rhetoric and, as an attorney, was led by it to the obvious conclusion. If the current government was corrupt, and in violation of the Constitution, then it was illegal, and the people had a right to overthrow it, and according to the Second Amendment they had the right to bear arms, and according to the First Amendment they had the right of association, so they should just march into Washington with their guns, arrest Congress, try it for treason, and impose sentence. Treason is punishable by death.

Thompson proposed to arrest Congress on September 19, 1994. Being a lawyer, she knew she had to be specific about the nature of congressional treason. Members of Congress were to be tried for, among other things, failing to abolish the Federal Reserve System and the Internal Revenue Service, the Fourteenth, Sixteenth, and Seventeenth Amendments to the Constitution, the North American Free Trade Agreement, and the Brady Bill. The militia was supposed to show up "armed and in uniform. . . . The militia will arrest Congressmen who have failed to uphold their oaths of office, who will then be tried for Treason by citizens' courts." "We are at war right now," said Thompson. "Make no mistake about it."

The militia movement was divided on Thompson's "Ultimatum." Debate raced wild on Internet newsgroups such as alt.conspiracy and talk.-politics.guns. "Are you prepared for the next American War?" was a hot topic. Some thought it a good idea, others wondered whether Thompson was an agent provocateur. The John Birch Society—which shared many of the militia movement's conspiratorial premises—warned members to shy away from this armed march on Washington. The idea of arresting Congress at gunpoint was too much even for the *Spotlight*, which also encouraged its readers to stay clear.

Thompson called off her "Ultimatum" before September 19, 1994, but defended her actions: "Has anything in the history of this country, since the Revolutionary War, accomplished this much toward actually solving our current problems, mobilizing so many, so quickly or so effectively, or done so much to literally scare the absolute bejeebers out of the opposition as the public announcement, by a dumpy broad in Indianapolis, that, enough is enough, we are going to arrest the traitors, man the weapons?"

While the Internet heated up with talk of armed insurrection and political assassination by people who had the hardware to make the threat real, law enforcement turned a blind eye.

X   X   X

The militia movement was organized without much scrutiny, even by the media, despite stunts like Thompson's "Ultimatum." There were articles here and there, some of the best by British journalists. But law enforcement and government officials, for the most part, were quiet. The private armies were not. Some went from talking about war to preparing for battle with government, either as groups or "Leaderless Resistance" units.

In 1994 in California, Jim Rodgers, a leader of the Tehama County, California, militia, said, "If your board of supervisors tries to do something you don't like, show up. They're going to assume someone in the back has a rope." He also advised waiting until the proper moment for a more forceful attack. The *Sacramento Bee* reported Rodgers's justification for delay: If members practiced for guerrilla warfare now, they " 'would be throwing the gauntlet down to state agencies and they'll respond.' Instead, he urged, hold classes in search and rescue or hunter survival. 'It boils down to the same thing, you're just putting it under a different name. You're not in a position now to confront. A year from now you'll win, but not now.' "

Others thought the time for battle was nearer. In North Carolina, Albert Esposito headed a militia group called the Citizens for the Reinstatement of Constitutionalist Government. He preached that members should stockpile the "Four B's"—Bibles, bullets, bandages, and beans. With these supplies the group could "resist the coming New World Order . . . [r]emove treasonous politicians and corrupt judges from positions of authority . . . make the Holy Bible and the United States Constitution the law of the land . . . and return authority to the people." The group disseminated application forms for the "National Free and Sovereign Civilian Militia, North Carolina State Division." (The form inquired about the applicant's skills. "Reloading ammo," apparently, was an ability of some value.)

While the North Carolina group was accepting applicants, Robert Pummer's Florida State Militia (FSM), founded in 1994, published a handbook to get its 500 members ready for the imminent war. "BUY AMMO NOW!" the handbook urged. "YOU WILL NOT BE ABLE TO BUY IT LATER!" It also advocated a cell structure as a buffer to infiltration: "You still have your inner circle, and this the FBI, ATF, or any other federal scumbags cannot penetrate, if you keep up your guard." Possession of weapons and organization into a proper paramilitary structure were only part of the necessary preparation. To help members achieve a battle-ready attitude, the FSM promoted major white-supremacist and neo-Nazi publications including *Spotlight*, *The Truth at Last*, and *The National Educator*, as well as the Liberty Lobby–associated radio program *Radio Free America*.

Other groups made Pummer's look tame. Two members of the Minnesota Patriots Council plotted to use ricin, a biological poison, to murder law enforcement personnel and federal employees. They were convicted of conspiracy in March 1995. Another midwestern militia group, Citizens for Christ, had more traditional battle plans. In September 1994, authorities found a large supply of electric blasting caps, machine guns, ammunition, and dynamite at the group's property.

Throughout 1994 and into 1995, some private armies planned to hunt government officials. The Blue Ridge Hunt Club was a Virginia-based group led by James Roy Mullins. He and three others were arrested in 1994 and charged with firearms violations, including the sale of unregistered silencers and an illegal rifle. Searches uncovered thirteen guns, homemade silencers, explosives, fuses, blasting caps, hand grenades, and a computer disk, on which were detailed Mullins's terrorist plans:

> Hit and run tactics will be our method of fighting. . . . We will destroy targets such as telephone relay centers, bridges, fuel storage tanks, communications towers, radio stations, airports, etc. . . . human targets will be engaged . . . when it is beneficial to the cause to eliminate particular individuals who oppose us (troops, political figures, snitches, etc.).

The group reportedly had plans to increase its stockpile by a raid on the National Guard Armory in Pulaski, Virginia. According to the researcher Paul deArmond, the armory weapons were to be stolen "as a part of a plot to attack members of Congress." While in jail awaiting trial, Mullins wrote a letter asking a friend a favor. He needed to borrow a machine gun "to take care of unfinished business," reportedly with prosecution witnesses.

Judges were fair game for militia plans, too. A Tampa group demanded that four judges, along with some other officials, turn themselves in for trial in the group's "common law" court. A member of the American Citizen Alliance, another Florida militia, was heard discussing plans to assassinate federal judges and other federal officials. In February 1995, a militia leader was arrested for threatening a San Francisco federal judge.

As 1994 ended and the spring of 1995 approached, America was asleep to the dangers of the militia movement—which was doing even more than making plans for battle, stockpiling weapons, and selecting targets. Some members were shooting at police. In September 1994, a Missouri state trooper was shot and wounded by a man whom the ATF termed a "white supremacist with militia leanings." In November 1994, a Tennessee man gathered an arsenal in preparation for war with the government. Pulled over for drunk driving, he wounded two officers before he was shot and killed. In February 1995, a young Oregonian with militia connections shot Oregon State Police Trooper Lisa Boe and Explorer Manolo Herrera, who were inside a patrol car. Bullets struck them both in the back. Luckily, they were wearing bulletproof vests.

This was only weeks before the Oklahoma City bombing. Even then, FBI, ATF, state, and local officials were still insisting that the militias posed no law enforcement problem.

13 Paranoia and the New World Order

WHEN THIS BLOWS, A LOT OF US WILL DIE, A LOT
OF US WILL BE INJURED FOR LIFE, AND A LOT OF
US WILL BE IN JAIL. BUT ALL OF US WILL BE FREE
AGAIN.

JAMES JOHNSON, Ohio Unorganized Militia

Seven months to the day before the Oklahoma City federal building was bombed, some "patriots" who approved of Thompson's "Ultimatum" were prepared to see members of Congress hanged, even if they were not willing to do the hanging themselves. The fact that thousands of Americans would seriously debate—on the Internet and elsewhere—whether arresting Congress at gunpoint was a good idea, offered a window on the thinking of militia groups across America. What could have led people to the point where a "good American" no longer wanted to vote the bastards out but to shoot the bastards dead?

People were attracted to the militias because of concern about particular issues—guns, the environment, federal intrusiveness, abortion, bigotry. But there is a bright line between traditional redress of political grievance—electing different representatives or supporting a third-party candidate—and armed revolution. Waco, Ruby Ridge, the Brady Bill were all things Americans could point to, if the facts were distorted just enough, to suggest that the government was coming after them. Taken out of context, Waco and Ruby Ridge both had the feel of military assaults against civilians. And the Brady Bill had the flavor of a first step toward the "Cohen Act," the fictional legislation in The Turner Diaries that outlaws private gun ownership and starts a revolution that inspired both the Order and Timothy McVeigh.

Drawn into the militia movement, many Americans felt liberated. Here was a new way to see the world in which everything made perfect sense, in which there was an answer for every question, in which, as Bob Fletcher put it, there were no liberals or conservatives, no Democrats or Republicans, just good guys and bad guys. And, with few exceptions, the people who made up government were the bad guys.

✗ ✗ ✗

Jane Wallace, an excellent interviewer, had Bob Fletcher of the Militia of Montana on her cable TV show. He was patched in by phone from Noxon, Montana; she was sitting behind her polished dark wood desk in a library-style set. He was serious. She was snickering. She had asked him whether news accounts of his conspiratorial worldview were correct—for example, did he believe in a government plot to control the weather? The news reports were correct, he said, and then he started to explain. Jane Wallace couldn't keep a straight face as she cross-examined Fletcher about his lunacy.

It was easy to make fun of such views. But stop for a minute, and wonder how you would see the world if you accepted Fletcher's premise. What if you believed that government was a powerful, evil entity that did things like control the weather in order to harass ordinary citizens? What if you believed that Gurkha troops were really being trained so that they would come into every American's house, without a warrant or notice, and search every crack and crevice not only for guns but for evidence of gun ownership? What if you believed that your security and heritage had been sold out to foreign interests, which were, right now, massing at the borders to invade? What if you believed that numbers on the back of road signs in your neighborhood corresponded with the concentration camp to which the government was preparing to take you—that it was only a matter of time? If you really believed these things, you, too, might think you'd have to take up guns to protect not only yourself, but America—from the American government.

Where did such ideas come from? The larger answer—explored in the next chapters—is they have always been with us. A narrower answer— the source of the specific ideas that drove many of the militias' theories—

was the anticommunism of the 1950s, popularized by Senator Joseph McCarthy and, especially, the John Birch Society.

America, of course, had reason to be concerned about communism. Although World War II saw Americans fighting in alliance with the Russians, by the late 1940s and early 1950s the Soviet Union was America's most dangerous enemy. Eastern Europe was under Soviet domination, the Cold War had begun, the Soviets had developed the atomic bomb, and Americans Ethel and Julius Rosenberg had been convicted of spying for the U.S.S.R. Senator Joseph McCarthy and the House Un-American Activities Committee, however, took the realistic American concern with communism and made it into a paranoid witch-hunt. They tarred innocent people, destroyed careers, and used the power of government to chill dissent and empower conspiracy theories.

In 1951 Senator McCarthy said:

> How can we account for our present situation unless we believe that men high in this government are concerting to deliver us to disaster? This must be a project of a great conspiracy, a conspiracy on such a scale so immense as to dwarf any previous such venture in the history of man. A conspiracy of infamy so black that, when it is finally exposed, its principals shall be forever deserving of the maledictions of all honest men. . . . What can be made of this unbroken series of decisions and acts contributing to the strategy of defeat? They cannot be attributed to incompetence. . . . The laws of probability would dictate that part of [the] decisions would serve this country's interest.

McCarthy's pursuit of Communists under, it seemed, every conceivable rock ultimately cost him his credibility. But his feverish conspiracy theories were taken up anew, and expanded upon, by Robert Welch of the John Birch Society. Welch wrote that not only John Foster Dulles, but President Dwight D. Eisenhower himself was "a dedicated, conscious agent of the Communist conspiracy." His proof, he said, was "so extensive and so palpable that it seems to put this conviction beyond any doubt." And so vast was the Communist conspiracy, Eisenhower as president was not even the head American Communist. *That* was his brother, Milton, from whom Dwight took his orders.

Welch, a candy manufacturer, founded the John Birch Society in 1958. He named it for "a young fundamentalist Baptist preacher from Macon, Georgia, [who at twenty-six was] the first American casualty in World War III." Birch, it was claimed, had been "murdered by the Chinese Communists at the first opportunity after the war because of the powerful resistance he would have been able to inspire against them."

In 1966 Welch authored a thirty-page treatise entitled "The Truth in Time," which laid out his thinking. He wrote about "the gradual integration of evil forces into what has now become the communist conspiracy, from its amorphous beginnings in the Eighteenth Century up to its present worldwide reach with tentacles of steel." Welch traced the Communists' plans to take over America all the way back to a Bavarian group called the Illuminati, which was founded in 1776, before Karl Marx was born. Illuminism was a reaction to the staunchly conservative social and religious forces of its time and place. It preached rationalism, reason, and an anticlerical view that seems mild and naive today, but that was embraced two centuries ago by many Masonic lodges.

Welch, by drawing a line from the Illuminati and the Freemasons all the way up to the twentieth-century Communist Party, created the image of an America that had always struggled to survive, having to fend off secret internal enemies. In the 1960s, of course, Welch believed America was in its deepest peril yet. As Arnold Forster and Benjamin Epstein described in their 1964 book, *Danger on the Right*, the Birchers argued that "time is running out and that it is almost zero hour in the fight to save America from an internal Communist takeover."

G. Edward Griffin, a California Bircher, wrote a book called *The Fearful Master*, which argued that the Communists were using the U.N. as part of a plot to shift Americans' allegiance from the United States to global communism. America had "abandoned the secure ground of national strength and independence," wrote Griffin, "to leap into the boiling waters of internationalism." Since the Birch Society believed America was being run by Communists, it argued for changes in government to counter that influence. It also agitated for the impeachment of liberal U.S. Supreme Court Chief Justice Earl Warren and for the repeal of the federal income tax.

On July 21, 1963, *The New York Times* summarized some of the Birch Society's more delusionary assertions:

> Some of the more memorable "plots" that come to mind include these: 35,000 Communist Chinese troops bearing arms and wearing deceptively dyed powder-blue uniforms, are poised on the Mexican border, about to invade San Diego; the United States has turned over—or will at any moment—its Army, Navy and Air Force to the command of a Russian colonel in the United Nations; almost every well-known American or free-world leader is, in reality, a top Communist agent; a United States Army guerrilla-warfare exercise in Georgia, called Water Moccasin III, is in actuality a United Nations operation preparing to take over our country.

Active members of the John Birch Society included Robert DePugh, later of the Minutemen; Gordon Kahl, later of the Posse Comitatus; Robert Mathews, later of the Order; and Willis Carto, later of the Liberty Lobby. All split off because the Birchers were either insufficiently militant, or insufficiently anti-Semitic, or both. But their organizations and publications continued to sport the type of conspiracy theory the Birchers popularized.

Today, these same theories resonate in the militia groups, adapted for a post-Soviet world. The political historian Richard Hofstadter, writing in 1965, explained the basic ideological premises that empower America's private armies of the 1990s:

> The central image is that of a vast and sinister conspiracy, a gigantic and yet subtle machinery of influence set in motion to undermine and destroy a way of life. One may object that there *are* conspiratorial acts in history, and there is nothing paranoid about taking note of them. This is true. All political behavior requires strategy, many strategic acts depend for their effect upon a period of secrecy, and anything that is secret may be described, often with but little exaggeration, as conspiratorial. The distinguishing thing about the paranoid style is not that its exponents see conspiracies or plots here and there in history, but that they regard a "vast" or "gigantic" conspiracy as *the motive force* in historical events. History *is* a conspiracy, set in motion by demonic forces of almost transcendent power, and what is felt to be needed to defeat it is not the usual methods of political give-and-take, but an all-out crusade. The paranoid spokesman sees the fate of this conspiracy in apocalyptic terms. . . . Time is forever just running out. . . . He does not see social conflict as something to be mediated and compromised. . . . Since what is at stake is always a conflict between absolute good and absolute evil, the quality needed is not a willingness to compromise but the will to fight things out to the finish. . . . This demand for unqualified victories leads to the formation of hopelessly demanding and unrealistic goals, and since these goals are not even remotely attainable, failure constantly heightens the paranoid's frustration.

With the fall of the Soviet Union, anticommunist conspiracy theories had no "evil empire" to target. For the first time in memory, America had no "logical" enemy. The paranoia became internally focused. Washington, more accessible than Moscow, became the new manifestation of evil.

Adding fuel to this inward paranoia was the "mainstreaming" of similar ideas by Pat Robertson's Christian Coalition. In his 1991 book, *The New World Order*, Robertson wondered, as militia members did, about "the government of the United States [deferring] to the United Nations." He asserted that "our constitutional right to keep and bear arms would be one of the very first casualties." Robertson also picked up the conspiratorial language in which the John Birch Society and militia members indulged, writing of "a single thread that runs from the [Bush] White House to the State Department to the Council on Foreign Relations to the Trilateral Commission."

Despite the rhetorical overlap between the Christian Coalition and the militia movement, they differed fundamentally. The Christian Coalition's strategy was to take over the system; the militias' was to use guns to make war against it. But their use of similar ideas gave strength to both groups. In the aftermath of the Oklahoma City bombing, an installment of Robertson's TV program, *The 700 Club*, while condemning the carnage, virtually endorsed militia ideology.

✗ ✗ ✗

The anticommunist fear of the McCarthy era, premised on the idea that America was being taken over by outside forces with the help of those inside government, was rewound and replayed by the 1990s militia movement. As in the 1950s, such fears could be seductive—especially if your neighbors shared them.

Imagine yourself as someone who, in 1994, became attracted to a militia because of the importance of gun ownership in your life. You have gone to a few meetings when you start to understand that there is more to this than a few troubling bills making their way through Congress. The government is against you, coming to take your guns on behalf of hidden forces—Illuminati, elites, bankers, Jews, whoever—that are really in control. Gun control is only the first step in their elaborate plot to take away your guns, then your rights, then your freedoms. This premise might sound preposterous, but there was a mountain of material on video, on radio, on the Internet, and in print that "proved" the claims. Black helicopters. Road signs for invading armies. Concentration camps. All "fully documented," militia members—neighbors—said. Their material had enough "truth" in it that you started to wonder. Once you wonder, you've taken the first leap of faith toward political delusion. Armloads of documents follow to keep you moving further into the militias' funnel of paranoia.

Of all the groups that were born in 1994–1995, the Militia of Montana could best serve all your paranoiac needs. Did you want to know more about One World Government? You'd get a copy of a 1977 document from the World Constitution and Parliament Association entitled "A Constitution for the Federation of Earth." The preamble read, in part, "Humanity today has come to a turning point in history. . . . [W]e are on the threshold of a new world order which promises to usher in an era of peace, prosperity, justice and harmony." The fifty-six-page pamphlet described what a democratic world government would look like, with courts, a parliament, an executive branch. To MOM this was evidence of "the plan," existing long before President George Bush popularized the phrase "New World Order" in a speech. To those without the conspiracy bug it read like a hippie-era peace-and-justice platform, which it was. The World Constitution and Parliament Association was founded in 1958 by a World War II conscientious objector named Philip Isely and his wife, Margaret, whom the London *Daily Telegraph* once called "aged but engaging American hippies." The Iselys convened "world federation" meetings from time to time into the 1990s. Even though these were large events that no doubt took them away from their Colorado vitamin business, none of the attendees was a representative of any government. Their intentions were good, but had nothing to do with reality, had no effect on the real world. Yet, to the militia movement, here was proof that the evil One World Government and New World Order planned and plotted to take away America's liberty.

The New World Order was the overall plan. MOM could also provide you with specifics. On April 19, 1994, the Militia of Montana issued an intelligence report from "Louisiana-Mississippi" about mysterious shots fired at fishermen, and a staging area for Soviet-made vehicles refitted as U.N. combat equipment. The name of the intelligence reporter was changed to protect his identity, of course, but MOM was still impressed with the information, apparently not troubled by the fact that the reporter was only semiliterate (though he or she claimed military experience), or by the assertion that three people were permitted to enter a NASA base without having their identification checked and were told, among other things, that a "building was of top secret nature and that there was [work on] a top secret UFO (unidentified flying object) going on inside that building and that it was top secret but we would be informed later as to any activity that were, [sic] could be informed about." *This* was the evil government about which MOM worried—one that would admit disguised trespassers to a base and tell them about secret UFOs?

Not convinced? There was much more. MOM would offer you one page of a 960-page report on the Violent Crime Control and Enforcement Act, dated December 23, 1993. This was the draft language (at page 843) for the recruitment of former "Royal Hong Kong Police officers into Federal Law Enforcement positions." On the margins were MOM's editorial comments: "April 19th—1993 Waco Burned. 1943 Warsaw Burned. 1775 Lexington Burned. 1775 They (The NWO) tried to take our arms the first time. British Flew Recon over Waco. British Interpol Controls US Federal Law Enforcement thru 22 USC 263 A." Next to the words "Royal Hong Kong" were MOM's marginal comments: "Still British" and "What Color Will the Coats Be This Time?" What was this all about? Republican Senator William Roth of Delaware had suggested that the government study the idea of hiring a small number of Hong Kong troops as consultants to help federal officials in their investigation of Asian drug gangs. The idea was never adopted. Of course, MOM saw the fine hand of the New World Order here.

MOM would also sell you a book, Item Number 415 in its catalogue: "Paul D. Wilcher (Attorney) Letter to Janet Reno." The letter ran more than a hundred pages. It "exposes the SHADOW GOVERNMENT within the CIA and how it has been using 'MIND CONTROL' on people including David Koresh and six of his men. Shortly after sending this letter, Mr. Wilcher was found dead, sitting naked on his toilet—the death was ruled suicide. His death was followed by another 'suicide' of Vincent Foster, another attorney, who was one of Bill Clinton's White House Counsels. The proofs are conclusive that both of these Attorney's [sic] were MURDERED by the Shadow Government."

Foreign armaments on American soil? MOM would send you an unsigned "Observation Report," dated "12 June 1994 . . . Time: 1325 hours." Someone apparently had spotted a T 72 Russian tank on a flatbed truck at an Exxon station in western Texas. The report bore a rubber stamped logo on the upper right-hand corner: "Say 'No!' to the 'NEW WORLD ORDER'—KEEP AMERICA INDEPENDENT."

MOM could also supply you with fuzzy pictures of alleged Russian and German trucks, some repainted white, behind barbed-wire fences complete with a "Beware of Dog" sign. The caption: "These Russian and German trucks are parked at a compound in Saucier, Miss. Patriots fear that these trucks may be used against United States Citizens, in a United Nations operation." No doubt the "patriots" did fear this, but their paranoia was so involved that even the *internal* illogic of their own delusions did not trouble them. For example, if the New World Order was really about to clamp down on Americans, disarm some, kill others, remove them to concentration camps, why would it need foreign machinery to do so? Wouldn't American trucks and tanks be preferable—for example, less suspicious, easier to get parts for? Or at least wouldn't it have been smarter to repaint the foreign equipment with U.S. markings, to render people complacent?

MOM's Bob Fletcher saw conspiracies wherever he looked and, on videotape or in person, he was pleased to share his views with you. "While I was in the military," he said, "I was sent to Cuba, back during the missile crisis. They say the missiles were leaving. But I didn't believe they were. I saw what I believe were decoys. And I think those missiles are there to this day."

Fletcher also had theories about the weather and, as with most conspiracy theories, there was a kernel of truth in them. Humans *can* affect climate. Cloud seeding is nothing new, nor is the idea that smog and escaped Freon from air conditioners and acid rain from industrial pollution can have an impact on weather, but if you asked Mr. Fletcher about weather modification, he would provide you with a series of documents purporting to show that the government does more than seed clouds; it manufactures earthquakes at will. His proof? A sixty-year-old newspaper clipping.

In the MOM video *Invasion and Betrayal* Fletcher said:

> In the last year there literally have been hundreds of earthquakes in several parts of the United States. They're not even reporting all the earthquakes that are taking place. . . . and you look at the quake that took place in Kobe, Japan, and you look at the weather controls that have created floods up the Mississippi and flooding and droughts in other areas, if you look at Ethiopia where originally, matter of fact I must point this out, in Ethiopia where they're having [a] drought . . . they've killed seven or eight million people . . . within the last year in Ethiopia, and a famine is taken [*sic*] place. Part of a plan done by the New World Order advocates many years ago specifically specified that by the year 2000 to maintain proper control there must be an eradication of billions of people from the face of the earth in one way shape or manner or another. . . . It was called the plan 2000. We have five years and they will be at the 2000 point. . . . Talking about weather control . . . You can do devastating things worldwide when you control the weather.

It is unclear why, if—as Fletcher and Trochmann believe—the government was targeting militia groups, there have been earthquakes in Palm Springs and Los Angeles, California, rather than Noxon, Montana; Decker, Michigan; and Hayden Lake, Idaho.

14 Conspiracy and Black Helicopters

IF I DIDN'T BELIEVE IT WITH MY OWN MIND,

I NEVER WOULD HAVE SEEN IT.

GRAFFITO, Bard College, circa 1971

Books of fiction sometimes fuel conspiracy theories. The *Protocols of the Elders of Zion*, for example, was a forgery based on a nineteenth-century French novel. Millions believe in Jewish conspiracies because of the *Protocols*.

The militia movement took sustenance from another work of fiction, the 109-page *Report from Iron Mountain on the Possibility and Desirability of Peace*. Written in 1967 by Leonard C. Lewin as political satire, *Iron Mountain* presented itself as authored by a "John Doe" who, along with fourteen other scholars, had formed a "Special Study Group." Supposedly the authors had spent a summer hiding in a bomb shelter, then took two years to finish their work.

Lewin intended the book to answer the Vietnam-era antiwar protests. Its premise was that, if we had no war, what would "permanent peace" bring? War, "John Doe" concluded, was essential for stability. It fueled the economy and helped people retain allegiance to government and its leaders. To have the benefits of war during peace, the report asserted, the government might manufacture "alternative enemies." Suggestions included horrendous pollution and false extraterrestrial invaders. Also discussed was the idea of contaminating water with drugs to control Americans.

When the book was released it attracted speculation as to whether it was really a government-instigated analysis and, if so, who wrote it. By the 1980s it was out of print. But in the 1990s Willis Carto's Liberty Lobby was selling an unauthorized version through its newspaper, *Spotlight*, and through Carto's Noontide Press. It became important literature in the militia movement. Samuel Sherwood of the United States Militia Association saw it as proof of the New World Order. "A group of people got together and said, 'Here is our blueprint for America,'" said Sherwood. "It has caused a great deal of alarm."

✗ ✗ ✗

Some militia members must have become nervous while waiting in the express lines of their local supermarkets. Such authoritative journals as the *National Enquirer* and the *Star* confirmed what many in America's private armies believed: UFOs existed. Of course to these militia members, UFOs were not funny flying saucers, relatives of ET, or aliens searching for Elvis—they were part of the plot to take over the country.

UFOs have long been part of the tapestry of American conspiracy theory. Unidentified flying objects were, by definition, unidentified. Sometimes people's eyes played tricks, or some atmospheric condition not commonly understood may have been responsible for what people claimed to see. As with stories of the Loch Ness Monster, Bigfoot, the nine lives of Elvis, or sex with aliens, logic tells us that, especially in the days of video cameras and television newsmagazine shows, some convincing proof would have appeared if the stories were true. Reasonable people reject these myths.

Conspiratorialists make the opposite presumption: that the phenomenon is real. Therefore, they argue, the proof must exist; so why is what *they* know not generally known? Certainly the media should have documented it; government should have admitted it. Therefore, there must be a conspiracy of silence. To believe in UFOs you must believe in conspiracy.

With wild conspiratorial paranoia so large a part of the militia movement, why should it not borrow from UFO lore? Rather than imagine *Star Trek*–style technology, it saw conspiracy in an existing flying machine: the helicopter.

Through *Spotlight*, the Liberty Lobby hawked *Black Helicopters over America: Strikeforce for the New World Order*, by Kim Keith. In 155 pages this book provided "a chronology of the mysterious unmarked chopper appearing nation-wide in ever-increasing numbers. . . . The first documented sightings were in 1971, in Lake County, Colorado, when 40 sheep were found dead and 'blistered' in some unknown manner, after a rancher observed a helicopter flying over the animals. . . . By 1993, there were almost too many 'black helicopter' incidents to count."

According to *The Washington Post*, "the helicopters are piloted by state wildlife officers patrolling for poachers. Elsewhere in the West, they belong to the National Guard, which has been conducting surveillance on marijuana farmers in many states for years." Militia folks, of course, don't believe these explanations. They think the helicopters are part of a plot to enslave Americans. The myth of the black helicopter was so strong in militia circles that Helen Chenoweth even held congressional hearings about them.

There was at least one militia opinion molder who was not satisfied to transfer the lore of UFOs onto helicopters. William Cooper saw a connection between "traditional" UFOs and the New World Order. In his book *Behold a Pale Horse*, Cooper related his longtime experience with UFOs. He had heard about them in military training and saw one when he was assigned to a submarine. "The whole time I was in Vietnam," he wrote, ". . . I noticed there was a lot of UFO activity. . . . UFOs, I was told, were definitely sensitive information. I learned exactly how sensitive when all the people of an entire village disappeared after UFOs were seen hovering above their huts."

Cooper also believed in the "Secret Government," which he traced to 1947. What was its genesis? "16 crashed or downed alien aircraft . . . 65 alien bodies and 1 live alien were recovered [between 1947 and 1952]." More flying saucers came in 1953—twenty-six dead and four live aliens were found, Cooper claimed. President Eisenhower, with the help of Nelson Rockefeller, developed a strategy to "wrestle and beat the alien problem."

The aliens kept coming. One was even recognized as an ambassador by Eisenhower. Treaties were signed. Groups that right-wing conspiratorialists know well—the Trilateral Commission and the Bilderbergers—were created because of the need to deal with aliens. "The name of the Trilateral Commission," Cooper asserted, "was taken from the alien flag known as the Trilateral Insignia." If you wondered who else might have been involved, Cooper's book included a reprint of the *Protocols of the Elders of Zion*—with instructions to substitute "Illuminati" for "Jews."

Cooper had distinctive views of many landmark events of the twentieth century. For example, President Kennedy was assassinated, Cooper claimed, because he was going to let the American people know about the aliens. "The Secret Service agent driving the limo . . . shot Kennedy in the head," Cooper said.

Cooper may sound like a nut, but he broadcast across the globe five nights a week on shortwave station WWCR. He was a talk-radio star for many in the militia movement, and he apparently had an impact. In the widely promoted Militia of Montana video *Invasion and Betrayal*, Bob Fletcher sounded like William Cooper. "When JFK was shot," Fletcher said, "I watched it on TV, and I was convinced it came from the car. How else would you explain Mrs. Kennedy trying to climb out of the car as soon as the shots hit her husband?"

✗ ✗ ✗

On January 23, 1995, the *Spotlight* ran a border-to-border headline: "Arizona Desert May Hold Secret of Foreign Military Equipment: For Use Against Americans?" It announced the "appearance of two Soviet Hind-series attack helicopters at a remote desert airport." The helicopters were "strangely equipped with English language instrumentation." How did the *Spotlight* know? "The Hinds were spotted by three area men, who were accompanied by two small boys, age 4 and 6. . . . [They] asked if the children could see the helicopters. The pilots [agreed] and allowed the men and boys to look inside."

A companion article alleged that "The National Guard is being subverted from its intended purpose and turned into a part of a New World Order force. . . . The White House has been methodically destroying the effectiveness of guard forces to face foreign enemies." The proof? Some guard units were having their M-60 tanks replaced by newer M-1 Abrams tanks that were experiencing maintenance and equipment problems.

On March 20, 1995, with another border-to-border headline, the *Spotlight* wrote of Russian troops in America. Motorists apparently had seen a disabled Russian military vehicle on the side of a road; a half-dozen men who appeared to be Russian soldiers were spotted eating at a restaurant near the Fort Indiantown Gap Army base—a report "confirmed" by a waitress at Funk's Chicken Lickin'. "Perhaps most disquieting," the *Spotlight* asserted, "was that the soldiers, when approached by curious customers and employees of the restaurant, indicated they were Americans training as OPFORS (opposing forces) at the base in conjunction with an ROTC (Reserve Officers Training Corps) exercise."

The *Spotlight* apparently was not bothered by the illogic that secret Russian invaders—who presumably would not want to draw attention to themselves—would risk all by a meal at the Chicken Lickin'. And what did the *Spotlight* think about the fact that these gentlemen spoke English? This, apparently, just confirmed the *Spotlight*'s suspicion. "*Spesnaz* [special operations] troops," the *Spotlight* said, "are trained to speak fluent English, even with U.S. regional accents." All right—assume you're a Russian agent, and you've been found out, despite your years of practice to acquire perfect American English. What is the last thing you do? "The following day," the *Spotlight* continued, "the National Guard officer told the *Spotlight*, he made a point of returning to the restaurant and found the same soldiers there again."

Many of us tend to think that only uneducated or dim people are prone to conspiracy theories like these. That's not so; all forms of bigotry, for example, are palpably stupid, yet millions harbor bigoted thoughts. Bob Stevens, the sheriff of Meadville, Pennsylvania, said, "It's some pretty intelligent people who believe [these conspiracy theories]. I'm talking college graduates and like that, telling me the U.N. is going to fly in here in black helicopters and take over." Tony Horwitz, writing in *The Wall Street Journal*, told of a college-educated man who held strong antigovernment views. "Once you've abandoned the conventional world," the man said, "you can't go back. I don't want to sound as though I've drifted into the Twilight Zone, but you see things in a new way. I feel like I'm in 'Invasion of the Body Snatchers,' fighting people who do things that have been programmed into them by Hollywood or Madison Avenue or some college professor. They think I'm crazy, but I think it's the other way around."

✗ ✗ ✗

All these ideas may seem bizarre in isolation, but they are reinforced by the core structure of the militia ideology—the belief that government has been taken over by evil forces. If you believe that, then plans to attack people with religious beliefs who are also gun owners (as at Ruby Ridge and Waco) made sense: Who else would the New World order go after? Concentration camps make sense: You have to put loyal Americans somewhere. The U.N.–Russian–German–Gurkha–street gang troops make sense: You couldn't count on the military to round up loyal Americans. The numbers on the backs of road signs make sense: The attack is being prepared; it can happen anytime, and the foreign troops need to know where to go. GATT and NAFTA and U.S. support for the United Nations make sense: They were steps along the steady slope of giving up sovereignty to One World Government. Certainly they couldn't have been intended to increase American security and trade through international cooperation.

Once people are trained to see things a certain way with passion, what they see changes. Talk to a recent law school graduate immersed in study for the bar and he or she will be able to discuss the legal principles applicable to a speck of dust floating by. Watch the evening news with a medical resident and hear a running diagnosis of the ailments afflicting newsmakers. Talk to a Bob Fletcher or a Norman Olson or any other committed militia leader, and everything is recast as part of the New World Order's assault on America from within.

For example, militia leaders point to a forty-six-question "Combat Arms Survey" that was given to three hundred California-based marines. They say this survey was part of a plan to prepare federal troops to take away America's guns. Part of a graduate thesis, the questionnaire asked how the soldiers would feel about being used in various situations, including drug law enforcement, environmental disaster, and a U.N. mission. The survey's last question asked whether the marine would "fire upon U.S. citizens who refuse or resist confiscation of firearms banned by the U.S. government."

According to a spokeswoman for the Naval Postgraduate School, the question presented an example of an unlawful order, the point being to ascertain whether marines understood the Uniform Code of Military Justice and the U.S. Constitution. Militia members were not persuaded. "They are masters of deceit and fear and negative propaganda," said Norman Olson. "Their disinformation and lies are aided and abetted by the media."

Ask a militia member for proof that the New World Order is really in charge, and he may take out a dollar bill. Turning it over, "Notice the pyramid with the eye hovering above?" he'd ask. "That is a sign that the United States is connected to the Illuminati." Some may say pyramid and eye signify the Freemasons, or are the devilish mark of the Federal Reserve, but in any case they know it is a secret signal that America has been taken over by secret forces. Ask the Department of the Treasury about the pyramid, part of the Great Seal of the United States, and you will be told that the seal was adopted in 1782, that the pyramid depicts "permanence and strength," that it is incomplete because "the United States will always grow," and that the eye stands for "education and freedom and knowledge."

The militias' conspiratorial ideas went way beyond pointing at military vehicles or questionnaires or strange markings on currency. If you believed the New World Order was really poised to take over America, you would also think it must be working on many fronts, infiltrating all aspects of American life. Why was American education a problem? Simple. Edward L. Brown, leader of the New Hampshire–based Constitution Defense Militia, saw a conspiracy. "The NEA [National Education Association]," he said, "takes their orders from UNESCO [United Nations Educational, Scientific and Cultural Organization], which takes their orders from the United Nations to dumb down the kids."

Look at "all the U.N. troops and equipment in this country," said a California militia member, "and how easily they could be used by a government gone tyrannical or whatever to disarm the people. In fact that seems to be what they're training for. The government won't give you a figure. We've received figures from people in the military that they say they know of up to 800,000 here. And I don't think there's that many. The closest approximation is up to 300,000."

Many who know the United Nations are amazed that anyone thinks the organization is capable of accomplishing anything, let alone world conquest. As many have noted, serving meals on time in the U.N. cafeteria would be a more realistic goal. But militia members see signs everywhere. In fact, there is a sign at Yellowstone National Park acknowledging that UNESCO has designated the park a "World Heritage Site." After someone mentioned this on a talk-radio show, the park was deluged by callers inquiring whether the U.N. was now in charge. Asked about the claim that the U.N. had acquired jurisdiction over Yellowstone, David Trochmann said, "What makes you think it hasn't?"

✗ ✗ ✗

Many militia members claimed that they were the true defenders of American tradition and liberty. That perception—that they alone were saving American society, with guns if necessary—was a driving force for the movement. "It all started when I read the Declaration of Independence," said James Johnson of the Ohio militia, "and I realized the grievances they had against the king were the same as we've got today. I firmly believe the U.S. government today holds our Constitution under contempt. . . . We're not a bunch of hotheaded rednecks, but we have to defend our Constitution."

"This whole King George thing is very important," said militia spokesman Ed Brown. "He wanted ten percent, and we went to war. These are citizens who just want to be left alone. They have answered a call to arms to defend their families, their homes, and their Constitution from some foreign power that threatened to take away, above all, their beloved guns."

The use of patriotic images to malign American government allows militia members to reject the notion that they are being treasonous— rather, it is government that has forsaken America and her Constitution. Defense of the Constitution—that is, up to the first ten amendments— with citations to chapter and verse became not only an assertion of loyalty, but almost a religious exercise. Those who are treasonous, said Norman Olson, are those who would "break" the Constitution.

Religious images also play a role in the conspiracy model. Some fundamentalists believe that the New World Order was described in the Book of Revelations. It was Satan's kingdom, during which "the mark of the beast" would be placed on everyone's right hand and forehead. Some militia members believed the New World Order would force everyone to bear Universal Product Codes. A militia member in California had reservations about President Clinton's initial health plan because of such beliefs. The plan's suggested I.D. card had 18 digits; $6 + 6 + 6 = 18$; 666 is the devil's number. Some militia members believe that, as technology improves, people will be forced to have biochips implanted in them as the "mark of the beast."

When will the full implementation of this New World Order happen? People had different ideas. Fletcher said 1996. Some gave it a little longer. A flyer from the 7th Regiment, a Highlands County, Florida, militia, read: "Mystery Babylon the Great Harlot (The New World Order) has set her goal of total world conquest by August 1997." The *Spotlight* said the Bilderberger group, which supposedly includes David Rockefeller, Henry Kissinger, Katharine Graham, and "international financiers and bankers," had a "timetable for world government [that is] looming—the year 2002."

Like cults that predict the end of the world, wait, lose members when the date passes, then revive after the revelation of a new date, the militias will survive any inaccurate projections of the New World Order's coming. Margaret Thaler Singer, a psychologist, also notes that the millennium is approaching. "Every time a century ends," she said, "people are running up and down the streets, predicting the end of the world." This time, unfortunately, they are well armed.

✗ ✗ ✗

Belief in the rich conspiracy theories of the militia movement can lead people to strange behavior. Catherine Crabill was a thirty-eight-year-old housewife, living in Reserve, New Mexico. FBI agents and National Guard members had arrived to help local authorities look for the body of someone who had been reported murdered the year before in the mountains outside town. Fearful, Crabill took her four small children and left home for a few nights. Despite assurances from the county sheriff, others left their homes, too. They were members of a newly formed militia group, who feared that the government was preparing to attack them.

Militia members from around the country showed support for the local group. Rumors were flying, partly because a local resident erroneously told a California talk-radio program that five thousand troops were coming to Reserve. (The search party consisted of twelve National Guardsmen and two FBI agents.) The *Albuquerque Tribune* quoted a Militia of Montana member saying, "We got reports that a half-dozen to a dozen people wouldn't spend Saturday and Sunday nights in their homes. I think this is unusual, but I don't think it's crazy. I think this is something people should have a watch over, after what the federal government did at Waco."

At least one conspiracy theory has been investigated, and debunked, by militia members. Doug Fales of the Placer County (California) Militia said: "There was a myth that when Mather air field was an air field the barbed wire was facing outward and now it's facing inward to suggest that there is some sort of concentration camp in there. We drove by and checked it out, and it's not true."

But what about the other rumored camps? A Florida-based militia group, the 7th Regiment, put out a flyer claiming "23 concentration camps for the housing of Christians and other dissidents already have been built in America and 20-plus more are under construction." How do you drive past the New World Order to debunk it?

Conspiracies and guns make a dangerous mix. What do you do when there are armed people in your community who believe that a zoning ordinance is not a zoning ordinance, but part of a plot to take their guns, seize their land, and pack them off to a concentration camp? In the extreme, how dangerous can such ideas be? Ingo Hasselbach, who used to lead a neo-Nazi group in Europe, asserted that "enough militant ideology and conspiracy thinking can destroy even the most basic human sympathy."

15 Corporal Captains

WE'RE NOT GOING TO BE OUTGUNNED BY THE
GOVERNMENT, BECAUSE EVERYTHING THEY'VE
GOT IS OURS. WE HAVE TREMENDOUS NUMBERS
OF PEOPLE INSIDE THE NATIONAL GUARD, NAVY,
ARMY, MARINES WHO WOULD TURN ON THE
GOVERNMENT IF THEY STARTED SOMETHING.

M. J. "RED" BECKMAN

Many in and around the militia movement—Bo Gritz, Linda Thompson, William Cooper, Timothy McVeigh, Terry Nichols—have military experience. Thompson says she served as "Assistant to the U.S. Army Commanding General, NATO, Allied Forces Central Europe." Her training, she claimed, included an "Adjutant General Officer Basic Course," which presumably prepared her for her present role as self-proclaimed "Acting Adjutant General of the Unorganized Militia."

Most of the leaders of the Michigan militia have had military experience, too. Reporter Charles Laurence called them "corporals re-styled as colonels and captains." Whether people with military expertise were especially drawn to paramilitary groups for some reason—the familiar organizational structure, for example—is not known. However, militias have put great effort into recruiting those with military and law enforcement backgrounds. Through such members they gain legitimacy, weapons experience, and leadership.

When members of the Texas Constitutional Militia spoke with a reporter for the London-based *Sunday Telegraph* in late 1994, they stressed their military connections. "We have penetrated the government's electronic intelligence system and turned it against them," said Jon Roland, one of the group's founders. Militias were prepared to use their members' military skills to fight the government that had trained them.

The *Telegraph* reported that many local law enforcement officers, National Guard reserves, and even active-duty service members were part of the militias. A group called the Texas Light Infantry was supposedly of three-battalion strength and made up of former State Guardsmen. Another, Big Star One, was division-sized, included many active-duty officers, and operated in Texas, Oklahoma, and New Mexico. "Weaponry," the *Telegraph* asserted, "has been leaking like a sieve from U.S. armouries." "There will be no Waco in this area," claimed the *Telegraph*'s source. "If the shit hits the fan they'll find that the regular army and the militia are in cahoots."

The boasts of the Texas militia members sound grossly exaggerated, but the *Telegraph* also quoted a captain in the Texas State Guard, who acknowledged, "There's a Rambo group up in Wichita Falls that's entirely outside the chain of command." The sad fact is that no one knows how many active-duty military people are connected to the militia movement or how much ordnance has been pilfered. Even after the Oklahoma City bombing, and despite repeated prodding from experts stressing the urgency of this question, neither the media nor, it appears, government officials have been quick to investigate the problem. Perhaps it is no coincidence that reporting on the military connection has come primarily from the foreign press. Americans tend to presume that all military personnel are loyal patriots. The citizens of other countries know there is no such guarantee. Americans ought to know that now, too: Timothy McVeigh was a model soldier.

$$X \quad X \quad X$$

Gerald "Jack" McLamb—Bo Gritz's associate who helped negotiate the end of the Ruby Ridge siege—has tried harder than anyone else to attract uniformed personnel into the Patriot movement. He has spoken all over the country, while in police uniform, of the New World Order and the "coming storm." Viewing the federal government as evil incarnate, he has said that local officers do their duty when they *do not* enforce the law.

McLamb is a retired police officer from Phoenix, Arizona. He was a founder (in the early 1980s) of the American Citizens and Lawmen Association (ACLA), and executive editor of its *Aid and Abet Police Newsletter*. He also edited the seventy-five-page "Operation Vampire Killer 2000:

American Police Action Plan for Stopping World Government Rule," a publication of Police Against the New World Order (PANWO). *Aid and Abet* described "Operation Vampire Killer 2000" as a "step by step plan to re-educate our fellow law enforcement officers to the plans of the global elite such as Bush, Clinton and Perot." Some claim that the "Vampire" to be killed stands for police officers who follow the law.

The Coalition for Human Dignity reported on a 1993 lecture McLamb presented at the Seattle Preparedness Expo, entitled "National and U.N. Police Forces Within the U.S.".: "He carefully explains . . . his views of the great conspiracy. . . . [T]he 1992 Los Angeles riots were orchestrated by the Federal Emergency Management Agency (FEMA) to test American reactions to the imposition of martial law. . . . He also speculates that the Crips and the Bloods will be used as SA-style storm troopers to take away guns from Americans who refused to surrender their weapons to federal authorities."

McLamb's "Operation Vampire Killer 2000" also defined the New World Order as a plan "for an oligarchy of the world's richest families to place 1/2 the masses of the earth in servitude under their complete control, administered from behind the false front of the United Nations. To facilitate management capabilities, the plan calls for the elimination of the other 2.5 billion people through war, disease, abortion and famine by the year 2000. . . . Their plan . . . is well established and under way."

McLamb's answer to this New World Order plot was simple. "Who is dispossessing the American people of their land, homes, businesses, trucks, cars and personal freedom???" he wrote. "Is it the TRAITORS AND THIEVES in government leadership? No!!! Is it those treacherous demonic Elitists who own the Federal Reserve? No! . . . Your local *POLICE OFFICERS* do the actual deed. (Yes, of course, we are only following the dictates of those that I just mentioned. . . . IF OFFICERS DON'T ENFORCE TREASON, IT WON'T GET ENFORCED.)"

McLamb also believed that local officers should do more than refuse to enforce the law: They should be aligned with militias. "If you don't have one here," he told a group at the Seattle Preparedness Expo '94, "or you want to start one of your own . . . get a hold of us. . . . If you have militia material, send it. [We'll] keep it on file and help spread this wonderful, legal concept across this nation." McLamb also shared his material with the Constitutionalists Networking Center, Evan Mecham's white supremacist group. CNC said it would distribute copies of "Operation Vampire Killer 2000" to members of the military, and to every law enforcement officer in the country.

✗ ✗ ✗

The Resister described itself as the "Official Publication of the Special Forces Underground." It recast the antigovernment conspiracy theories of the militia movement into a form palatable to service members. One article, for example, started with a discussion of military history and the disfavor in which "standing armies [were held because during colonial times they were] used domestically to enforce unpopular laws and keep the population subjugated to the dictates of the central government."

The Resister saw parallels today: "The increasing militarization of federal, state and local law enforcement agencies, aided by the duplicity of the Department of Defense," it asserted, "has created the very beast feared by the founders generally and the antifederalists specifically; an armed force under the exclusive control of the executive branch of the federal government. These federal agencies have no purpose other than the enforcement of arbitrary, undefined, whim-based federal 'laws.'"

Building upon a rational concern—the extent to which the military has been "helping" local law enforcement on matters such as drug interdiction—*The Resister* painted a conspiratorial scheme:

> There is no single atrocity that illustrates this obscenity better than the BATF assault on . . . Waco. This operation was directly supported by Company C, 3d Battalion, 3d Special Forces Group (Airborne). . . . Operation Alliance, in an attempt to secure DOD support . . . forwarded a completely fictitious report through military channels that there was a suspected methamphetamine lab at the Waco compound. . . .
>
> If the federal government was serious about the "threat to national security" posed by the drug trade . . . it would have invaded, reduced to rubble, and occupied as subject colonies the drug trafficking states of Mexico, Colombia, Peru and Bolivia. It causes you [to] wonder who is benefitting by not doing so. . . . Is the "war on drugs" simply another front in the socialist war on the Constitution?

The spring 1995 issue of *The Resister* contained an "Open Letter to our Readers: On Militia":

> The Coordinating Staff of the Special Forces Underground . . . believes that our current federal, state, and local government represent the antithesis of everything we hold true. The only secure way to communicate our beliefs within the military is by . . . clandestine publishing. Thus *The Resister*.
>
> One uncontrollable consequence of publishing *The Resister* was its spread outside the Special Forces into the patriot movement. . . . Our support for the concept of the unorganized militia in general is unqualified. Our support for particular militia groups is very much qualified.

Where was the militia when the Supreme Court usurped the power to interpret the Constitution? Where was the militia when the Anti-Trust laws were passed? Did the militia mobilize to oppose *any* of the following? Democracy; the Federal Reserve Bank; direct taxation; popular election of Senators; universal suffrage; compulsory education; prohibition; the formation of federal law enforcement; regulatory, or social agencies; the War Powers Act; labor laws; social security; the formation of the U.N.; the Marshal Plan; so-called "civil rights"; Lyndon Johnson's blatantly Marxist "Great Society" programs; environmental laws; lowering the voting age; equal opportunity; affirmative actions [*sic*]; forfeiture laws; or *any* other statist, socialist or Marxist legislation. The answer is: NO.

. . . You cannot reasonably expect to form a militia, voice your opposition to the federal government and its rights abrogating domestic policies and expect to remain untargeted by its internal security apparatus. Any attempt to restore the Constitution, as written, threatens extinction to the federal bureaucracy and the pull-politics [*sic*] beast it rides. The federal government's eradication of the Seventh Day Adventists in Waco had nothing to do with religion, alleged firearms violation, or alleged child abuse. It was a message to the American people from our socialist federal government, delivered by their errand boys in the BATF and FBI. It is the universal message of all tyrannies: if you are defiant, we will kill you.

The "Open Letter" said that, if a militia group was sufficiently disciplined and ideologically attuned to *The Resister*'s agenda, the Special Forces Underground would work with it.

The question of how involved American police and military personnel are in the militia movement has not yet been answered. That former officers are members of militias is clear; but for active-duty police and, especially, military officers to become involved means that they accept some risk of losing their jobs or at least harming their careers. It would be gratifying to know that there are safeguards in National Guard armories and other military supply locations sufficient to ensure that the temptation to "appropriate" is not easily satisfied. Before April 19, 1995, some militia members boasted of how easy it was to obtain these weapons. America's military, of course, is not like that of Mexico or Panama. But Canada and Australia have had recent problems with far-right cells in their armies too. It is a danger that should not be ignored in America.

✗ ✗ ✗

Militias, of course, did not need to rely on pilfered army supplies. They also bought or made their weaponry. Gun shows around the country attracted hobbyists, but also those who wanted to arm themselves for political purposes. Timothy McVeigh, for example, spent a good deal of time around gun shows.

And, even more startling, people did not have to go out of their home in search of weapons; the information about how to make them came with the click of a button or the turn of a page. The day of the Oklahoma City explosion, a New York City television station also ran a story about two twelve-year-olds who had downloaded the recipe for napalm from the Internet, made a batch, and brought it to class for show-and-tell.

Americans seem surprised, again, that recipes abound for making explosives out of common material. Some went apoplectic in the Vietnam War years when the *Anarchist Cookbook* was on bookshelves. Molotov cocktails, it turned out, were easier to prepare than Alice B. Toklas cookies—and all the former's ingredients were legal. The twelve-year-olds who made napalm were downloading child's play. "The day may come," one posting of "Books and Videotapes on Explosives and Demolitions" on the Internet said, "when [people might] need something more powerful than commercial dynamite or common improvised explosives. For blowing bridges, shattering steel and derailing tanks, they need C-4. But . . . C-4 is not legally available to civilians and is hard to come by on the black market." For $13.95 one could order—"FOR ACADEMIC STUDY"—"the step-by-step directions . . . for homemade C-4." The directions promised not only to show you how to make the explosive from "just three ingredients, all legal, common and inexpensive," but also how to "survive" making it.

Also offered for "FOR ACADEMIC STUDY" were the *Improvised Munitions Black Book*, volumes one and two; *The Big Bang*; the *Black Book Companion* ("a further study into the dark art of improvised explosives"); *Boobytraps*; *Improvised Explosives*; *Professional Standards for Preparing, Handling and Using Explosives*; *Guerrilla's Arsenal*; *Ragnar's Homemade Detonators*; *Homemade Semtex: C-4's Ugly Sister* ("Semtex is the plastique most widely used by terrorists around the world"); *The Anarchist Arsenal* (which "offers a fresh approach to explosives [including] Semtex, C-4, land mines . . . syringe fuses, car bombs, contact explosives and many more"); *The Advanced Anarchist Arsenal* (the author "takes up where he left off"); *Smart Bombs*; *Explosive Principles*; and *Pyrotechnics*.

Many of these books cost less than ten dollars. The most expensive (*Homemade Semtex: C-4's Ugly Sister* and *The Advanced Anarchist Arsenal*) were $14.95. A "best buy" might have been *Improvised Radio Detonation Techniques*, which for $11.95 told you all you needed to know about "radio-controlled detonation." Detonation by radio of "strategically placed explosives is a great way to strike anonymously in an unconventional warfare situation," the descriptive copy read. People engaged in such activity "often only have the most common items to work with in their area of operations. How to still be effective with the simplest of tools? This manual outlines how . . . common consumer electronic devices can be modified to work as radio-controlled detonation devices." What could today's unconventional warrior turn into a remote-controlled bomb? "Cordless electronic touch tone phones, radio paging systems, cellular mobile phones," even "children's toy walkie talkies."

Don't want to surf the Internet? Order from a catalogue. Delta Press, Ltd., puts out an eighty-page, multicolored list. Volume 35, for the spring of 1995, not only had books on "the 'New World Order' and how it threatens your freedom," but also literature on bombs (including books on "how to use agricultural type ammonium nitrate as a high explosive" and the twenty-ninth printing of the *Anarchist Cookbook*). There were books on urban warfare, poisons, mines, hand grenades, sabotage devices, terrorism ("One lone individual with a .22 rifle can disrupt electrical power for an entire city"), terrorist explosives, high explosives, two-component high explosives, flamethrowers, shaped charges, assassination (including "plans for a .22 caliber cigarette lighter"), homemade grenade launchers, pipe bombs, firebombs, "backyard rocketry," assault rifles, street sweepers, submachine guns, sniping, how to convert guns to fully automatic weapons, and how to make silencers.

There were also guidebooks on "disappearing and new identity" including *Criminal Use of False I.D.* ("This manual shows all the loopholes that exist in our current system. . . . What will you say when they come looking for YOUR guns?"); *Counterfeit I.D. Made Easy* and *Reborn in the U.S.A.* Need "self protection"? You can buy the "Executive Ice Scraper." "Caution," the instructions warned. "Under no circumstances should you ever strike someone with this ice scraper . . . made of heavy duty plastic. It will produce a particularly nasty cut requiring about 20 stitches to close." The "heavy duty plastic" model was $4.95. Directly under the words of caution, in red, were the words "Also Available in Metal," for $12.00.

Also offered for sale were the "Pager Holster" and the "Stealth Hacksaw" ("Put it on your key ring, sew it into your jacket lining, slip it in your sock. Just don't get caught without it"). There was a wide choice of material for lock-picking. One book was entitled *How to Open Handcuffs Without Keys*, another *Successful Armed Robbery*. There were *Techniques of Safecracking, Techniques for Burglar Alarm Bypassing,* and *Credit Card Fraud*. There were books on surveillance: *How to Get Anything on Anybody* and *Be Your Own Dick*. Books on divorce: *Screw the Bitch*. Books on how to commit murder: *Hunting Humans* and *Execution: Tools and Techniques*. There were books on "Getting Around the System," including *Beat the Box*, *Getting Started in the Underground Economy*, and *Job Opportunities in the Black Market*.

Of course, a good way to collect weapons was to be a gun dealer. An entire "Super Pac" of five books about gun dealerships—including applications—cost only $13.50. The only suggestion in the eighty-page catalogue that you might get in trouble was a 128-page book ($16.95) entitled *Surviving in Prison*.

Posters were for sale, too. Many of these were more expensive than the books, but understandably so. There were "Genuine German Propaganda Poster Reproductions" which included posters of the Waffen SS and the "Hermann Göring Division." If you wanted Nazi books, no problem. These items, it was noted in red ink, were "for entertainment purposes only and do not express the political beliefs of the owners." Entertainment included *Nazi Regalia*, *Weapons of the Waffen-SS*, and what, at $59.95, must have been the most engrossing: *Forgotten Legions: Obscure Combat Formations of the Waffen-SS*.

Also for sale were books of interest to those who shared the militias' political paranoia. These included books by neo-Nazi William Pierce, including *Hunter* and *The Turner Diaries*. The latter, you may remember, was one of Timothy McVeigh's favorites.

PART FOUR **March Madness**

16 In Legislators' Faces

GO UP AND LOOK LEGISLATORS IN THE FACE,

BECAUSE SOMEDAY YOU MAY BE FORCED TO

BLOW IT OFF.

SAMUEL SHERWOOD, United States Militia Association

"Do you know why Jesus was killed?" Samuel Sherwood asked his audience. "There was no militia. Think of that for a moment. There was no one there to respond, to say, 'You can't do that.'"

Sherwood, head of the United States Militia Association, not only had opinions about Jesus, he had strong opinions about guns. "Gun ownership," he said, "is not a freedom or a liberty as much as it is a constitutional responsibility." Yet he did not own a firearm until 1994, when a son insisted so the family could hunt deer. Sherwood also said his name was Samuel, as in Samuel Adams. But he was born Mason Stanley Sherwood. On July 1, 1993, he changed his name to Michael Stanley Sherwood.

Sherwood's USMA was based in Blackfoot, Idaho. Its publications ran ads for John Birch Society titles and for the pro-militia fringe group "Jews for the Preservation of Firearms Ownership." Sherwood's literature made claims such as the following: "Bilderbergers . . . want America turned into a separate group of small nations like Europe so they can get rich off our internal wars" and "Bill Clinton is bringing up to 100,000 Hong Kong Chinese to America to . . . seize every gun in America." Sherwood said that President Clinton "was determined to seize your guns, steal your food, take your children away. In his term he will have killed more babies than Hitler, put more homosexuals in government than Sodom and Gomorrah, had the schools teach your children it is right and forced you to accept it." He also said Clinton was a "petty malcontent disloyal traitor," who had created a "heightened probability of military hostile activities within the United States by elements personally loyal to the president in actions against the citizens of this nation and the states."

Despite such cookie-cutter militia rhetoric, Samuel Sherwood was a unique figure in the movement. His ideology was just as antigovernment, just as laden with conspiracy theories as that of his neighbors in Montana. But Sherwood had another idea: Rather than stockpile weapons, he would stockpile politicians. The plan seemed simple. First his group would support certain politicians, including those running for election. Then he would call on these officials to speak to his group. Seeing this stamp of approval, people would flock to his militia. The politicians, now beholden to a significant and motivated voter bloc, would support legislation Sherwood proposed, giving his group legal recognition. So recognized, his militia could arm itself under the protection of state law. And once his militia was armed, there would be little it could not do to remake Idaho. This bizarre scheme worked remarkably well for a time. But as Sherwood would find out, it would prove difficult to use lawmakers to overthrow government.

✗ ✗ ✗

In 1992 Samuel Sherwood wrote a book entitled *The Little Republics*. Its premise was that a "political war" with Satan would destroy America, and that the country would have to be reborn. For that he had plans, which he would sell you. These included various constitutions. "Slavery contracts we call marriage licenses," for example, would be outlawed. And after the current government was gone, homosexuals, abortionists, rapists, disloyal politicians, and others would be executed. Tax evaders, however, would only forfeit library privileges. And Sherwood had other goals for the interim: Get rid of income taxes, Social Security, the Drug Enforcement Agency, the Bureau of Alcohol, Tobacco and Firearms, and the U.S. Departments of Labor, Health and Human Services, and Energy. He also suggested that every American should carry an automatic weapon to "decrease crime."

Sherwood claimed that his United States Militia Association had five hundred members in Idaho and five thousand others around the country. When they came to meetings, they were supposed to be dressed in proper military attire because their role, he said, was so important. Sherwood said that every state—in fact, every county—should have its own citizen militia. A well-armed militia.

"What we're seeking to do is organize people into organized militia units at the county level," he said. "The National Guard is organized at the state level. We're trying to organize them at the county level so that they can be a resource to the county sheriff and the county commissioners and whoever needs them."

Sherwood said that more than half of Idaho's sheriffs liked the idea of a citizen militia, which would be available to deal with riots such as that in Los Angeles and to protect the U.S. Constitution from threats both internal and external. His "hook" for gun lovers was that he planned to have his militia legally sanctioned by the state. Since it would then be a "well-regulated militia," as in the Second Amendment, Sherwood claimed, the arms and training would be legal—exempt from gun control laws. This exemption, of course, would cover weapons such as tanks and artillery. Should the government be concerned about people like Sherwood having tanks? He thought not. "The only threat could be from the government itself," he explained, "who, in the fear of its citizens feels that these arms would be used against it because of the unjust laws it has put in place."

"Let's sell all the people who believe *that* the Brooklyn Bridge," said Les Stanford, spokesperson for the BATF, deriding Sherwood's assertion that federal gun control laws would exempt militias. Nonetheless, Sherwood's claim that his militia would be an end run around gun control laws brought many people to his meetings in Idaho and elsewhere.

Sherwood's reach extended far beyond Idaho. The *Salt Lake Tribune* reported that "a reprint of one of Sherwood's publications showed up earlier this year in the Utah legislature during debate on anti–gun control laws. The article distributed to House members compared President Clinton to Adolf Hitler on gun control issues." Literature was also circulated in the Utah Senate reportedly suggesting, in the words of the *Tribune*, that lawmakers "should provide for organization and arming of a militia consisting of all Utah males between the ages of 18 and 45. The letter goes on to detail the arms that should be provided to the units, including machine guns, grenades, surface-to-air rockets and artillery." Utah Senate minority leader Scott Howell expressed the reaction of many Utah legislators to Sherwood's material. "It's sick," he said.

Even back on his home turf of Idaho, Sherwood's ideas seemed a bit much. According to Sheriff Greg Moffat of Madison County, Idaho, who is president of the Tri-County Sheriffs Association (which includes sheriffs from sixteen eastern Idaho counties), the sheriffs' group decided to "give absolutely no support to the idea of a militia" and passed a resolution against it. "We need help from the public, but not that kind of help," he said. "Their intent is to amass weapons, including automatic weapons, and go against the federal government.

"I'm a gun nut myself," said Moffat, "and if the federal government came in and wanted to confiscate weapons, you'd find me at the border of this county ready to fight to the death for the Second Amendment myself. But this group wants to be organized as a political entity to circumvent the Brady Bill, and I'm not in favor of that."

✗ ✗ ✗

The Idaho Liberty Network held a conference in Coeur d'Alene, Idaho, on April 23, 1994. It was organized by E. Tom Stetson, a member of Concerned Citizens of Idaho and a contributor to *Jubilee*, the Christian Identity newspaper. Speakers included Dick Carver, the county commissioner who became a hero to the Wise Use and militia movements with his well-publicized confrontation with federal officials in Nye County, Nevada. Also appearing were Samuel Sherwood, Lionel Koon, a former Madison County, Idaho, sheriff, and Pete Cenarussa, Idaho's secretary of state. According to the Coalition for Human Dignity, the meeting was a Christian Patriot "festival," which helped promote militias.

Sherwood, keeping to his game plan of co-opting politicians, used the opportunity to commend Secretary of State Cenarussa: "Boy, wouldn't the press love to fry him. I mean, come on, if they were smart they'd be here. Tomorrow the Boise, Idaho, *Statesman* or whatever that stupid paper from down there is: 'Secretary of State meets with radicals in Coeur d'Alene.' Right, yeah we're real radicals. We just want our freedom, you know, that's all."

Sherwood's plan to court government and have it bestow legal status on his militia was gaining momentum. The March 1995 edition of *Aide-de-Camp*, USMA's newsletter, had a front-page quote from Idaho Secretary of State Cenarussa: "We need to figure out a way to call you out as the militia and get you recognized."

Sherwood had persuaded other key Idaho politicians, too. He claimed his organization worked to help elect Anne Fox state superintendent of public education. Fox, in turn, spoke at USMA meetings, as did Cenarussa and Lieutenant Governor Butch Otter. Sherwood's strategy might have succeeded, had he kept his eye on his goal—to gain legitimacy for his group—rather than trying to convert politicians to his point of view.

Sherwood's plan began to unravel the night of March 2, 1995, when Lieutenant Governor Otter was guest speaker at a USMA meeting in Boise. Otter's conservative stump speech didn't play well with Sherwood. First, the lieutenant governor believed that the Republican Party's success in Idaho's 1994 elections was due, in large measure, to the National Rifle Association. Sherwood's USMA did not support the NRA; rather, it promoted the more extreme views of Larry Pratt's Gun Owners of America. Second, Otter was a supporter of the Conference of States, an idea that should have attracted militia groups such as Sherwood's. Scheduled for the fall of 1995, the COS meeting was organized by promoters of the Tenth Amendment: "The powers not delegated to the United States by the Constitution, nor prohibited by it to the States, are reserved to the States, respectively, or to the people." In 1994, fifteen states had passed resolutions reaffirming that sentiment; the meeting was designed as an opportunity for states to strategize to transfer power from the federal government and to themselves. Knowing the militias' antifederal venom, Otter probably thought this was a safe crowd in which to talk about his participation in the conference. What he apparently did not know was that the militia movement had become alarmed about the Conference of States. For one thing, the scheduled date was troubling to people who believed the U.N. was poised to take over America as part of One World Government. Not only was the year, 1995, the fiftieth anniversary of the U.N.'s founding, but the meeting was set for October 23–25. October 24 was United Nations Day.

What was more, a key "patriot" politician, who shared militialike beliefs about the New World Order, the "tyrants" who run "the puppets in Washington," and the power of the Tenth Amendment, set out to kill the conference. Colorado state senator Charlie Duke, who called himself "a real Republican, as opposed to that nonsense we see in Washington," went on radio, met with state legislators, and sent faxes, all to spread the message. "If the people who would destroy our Constitution were to gain control of [the conference]," he said, "then we see that the potential for the destruction of our Constitution is very high."

The militias and others who defined themselves as "patriots" flooded state legislatures with messages railing against the conference. They were ultimately to succeed in canceling it, but in early March 1995 the conference was still on, and Otter defended it. According to Idaho resident Dan Yurman, "militia members verbally pounded Otter for ninety minutes with their fears about a planned takeover of the U.S. Government. They told him a Conference of States . . . would not enhance states' rights, but was a conspiracy to overthrow government. When Otter defended his participation in the meeting, Sherwood [reportedly] told him, 'You've been tricked, Butch. You've been tricked. A lot of you have been tricked.'"

A reporter from the *Boise Weekly* attended that meeting. After the heated debate with Otter, Sherwood was quoted as saying that there may be a civil war in the United States, and that people should "go up and look legislators in the face, because someday you may be forced to blow it off." Asked by the Associated Press whether that quote was accurate, Sherwood answered: "I said something about, 'You may have to be shooting them in the face,' and that may well happen." According to *The Washington Post*, "Sherwood told the AP that some Idaho lawmakers may betray Idaho and cling to Washington, so there'll be a need to shoot them." He also confirmed the statement to Twin Falls and Lewiston, Idaho, papers at the time, although he later denied making it.

Key Idaho elected officials, including Governor Phil Batt, Lieutenant Governor Otter, and State Attorney General Alan Lance, blasted what became known as Sherwood's "shooter" statement. State legislator Wendy Jaquet called it "extremism at its worst." State Senator Ron Beck said it was "frightening and uncivilized."

On March 8, 1995, the Idaho Falls *Post Register* editorialized about the militia, whose "influence and membership is growing at a frightening pace" and which "should not be taken lightly."

On March 13, 1995, both houses of the Idaho legislature passed a resolution. Recognizing the right of free speech, it noted that "public statements threatening civil war and the infliction of bodily harm upon public officials are outside the realm of those rights . . . and are abhorrent to a civilized society."

17 Militia Alert!

THE RUMORS ARE FLYING ABOUT PENDING

ATTACKS ON "MILITIAS" IN MONTANA, FLORIDA,

AND MICHIGAN. THE RUMOR MILL WON'T STOP,

AND SOONER OR LATER THE "COLD WAR"

BETWEEN THE FEDERAL BUREAUCRACY AND THE

STATES WILL ESCALATE INTO A SHOOTING WAR.

SAMUEL SHERWOOD, March 1995

In early 1995, *The Resister* published what it claimed was an intercepted ATF telex. National raids of militia groups were supposedly in the offing. Federal officers were alleged to be training for the exercise at Fort Bliss, Texas.

The *Resister* telex spread like wildfire over the Internet. In Usenet forums such as alt.conspiracy and talk.politics.guns, the debate raged. Was this real? A hoax? Was this attempted disinformation? When was the feared government crackdown going to start? Would there be Wacos all over the United States?

Conspiracy theorists all, the militias reacted to the March rumors in two ways. Either they believed the raid was going to happen or, as the White Mountain Militia Information Service posted on the Internet, "recent reports of a possible BATF raid on unorganized militia are disinformation. The obvious goal of the enemie [*sic*] is to create paranoia and stress that may lead to the precipitation of a conflict." Either way, of course, militias believed the government was responsible for the alleged teletype, and that it was part of a plan to eradicate them.

Key militia leaders' opinions were split, too. Linda Thompson denounced the rumor as hoax. Jon Roland, leader of the Texas Constitutional Militia, seemed to think the raid might be real. He posted the following on the Internet:

> Concerning the possible mass arrest of militia leaders and patriots. We continue to get confirming reports, but so far no hard evidence, of a mass arrest, with the date March 25 being most often mentioned. We have the NRA, other civil rights organizations, and at least six U.S. Senators inquiring into the matter.
>
> To the basic reports have come several unconfirmed reports as to what the targets might be and what offenses might be staged to be blamed on militia activities. . . . We have several reports of possible plans for atrocities to be committed by agents against innocent persons and blamed on militia activists. The atrocity targets include the following, with many variants possible:
>
> (1) The homes and family of "straight" government agents, judges, and elected officials. This would provide a pretext for labeling militiamen "terrorists." . . .
>
> (2) "Straight" local law enforcement personnel asked to either serve warrants on militia leaders or to accompany federal agents while they do so. The local officials and militiamen would be killed and the killings made to look like they were done by the militiamen.
>
> (3) Crowded public places, to be bombed, and the bombings blamed on militia leaders, with evidence to later be planted on them.

Even though March 25 was the target date, other March events ratcheted up tension throughout the militia movement. The arrest of John Trochmann and others at the Montana courthouse terrified many. Was this an early start to the crackdown, or just coincidence? Newsletters, faxes, Internet postings frenetically debating every possible explanation made the anxiety palpable. The *Spotlight* wrote that Trochmann's arrest might mark "the start of a well-orchestrated crackdown on militias and other patriotic groups all across America."

On March 4, 1995, a Texas militia group faxed the following message: "All militias across the country are on alert status, based on unconfirmed reports that federal and state officials were planning a mass arrest of militia leaders and other patriots, and that this arrest of . . . militia activists is seen by many as a possible prelude to such an attempt to repress political dissidents."

"It remains our position," said the White Mountain group on the Internet, "that the enemy MUST provoke hostile actions if they are to legitemize [sic] any attack on The People. Unless and until the federal thugs attain Waco, we MUST remain calm, calculating and cool headed. Once an overt, demonstrable, criminal attack on citizens occurs the entire situation changes. At that point, we are moraly [sic] obligated to go to the aid of our fellows and repel the violent onslaught by whatever means are available."

On the March 7, 1995, installment of his talk show, *Progress Report with Newt Gingrich*, the House Speaker's guest was the Librarian of Congress. They were discussing new technology and the "national digital library." The third caller began talking about that subject, then switched to another:

> The following inside information is dated Washington, D.C., 7th of February, 1995: "All leaves of absence of BATF-NETGOV personnel are cancelled in preparation for federal action against U.S. citizen militia groups and organizations. Actions may be scheduled for late February or early March. Possible areas of operation are Arizona, Florida, Montana. But no area should be considered excluded for possible engagement by federal agents. These actions may or may not proceed a Presidential or Attorney General order to disarm militia and confiscate arms."
>
> Now, we thought with the Republican revolution that these violations of Article II and the rest of the rights that have been violated, such as in Waco and Ruby Ridge with the Weaver family, would stop.

Gingrich had no reply to this part of the caller's question. On March 21, 1995, alt.conspiracy offered the following posting:

> The slaughter of dozens of women and children in Waco by government storm troopers under the command of Field Marshall [sic] Reno may pale in comparison to what has been planned for late March: a nationwide BATF/FBI assault on private militias as the prelude to a possible declaration of martial law throughout the United States. All leaves and vacations have been canceled for BATF/FBI personnel, and for various State Police and National Guards such as California's. The Army's infamous Joint Task Force Six (which did the training for Waco) has been training BATF jackbooters with Bradley Assault Vehicles at Ft. Bliss, Texas. Government agent provocateurs are set to plant fully automatic and heavy weapons, like rocket launchers, on the property of militia leaders. Every militia in the coun-

try—and there are dozens, many of which are well-armed and well-led by former or even active-duty officers—is on a state of Red Alert. Should Reno be stupid enough to actually attack them militarily, there is going to be a lot of blood.

The establishment media is [sic] programmed to immediately thereafter thunderously bellow for nationwide gun confiscation and even martial law. The Senate Armed Forces Committee has been alerted and is questioning key Defense and Justice people behind closed doors.

On March 22, 1995, a frantic "Patriot WARNING!!!" appeared in alt.conspiracy:

Our network has obtained information about a planned move by a joint ATF/MJTF task force against "domestic terrorist organizations" scheduled to occur on 3/25/95 at 0400 (4 am).

Patriot Organizations: THIS MEANS YOU! . . .

They are getting us ready with the propaganda about "terrorists" in the wake of events in Japan. Pay attention to the hype on the TV. They are now telling us to be prepared for something like what happened in Japan (Nerve gas/Subway). . . . Just tonight KTLA in Los Angeles finally admitted that FEMA would be involved with a similar incident within the United States. What was FEMA set up to deal with??? Hurricanes and earthquakes, right?

Ok. You should all get the point. If you have no idea what I'm talking about, its [sic] too late for you. For those of you who have been preparing, keep your heads up. We have no choice.

On March 22, 1995, U.S. Representative Steve Stockman (a Texas Republican) sent the following letter to Attorney General Janet Reno:

It has come to my attention through a number of reliable sources that an impending raid, by several Federal agencies, against the "citizen's militias" groups, is scheduled for March 25 or 26 at 4:00 A.M. A paramilitary style attack against Americans who pose no risk to others, even if violations of criminal law might be imputed to them, would run the risk of an irreparable breach between the Federal government and the public; especially if it turned out to be an ill considered, poorly planned, but bloody fiasco like Waco.

While information is scarce, it is known that Joint Task Force Six, with headquarters at Fort Bliss, Texas, is co-ordinating the military training, including the use of tanks and other armored vehicles, for certain Federal Law Enforcement agencies in possible violation of the Posse Comitatus Law, 18 U.S.C. 1385. Any possible impending military action against American citizens might be forestalled by, among other things, simply asking for a complete explanation of all training activities of JTF-6 for the last three years, including the individuals, agencies, who authorized the training, what military equipment was used, what apparent purpose was served by the training, and copies of all legal opinions as to the legality of such training.

I will be eagerly awaiting your response to these questions.

On March 24, 1995, the NRA sent an "Alert" to its members on the Internet, saying that it could neither confirm nor deny the rumors of an impending attack on militias. It also posted Congressman Stockman's letter as part of the "Alert."

✗ ✗ ✗

Tension in the militia movement built all through February and March. The persistent rumors of an ATF crackdown were only the beginning. Calvin Greenup called the militia out in order to try to shoot down a National Guard helicopter should it return to overfly his Montana property. A young man with ties to the militia movement shot an Oregon State Police trooper and her passenger. Sherwood made his "shooter" statement about Idaho legislators. A bomb went off in the Carson City, Nevada, Forest Service office, which covered the Toiyabe National Forest. Trochmann and others were arrested at the Roundup courthouse with weapons, armor-piercing bullets, and other equipment.

Local authorities were concerned, too. On March 6, 1995, the U.S. Marshals Service told Musselshell County, Montana, attorney John Bohlman that "20 men were leaving Medford, Ore., to protest the arraignment [of Trochmann and the others arrested on March 3], and to blow up a power station." Power plants across the Northwest, even in North and South Dakota, heightened their security. A March 13, 1995, Army Corps of Engineers memo stated that "[t]hough the threat is generic . . . it should not be viewed lightly. It would be prudent to notify your project managers and suggest vigilance and to report . . . any suspicious activity."

As March drew to a close, militia members grew even more anxious. Jim Barnett, leader of the Pensacola-based Escambia County Militia's Alligator Chapter, was deluged with calls from friends offering to hide him. March 25, 1995, they had heard, was the date the "feds" were coming to arrest all militia leaders.

Whether one was in the militia or just monitoring it through the Internet, the fear became tangible as March 25 approached. The computer keyboard seemed to relay emotions, and those emotions were panic and paranoia. When March 25 passed with no ATF crackdown, it was as if a balloon on the verge of overinflation had had a temporary reprieve. Yet the militia movement still appeared ready to blow.

Those who watched the militias and knew about "Leaderless Resistance" were concerned. The next date on the militias' unofficial calendar, and the most important day to all who shared their violent and delusional antigovernment ideology, was April 19, the anniversary of Waco.

PART FIVE **Oklahoma**

---

18 April 19, 1995: "Balancing" the Scales

THERE IS NO JUSTIFICATION FOR BRUTALITY

MEETING BRUTALITY. BUT WHEN A TYRANT'S

BRUTALITY IS NOT REINED IN BY JUSTICE, YOU

WILL HAVE SOMEBODY OUT THERE WHO TAKES

IT UPON HIMSELF, DERANGED THOUGH HE

MAY BE, TO BALANCE THE SCALES OF JUSTICE.

NORMAN OLSON, Michigan Militia

At 9:02 A.M. on April 19, 1995, the Alfred P. Murrah Building was torn apart by a massive truck bomb. Rubble, debris, glass, blood, smoke, screams, terror replaced the calm of moments before. Immediately after the explosion Tony Lippe, a nurse, held tiny Colton Smith. "It was like a final breath," he said. "I say whimper, but it was more like a wheeze. One solid breath and that was it. That kind of put me in shock, and I just sat there and held him. . . . I keep seeing the little boy's face and seeing my son."

Chase and Colton Smith were so close in age—Chase was three and Colton two—that they were destined to be best friends. They were buried in a single white coffin, holding hands, with stuffed animals and their favorite book, *Animal Sounds*.

Laura Garrison, aged sixty-one, was planning to retire in July 1995. She picked Wednesday morning, April 19, to go to the Social Security office to prepare. Her niece, Doris Washington, waited anxiously at the Red

Cross center, hoping for news. "She's not on any list," Mrs. Washington said. "We're assuming she's still in the rubble somewhere. She has a brother in a wheelchair and she calls him two or three times a day. She hasn't called."

Luther Treanor, also aged sixty-one, had gone to the Social Security office to plan his retirement too. He had brought along his wife, LaRue, and their four-year-old granddaughter, Ashley Eckles. All three died.

Sergeant John Avera said, "I heard a baby crying and we started moving bricks and rocks . . . and we found two babies. The officer I was with took one down one hallway and I took my baby out the other way." Avera's baby—Baylee Almon—became America's baby. Newspapers around the country had bloody front-page photographs of Baylee being handed to a firefighter. Baylee died. She had celebrated her first birthday the day before the explosion.

The blast was so powerful that ten nearby buildings were also destroyed. About two hundred other buildings—and 312 neighborhood houses—suffered structural damage. The bomb actually pushed the floors of the Murrah Building up, a stress they were not designed to sustain; then they came down on each other, in rubble.

Governor Keating rushed to the scene. He thanked a firefighter for taking part in the search for survivors. The firefighter said, "You find whoever did this. All I've found in here are a baby's finger and an American flag."

For the first two days the rescue effort was frantic. Despite the obvious scope of the tragedy, evidenced by the gaping hole that was once the front of the building, the hope that someone was still alive, trapped, waiting for deliverance, kept the workers going. The instability of the structure, however, slowed the search. The bomb had blown away key support columns. "Columns that were only built to support one floor are suddenly supporting four times that," said Paul Ed Kirkpatrick, a structural engineer who had helped construct the building in 1977. "It's as if you had a tree that was supported by cables. If you put an elephant on the top of that tree, it could hold. But without the cables, the tree would buckle and break. That's what we may be facing here."

Debris was loaded into containers, and passed hand to hand, in order to clear the way. "It's really bucket by bucket until you get to a body," said Greg A. Stephens of the Oklahoma Air Guard. "Everything inside that place is confused. You find a body ahead of you and then a child's tennis shoe and then a Marine insignia and a pile of signed checks. . . . [In one office, bodies] lay all in a row as though those people were all lined up for something. . . . There's one wall where the photographs of President Clinton and Al Gore are still intact, as though nothing happened. It's all mixed up."

Rescuers were looking for pockets in which people might have survived, sandwiched between slabs of concrete. "Anything six inches and up is fair game," said Dr. Dario Gonzalez, associate medical director of New York City's Emergency Medical Service, who was part of the Federal Emergency Management Agency's urban search-and-rescue team.

More than five hundred people had been injured in the blast; 432 of them needed treatment, and seventy-two of these, including six children, required hospitalization. Twenty-one children, ranging in age from a few months to five years old, had been in the second-floor day care center that morning, as had three teachers. All the teachers and the other fifteen children were killed, including four infants who were in cribs next to the windows, so they could look outside. Many who used to walk past the building liked to look up and see the babies, who liked looking down. Some think the bomber would have seen the infants, too.

By April 21, two days after the terrorist attack, Dan Schroeder, of a California search-and-rescue squad, said, "Our sensors are detecting absolutely no sounds of survivors. Our cameras show only death." The corpses were decomposing. Rescuers had to wear masks to breathe and protective gear to guard them from blood and other bodily fluids present in the wreckage. When they left work, they had to be decontaminated.

On April 22, the search teams began to use a few pieces of heavy machinery, rather than just hands and buckets, to move the rubble. It was an admission of lost hope. By April 30, the rescue effort itself had contributed to the instability of the building. The removal of debris from the remnants of the support columns had made the structure weaker, much as the removal of sand from the base of a beach umbrella would make it victim to the softest breeze. The hope that there were additional survivors was now so remote that the risk of killing the rescuers outweighed the wisdom of continuing the search. Nonetheless, every day, the parking lot of the First Christian Church—where the families gathered to hear news from the Red Cross—was packed.

Throughout the rescue effort, teams that were part of FEMA's urban search-and-rescue response system kept coming from across America, then leaving; the work was so arduous that any group could only stay a week. On its seventh day the Fairfax County, Virginia, team could not face leaving the site on a bus. It decided to walk down the street as a tribute. An Oklahoma policeman hugged a Fairfax fireman. "We can't thank you enough," he said. Strangers on sidewalks stood still and applauded. A UPS driver, his truck stopped, stood and saluted.

The search for survivors was officially over at 11:50 P.M. on May 4, 1995. Three of the last bodies removed were those of infants who at 9:02 A.M. on April 19 had been peering out the day care center's windows from their cribs. The next day, May 5, people gathered to gaze at the bomb site. A bagpipe dirge played as part of the memorial service. Rescuers stood together, silently. As they marched away for the final time, spectators, many with tears streaming down their faces, applauded. They applauded for twenty minutes.

On May 23 the remnant of the Murrah Building was imploded. Watching was Edye Smith, the mother of three-year-old Chase and two-year-old Colton. "It's like reliving that day," she said. Asked if she talked to her children, she said, "I sure do. . . . I tell them I miss them, and I just pretend sometimes . . . like they're right here with you, you know, at home."

Three bodies were recovered at the end of May, as was a severed leg inside a military-style boot, two layers of socks, and an olive elastic strap. When the final count was completed, at least 168 people had died, including a nurse killed by debris that fell during the rescue.

✗ ✗ ✗

During the first hours, as bodies and body parts began to pile up at the Oklahoma City morgue, forensic experts from the FBI, the U.S. Army, and area police labs arrived at the Murrah Building and at the morgue. They retrieved samples of clothing, concrete, paint, glass, and metal as evidence, all to be tested at the FBI's laboratory for traces of the explosive.

Claims of responsibility poured in that first morning. Federal authorities said eight of those seemed plausible. Seven of the claimants were thought to have Middle Eastern connections. The eighth was a militia, which noted other events that took place on April 19, including the battle of Lexington and the end of the siege at Waco. "April 19," this message ended, "the Second American Revolution."

Some officials quoted in the media discounted the possibility that anyone associated with militia groups could be responsible. According to The New York Times, these officials thought militias lacked "the technical expertise to engage in bombings like the one today." ATF officials said the bomb—which left a hole twenty feet wide and eight feet deep—was likely built of ammonium nitrate and fuel oil and weighed between one thousand and twelve hundred pounds. (Days later the FBI would estimate the bomb's weight at approximately 4,800 pounds.)

CNN reported that authorities were tracking several "Middle Eastern–looking" men who had been seen driving away from the building right before the explosion. The El Paso Times wrote that authorities were looking for "two men of Middle Eastern appearance," who might have been wearing bloody clothes and heading toward the Mexican border in a Chevy Cavalier or Blazer. Late on April 19, three men described as "of Middle Eastern extraction" were detained to determine their immigration status, and were questioned about the bombing. A fourth, who was stopped in Britain after arriving from Chicago and was then returned to the U.S., was described by the Department of Justice as "a possible witness."

Experts on Middle Eastern terrorism were ubiquitous over the media. Steven Emerson, an expert on Islamic Jihad, said: "There is no smoking gun. But the modus operandi and circumstantial evidence leads in the direction of Islamic terrorism." He explained that radical Islamic groups had established a center in Oklahoma City, which had even hosted a 1992 convention at which six thousand people cheered calls for the murder of Jews and infidels. Terrorism expert Neil C. Livingston explained why Oklahoma City might have been targeted: "As we make it tougher for terrorists in New York and Washington, the terrorists are forced to go out and look for softer targets in places like Lincoln, Nebraska; Boise, Idaho; and Oklahoma City." Others speculated that drugs might have been involved. A Drug Enforcement Administration office was reportedly housed in the Murrah Building.

Bomb threats forced the evacuation of government buildings in New York; New Jersey; Philadelphia; Baltimore; Lawton, Oklahoma; Fort Worth; Rochester; Boston; Wilmington, Delaware; Boise, Idaho; and Portland, Oregon. At one of those buildings, which also housed a day care center, the sense of panic was so intense that a teacher did not conduct a head count until she was blocks away. One youngster had been left behind. (When the child came out of the bathroom, everyone in the building had seemingly disappeared.)

During those first hours, the FBI would be lucky. An axle bearing part of a vehicle identification number was found two blocks away. The number belonged to a Ryder rental truck that had been rented on Monday, April 17, from Elliott's Body Shop on Golden Belt Boulevard in Junction City, Kansas. The employees at the shop thought they remembered two men who had come for that truck, although only one had spoken with them. He had given the name "Robert D. Kling" and offered what turned out to be a phony South Dakota driver's license. It sported April 19, 1970, as "Kling's" date of birth and April 19, 1993, as the date of issue. "Kling" had requested a truck that could hold five thousand pounds.

Late in the afternoon of April 20, the FBI announced that it had issued warrants for two "John Does" who were "white males." Composite sketches were released. John Doe Number 2 was described as having a tattoo on his left arm. A $2 million reward was offered.

✗ ✗ ✗

On April 19, 1995, about eighty minutes after the bombing, Timothy James McVeigh was pulled over on Interstate 35 near Perry, Oklahoma, by Highway Patrolman Charles D. Hanger, who had noticed that McVeigh's yellow Mercury was missing a license plate. When he approached the car Hanger saw a bulge in McVeigh's jacket. It turned out to be a 9mm Glock semiautomatic pistol with Black Talon bullets, known as cop killers because they can penetrate bulletproof vests. McVeigh also had a six-inch knife.

"No sir," McVeigh said to the officer, "I did not intend to break your laws. I just carry the gun for protection." Hanger was suspicious: McVeigh had said he was driving cross-country, but he had no luggage. McVeigh was taken into custody on charges of carrying a concealed weapon, transporting a loaded weapon, driving without a license plate, and driving without insurance, all misdemeanors. On his ride to jail he left a business card behind in the patrol car. The name David was on it, as was handwriting stating that five more sticks of TNT were needed by May 1. The *Dallas Morning News* reported that other writing was found in McVeigh's Mercury; the subject: revenge for Waco.

Ordinarily, McVeigh would have been released on bond the following day. But the local judge had to postpone McVeigh's arraignment until Friday, April 21, because he was in the middle of hearing a divorce case. The FBI was lucky again. While McVeigh sat in jail it had received a tip from a co-worker of McVeigh's, who had recognized the composite sketch of John Doe Number 1. The co-worker had told the FBI that McVeigh's antigovernment politics were vitriolic and that he was obsessed by Waco. Because of that phone tip, the FBI put McVeigh's Social Security number into its computer to be "flagged." And since McVeigh was from out of state, the Noble County sheriff's office ran his Social Security number through the National Crime Information Center computer. The number hit, and the FBI called Sheriff Jerry Cook of Noble County, asking him to hold McVeigh, who was then only a half-hour from release.

Assistant District Attorney Mark Gibson went up to McVeigh in the courtroom, to tell him that he would not be freed, that the federal government would hold him on charges of blowing up the Murrah Building and killing scores of people. McVeigh's reaction "was like the dutiful soldier," Gibson said. "Emotions don't come into play, right and wrong don't come into play. My feeling was that, in his mind, that was the end of that portion of his life. . . . He exuded nothing. . . . His mission was accomplished." Later, McVeigh referred to himself as a prisoner of war. Authorities said he would only give his name, rank, and date of birth. According to sources quoted in *The New York Times*, he also sat emotionless when shown pictures of the children who died.

McVeigh was escorted out of the courthouse that afternoon, dressed in orange prison attire, handcuffed, and looking remarkably like the composite sketch of "John Doe Number 1." A crowd gathered near the courthouse. "Murderer!" some shouted. "Bastard!" "Baby-killer! Burn him!" One man yelled, "His children should be shot!"

McVeigh was flown by helicopter to Tinker Air Force Base, where a brief hearing was held. A bill of information filed by prosecutors quoted a former co-worker of McVeigh's as saying that the suspect had "extreme right-wing views" and was "particularly agitated" over Waco, so much so that he had even visited the site and expressed "extreme anger at the Federal Government." An affidavit filed said witnesses had seen someone fitting McVeigh's description at the Murrah Building shortly before the explosion. Also cited was an interview with an unnamed female relative of James Nichols (McVeigh had provided the name "James Nichols" as next of kin at his traffic arrest), saying that McVeigh had stayed on Nichols's farm, that sometime around November 1994 Nichols had been making bombs, and "that he [Nichols] possessed large quantities of fuel oil and fertilizer." After the hearing McVeigh was taken in a procession of military and police vehicles to the El Reno Federal Correction Center.

Once authorities had learned that it was McVeigh who had rented the truck, other investigative leads opened before them. They went to the Dreamland Motel near Junction City, Kansas, where they found his registration—under his own name. He had come to the motel in a 1977 Mercury, reportedly bearing Arizona plates. He later drove a Ryder truck to the motel, and parked it far from his room. He checked in on Friday, April 14, and out on Tuesday morning, April 18. McVeigh had listed an address on his real driver's license—3616 North Van Dyke, Decker, Michigan, the farm of James Nichols. Later, on April 21, agents armed with automatic weapons approached this house. James Nichols cooperated. Agents searched the farm for evidence of explosives. They said that Nichols and his brother, Terry, were at that time witnesses, not suspects. They also said the brothers had associations with the Michigan Militia.

Meanwhile, McVeigh's gun—the one he had when arrested—led investigators to Kingman, Arizona. Apparently, McVeigh had not been satisfied with the Glock handgun. He had written to the company, listing his address as the Mail Room, at 1711 Stockton Hill Road in Kingman. FBI teams swooped into Kingman on the evening of April 21. Among their leads was the fact that a right-wing paramilitary group, the Arizona Patriots, had used the desert outside town as a practice site. Members of that group had planned to blow up Arizona federal buildings in 1986, according to testimony that emerged in a 1987 weapons trial. And on February 27, 1995, near Kingman, a bomb had exploded, shattering windows and damaging a porch of a house near the Canyon West trailer park. Agents analyzed evidence from that blast, including bomb fragments. They also found that McVeigh, who had once lived in the Canyon West trailer park, was in Kingman on that date, and that the blast left ammonium nitrate residue.

Meanwhile, in Herington, Kansas, McVeigh's old army buddy Terry Nichols sat in his living room. He had purchased a television set in January, but had not called the cable company until April 21, 1995. He was hooked up that afternoon, and asked the technician to leave his set tuned to CNN. He watched for a while. Then Nichols gave his wife, Marife, some cash, left home, drove to the police station, and surrendered. When he was read his rights, Nichols complained that the procedure was reminiscent of "Nazi Germany."

19 Timothy McVeigh: Trading Armies

I AM BOUND TO GIVE ONLY NAME, RANK, AND
DATE OF BIRTH. I WILL EVADE ANSWERING
FURTHER QUESTIONS TO THE UTMOST OF MY
ABILITY.

Code of conduct for Michigan Militia members "captured" by federal government

Timothy McVeigh lived at the small end of Ken Toole's funnel. He
was not an active militia member like John Trochmann or Norman
Olson. But his antigovernment, violence-laden, racist, conspiratorial,
Waco-obsessed ideas mirrored those of the most committed militia member. And even though he went to few militia meetings, he was the essence
of what Louis Beam meant by the "Leaderless Resistance" the movement
and its literature was designed to produce.

McVeigh was born in Pendleton, New York, on April 23, 1968. After
high school he worked as a security guard. Jeff Camp, his partner on an
armored truck, remembered McVeigh as being in love with guns, and
odd. He frequently carried two or three firearms, and he "came to work
looking like Rambo," Camp recalled, complete with shotgun and bando-
liers making an X on his chest. McVeigh was irate that his boss would
not let him drive the truck in that attire.

In early 1988, McVeigh and his friend David A. Darlak bought ten acres of land for $7,000 in Cattaraugus County, New York. They used it for shooting. McVeigh would show up in camouflage and fire away. The gunfire was so extensive that neighbors called the state police.

On May 24, 1988, McVeigh enlisted in the Army for three years at a recruiting station in Buffalo. With about three hundred others, he went to Fort Benning, Georgia, for basic training. His unit was Echo Company, 4th Battalion, 36th Infantry Regiment, 2nd Training Brigade. Terry Nichols also enlisted on May 24, 1988, in Detroit. Robert Littleton, another member of the Echo Company, said, "Terry and Tim in boot camp went together like magnets." They had similar ideas, and both knew guns. However, Nichols left the military in the spring of 1989, having been discharged because of a "family emergency."

After basic training McVeigh was stationed at Fort Riley. His unit— Charlie Company, 2nd Battalion, 16th Infantry Regiment—was a mechanized infantry group. Charlie Company's First Platoon had four Bradley fighting vehicles, which were armored, rode on tracks, and were used for tanklike attacks and to ferry troops to battle. The Bradleys were equipped with a 7.62-millimeter machine gun and a 25-millimeter cannon. They could also fire missiles. McVeigh was a Bradley gunner with a "perfect" military attitude. "If he was given a mission and a target," said Sergeant James Ives, "it's gone."

McVeigh was also remembered for his reading material. He avidly read *Soldier of Fortune* magazine and, according to Todd A. Regier, a former infantryman, had subscriptions to "all the survivalist and gun magazines." Roger Barnett, who used to borrow McVeigh's *Soldier of Fortune*, said McVeigh also devoured futuristic novels about World War III. One book he particularly liked, and promoted to other soldiers, was *The Turner Diaries*.

In the fall of 1990, McVeigh was rewarded for his compulsive attentiveness to military duty. Ahead of all the others in his unit, he was promoted to sergeant. He used his newfound authority to harass the few blacks in the platoon. They were all specialists, but he gave them dirty work usually reserved for privates. When the black soldiers complained, McVeigh was reprimanded—the only blemish on his record. McVeigh was known as a racist. He used the word "nigger" and said that he thought blacks were inferior. Anthony K. Thigpen, a black sergeant, recalled: "If it came down to all of us sitting down conversing with one another, McVeigh wasn't in that crowd if there were African Americans there." McVeigh's company "as a whole had a problem with race," remembered Captain Terry A. Guild. "There was graffiti on the walls of the barracks bathroom: 'Nigger' or 'Honky, Get Out.' . . . [McVeigh's] platoon had some of the most serious race problems. It was pretty bad."

In January 1991, shortly after McVeigh had reenlisted for a four-year stint, he and his company were sent to the Middle East as part of Desert Storm. McVeigh was excited by the assignment. "He was a perfect gunner," Regier said. "He was the best gunner we had." He took part in a hundred-hour battle, the invasion of Kuwait, in which the Bradleys played a significant role. The Iraqis were dug in in trenches. Charlie Company's strategy was to bring tanks and trucks equipped with plows behind the Bradleys, and bury the Iraqis. That way American infantrymen would not need to jump in after them.

Although other platoons saw more action than McVeigh's, combat was still a heady experience for him. As McVeigh's Bradley came close to the Iraqi line, his unit saw an enemy vehicle approximately five hundred yards away. "Everyone wanted to shoot it," Thigpen remembered. "You know, first round, down range. McVeigh was, of course, the lieutenant's gunner so he received the opportunity to shoot the first round. I mean, he was just thrilled." Less so the Iraqis, who suffered a direct hit.

After the war, McVeigh would boast to Kerry Kling (whose last name McVeigh would later use on his phony South Dakota driver's license) about his shooting prowess with a 25-millimeter cannon. "He said when they were invading Iraq he saw an Iraqi soldier coming out of a bunker and that when the first round hit his head, it exploded. He was proud of that one shot. It was over eleven hundred meters, and shooting a guy in the head from that distance is impressive."

McVeigh's unit drew the assignment of protecting General H. Norman Schwarzkopf, Desert Storm commander, and remained in Saudi Arabia until May 1991. But McVeigh left on March 28 to pursue a dream: Green Beret training.

In early April 1991 he arrived in Fort Bragg, North Carolina. The physical and mental tests to be a Green Beret are rigorous; the process lasts twenty-one days, and fewer than half of the candidates are chosen. McVeigh marched for ninety minutes with a forty-five-pound pack. He swam fifty meters in battle dress including combat boots. He ran two miles. He did the required push-ups and sit-ups. He was prepared for, and passed, the physical tests. According to *The New York Times*, he failed the psychological test, and withdrew on the second day, although other sources say he withdrew because he claimed an injury.

"Everyone knew he was highly upset," Thigpen remembered. ". . . [H]e was definitely angry. He was upset, very upset." He told his Army colleagues that he had an injury to his leg or ankle. Captain Guild said McVeigh "became disgruntled after he didn't make it. It might have been the first time he ever failed at anything in the Army."

Others noticed a change, too, when the unit returned to Fort Riley. He became "fanatical and loved to collect guns, and he always had a gun with him," Kling said. "He was a calm, laid-back person. But he felt strongly about the right to bear arms and protecting the Second Amendment—he was fanatical about that."

McVeigh also spoke of his mistrust of government, and about how he wanted to stockpile guns, ammunition, and food in a bunker. "He was going to be ready if the Apocalypse hit," said Sheffield A. Anderson, who served with McVeigh. Another of McVeigh's associates remembered him saying that the Army had inserted a computer chip into his backside, so that it could monitor him, something McVeigh would later repeat to people he met in Decker, Michigan.

Later that spring, McVeigh moved out of Fort Riley's barracks, into a house in Herington, Kansas. In September 1991, he moved into another Herington house, which he shared with Sergeant Royal L. Witcher. Witcher recalled that McVeigh had at least ten guns, which were hidden throughout the residence. McVeigh was not a "talkative" kind of guy, but he expressed to Witcher his views on black people: Blacks were "inferior ... Not as smart as us," Witcher said. "He was a very racist person." McVeigh also talked politics. "I don't know if there's such a word," Witcher said, "but he was ill-political. There was at least one thing in the paper he read each day that the Government had something to do with that he took issue with. Like gays in the military. The Government getting involved in things he didn't really think it needed to be involved in, things dealing with weapons, like raids."

At the end of 1991, Sergeant James Ives heard, McVeigh had begun associating with local off-base right-wing antigovernment groups. "Cults," said Ives, "is what I call them."

It was during this period, toward the end of 1991, that McVeigh became disenchanted with the National Rifle Association. According to Witcher, McVeigh felt the organization was not strong enough in its opposition to the proposed assault weapons ban.

McVeigh left the Army at the end of 1991, when there was an opportunity for early discharge. He went back to New York State and joined the New York National Guard at Tonawanda. While there he wrote letters to the local newspaper, the Lockport *Union-Sun and Journal*. McVeigh said he thought a human being was, by nature, "a hunter, a predator." He also asked: "Is a civil war imminent? Do we have to shed blood to reform the current system? I hope it doesn't come to that, but it might ... [because democracy] seems to be headed down the same road [as communism]."

He left the unit in May 1992, but continued to work in the area as a security guard. McVeigh visited his old army buddy Terry Nichols and Terry's brother, James, at their Michigan farm in the summer of 1992.

Then he returned to New York. In April 1993, McVeigh traveled to Waco, Texas, to visit the site of the Branch Davidian siege. The FBI took pictures of the Davidian supporters who showed up at Waco—out of concern, it said, that they might engage in violence, especially after Linda Thompson's call for the "unorganized militia." One of those photographed was Timothy McVeigh. According to everyone who knew McVeigh, he was incensed over and obsessed by Waco.

✗ ✗ ✗

The Arizona Patriots, a right-wing, racist paramilitary group that had been active in the 1980s, was suspected of having planned "terrorist attacks, assassinations and . . . robberies," according to *The Washington Post*. In fact, the group had discussed killing then-Governor Bruce Babbitt, federal judge Paul Rosenblatt, and many others. In June 1984, the Arizona Patriots had issued an "indictment" of all elected Arizona government officials, calling on them to resign within thirty days or face a "grand jury inquest." In 1986 the FBI raided the group and found heavy ammunition, as well as evidence that the group had planned to bomb buildings belonging to a synagogue, the ADL, the Simon Wiesenthal Center, and the IRS. Members had also been arrested with blueprints of three dams in their possession. *The Washington Post* wrote that after the arrests the group became "even more clandestine than usual." One member of the group, Jack Oliphant, was sentenced to four years in jail. According to *USA Today*, while in prison Oliphant wrote a manuscript entitled "To Alter or Abolish Government," which preached "all-out, do or die, to the last man civil war." After his release from jail, Oliphant went home to Kingman, Arizona.

In June 1993, McVeigh moved to Kingman, Arizona, where he had another Army buddy, Michael Fortier. According to *The Washington Post*, Fortier had connections to members of the Arizona Patriots. And, echoing the militia paranoia concerning gun control, Fortier ranted about the government's "plans" not only to disarm Americans, but also to separate them, the men from the women and children. He had a reputation as a serious "patriot." His yard sported a "Don't Tread on Me" flag.

In Kingman, Fortier helped McVeigh get jobs. McVeigh worked as a security guard and, later, at a True Value Hardware store. At both places of employment he regularly wore Army fatigues. McVeigh would find many kindred spirits in Kingman. With Walter "Mac" McCarty, a seventy-two-year-old former marine—known for picketing the county attorney's office because public officials insisted he remove his pistols when he entered the county office to pay his taxes—McVeigh discussed Ruby Ridge, Waco, Janet Reno, the FBI, the ATF, the Council on Foreign

Relations, the Second Amendment, the United Nations, and One World Government. "I gathered," said McCarty, "that he was following the right-wing, survivalist, paramilitary type philosophy. I also got the sense that he was searching for meaning and acceptance." That search may have led McVeigh to the shortwave radio dial; according to a neighbor, he listened avidly. He joined the audience of Mark Koernke and other purveyors of hate and conspiracy. He also was drawn to the Liberty Lobby's *Spotlight*, which was to become the most significant right-wing publication promoting the militia movement. The Anti-Defamation League reported that, using the alias "T. Tuttle," McVeigh advertised to sell what the ADL termed "a military-style anti-tank launcher" in the August 16, 1993, *Spotlight*.

In the two years leading up to the Oklahoma bombing, McVeigh was a regular participant in gun shows, events at which people could find not only all sorts of weaponry but also reading material, including the *Spotlight* and other far-right and militia literature. McVeigh promoted *The Turner Diaries* at gun shows. "He carried the book all the time," said another gun collector who crossed paths with McVeigh. "He sold it at the shows. He'd have a few copies in the cargo pocket of his cammies. They were supposed to be $10, but he'd sell them for $5. It was like he was looking for converts." McVeigh also peddled a flare gun that easily could be altered to launch rockets that, it was suggested, could down an ATF helicopter. And he hawked baseball caps sporting the letters "ATF" marred by dark dots simulating bullet holes. Some remember McVeigh at a 1993 *Soldier of Fortune* convention in Phoenix. He distributed information for free: a sheet bearing the name and address of Lon Horiuchi, the FBI agent who had killed Vicki Weaver.

Among the people McVeigh tried to influence were old army friends. Staff Sergeant Albert Warnement was a shooting buddy of his. Warnement remembered McVeigh's political views from the time of the Randy Weaver siege. McVeigh had told him, "I should get up and go to Montana." Later, when Warnement was stationed in Germany, McVeigh sent him "a lot of newsletters and stuff from those groups he was involved in. There were newsletters from Bo Gritz's group, some other odd newsletters, some from the Patriots; then he sent that videotape 'The Big Lie' about Waco. He thought the Federal Government was getting too much power. He thought the ATF was out of control. . . . [W]hen Waco happened, he really felt the ATF was out of control. . . . He wasn't happy about Somalia, that if we could put the United States under basically U.N. command and send them to Somalia to disarm their citizens, then why couldn't they come do the same thing in the United States?" His old Army roommate, William "Dave" Dilly, put it succinctly: "He had all the same interests as . . . the militias."

McVeigh, trading in guns and far-right political theories, did not stay put in the Kingman area. Ken Kirkland, of the St. Lucie County, Florida, militia, remembered seeing him at a militia meeting in March 1994 (McVeigh denies this). According to Kirkland, McVeigh was present as one of Mark Koernke's bodyguards, was "really upset about Waco," and had come to the meeting because he "heard the Branch Davidians, the people who survived Waco, would be here." According to the ADL, Mark Koernke had become "a friend, perhaps even a mentor, of Timothy McVeigh." Although the extent of this relationship—which Koernke also denied—is not known, there is evidence that it may have been close. Mark Osterman had his own program on shortwave. His Rolodex listed McVeigh as the contact for Koernke. And, according to militia member Eric Maloney, both McVeigh and Koernke attended a late January 1995 meeting with him and other members of the "Oakland County Sixth Brigade" at a truck stop northwest of Detroit. Maloney said the group discussed photographs of Russian tanks at Camp Grayling, and the need to take action against what was believed to be a potential invasion.

McVeigh had other militia connections, too. He visited James and Terry Nichols in Decker, Michigan, a few times, and while there he reportedly attended at least one Michigan Militia gathering. People remember him from a January 1995 meeting in Jackson, Michigan. The agenda that night included a discussion of the importance of "doing something" about the ATF. That was just weeks after McVeigh, along with his friend Fortier, had cased the Oklahoma City federal building—which housed an ATF office—to assess it as a bomb target.

Two weeks before the Murrah Building was blown up, McVeigh also called someone in Elohim City, a Christian Identity compound straddling the Oklahoma–Arkansas border. Some of its residents had connections to a 1980s far-right paramilitary group known as the Covenant, Sword and Arm of the Lord.

McVeigh's casual conversation also reflected his militialike politics. A relative of David Darlak, who had owned the New York "shooting" acreage with McVeigh, remembered seeing McVeigh in the area in late 1994, after the November elections. "He brought it up," the man recalled. "Something about the government, that something had to be done. He had slowly deteriorated and turned into a paranoid person. He got stranger and stranger, more intense."

The Timothy McVeigh of 1994 and 1995 was a different person from the one who had gone off to Desert Storm. Perhaps his sister, Jennifer, noticed the difference most; he apparently converted her to his cause. Proud of her brother, she told friends that "something big is going to happen in March or April, and Tim's involved." This statement came from someone no one remembered as having any interest in politics in high school, someone who spent her energy developing a reputation as a Jell-O wrestler at the Crazy Horse Saloon. But soon after her brother returned from the Army, Jennifer McVeigh wrote to a newspaper (*The Union Sun and Journal*) echoing militia views. "If you don't think the Constitution is being perverted," she asserted, "I suggest you open your eyes and take a good look around. (Research constitutional rights violated in Weaver, Waco. Also 'Gun Control')."

The weekend after the Oklahoma bombing the FBI searched a house in Pensacola, Florida, where Jennifer McVeigh had stayed. That search, and another of Jennifer McVeigh's vehicle, produced tapes and printed material from militia groups. Among the literature: "You May Not Have a Country After 1995!," "Saving America," and Jack McLamb's "Operation Vampire Killer 2000." When the FBI spoke to her, she defended Timothy's political beliefs. She also had at least twenty letters her brother had written outlining his views: that the government was now the enemy, and that he was a soldier defending America from that foe.

Perhaps McVeigh's mother expressed it best. She told an acquaintance in 1994 that Timothy had "totally changed." "It was like he traded one Army for another," she said.

Terry Nichols: Common-Law Individual

I AM NO LONGER . . . A CITIZEN OF THE CORRUPT
POLITICAL CORPORATE STATE OF MICHIGAN AND
THE UNITED STATES OF AMERICA. . . . I AM A
"NON-RESIDENT ALIEN" . . . A NATURAL BORN
HUMAN BEING BORN IN THE AREA YOU CALL
MICHIGAN [AND] NOT THE CORPORATE STATE
OF MICHIGAN.

TERRY NICHOLS

Terry Nichols was a failure. He wanted to be a doctor, but didn't last a year in college. He tried different jobs: working on his brother's farm, selling real estate, hawking air and water filters, running a grain elevator. Nothing lasted. He was married for almost a decade, then divorced. He joined the Army in May 1988, at age thirty-three—where he met Timothy McVeigh on the first day of basic training—but left early to care for his son.

In 1990, Nichols traveled to the Philippines in search of a mail-order bride. He found Marife Torres, a seventeen-year-old high school student, who was eager to come to America. They married. Nichols told Marife's friend Vilma Elubaring that the quality he cherished most in a bride was faithfulness. Nichols returned to the United States, where it took seven months for the paperwork to clear before Marife could join him. She arrived six months pregnant. Nichols said he would treat the boy— fathered by Marife's old boyfriend—like his own son.

Nichols seemed to blame the government for the pregnancy. "That one episode soured Terry on government," his father, Robert, said. "He originally told me it would take six weeks for her to come here . . . but it was red tape, red tape, red tape." Two years later the boy died under tragic—some think suspicious—circumstances. By this time Nichols was also deeply in debt.

According to *The Washington Post* reporter Serge Kovaleski, Nichols "fell increasingly under the influence of the anti-tax Posse Comitatus and developed ties to Michigan members of the White Supremacist Aryan Nations." The philosophy of these groups helped him understand his troubles: They were the government's fault.

Terry Nichols accumulated $19,739 in debt on his Chase Manhattan Bank credit card. The company sued in civil court. He defended himself in a voice *The Washington Post* described as "full of defiance, contempt and sarcasm . . . with a shower of far-right rhetoric." He filed papers referring to himself in the third person and stating that he was "no longer one of your citizens of your de facto government. He is a nonresident alien, nonforeigner. Stranger." "For the record," he said in court, "I appear here as a common law individual. Should the court insist that I answer any questions, I will only do so under duress, threat and intimidation. Doesn't the Constitution of the United States and the constitution of the state of Michigan hold any water in this court?"

Nichols's "answers" to the courtroom questions were also full of Posse Comitatus–like "thinking." He claimed he had paid his Chase Manhattan debt with a "Certified Fractional Reserve Check," a worthless paper used by some associated with militias and other "patriots." Nichols explained why he didn't have to pay his debt in dollars: Chase Manhattan "knowingly and willingly know[s] how to make credit out of nothing and make interest on it and actually steal people's hard earned money. They gave me valueless nothing for something they want to take from me that has value. That's not right, is it?"

Nichols said he might sue the judge. He said the judge was without jurisdiction over a "common law individual." He continued to rail that Chase Manhattan Bank had not accepted the "check" he had offered, signed "Explicitly reserving all my rights, Terry L. Nichols." He insisted that the judge force the board of directors of the bank to come to the courtroom, so that he could confront them. He lost the case—and established a record showing his ideological affinity with other "sovereign citizens," people such as John Trochmann and Calvin Greenup. Twice Nichols filed court papers attempting to repudiate his U.S. citizenship.

He defended against a lawsuit by another credit card company—First Deposit National Bank—by claiming that he had sent it a letter in March

1992, removing his signature from the credit card contract. He said the bank was built on "fraud and misrepresentation, collusion, color of law, conspiracy, enticement, inducement, seduction, duress, coercion, mistake [and] bankruptcy." He filed countercharges, saying that he suffered "mental and emotional damage, loss of happiness and the unjust destroying of credit history . . . by wanton acts when no probable cause existed." He asked for $50,000 in cash, or 14,200 ounces of silver. The request for silver was no eccentricity. Like many on the far right, Nichols apparently believed that the monetary system was a sham, that the federal government had no right to print currency. The only real value, according to this doctrine, was in precious metals.

Terry Nichols also had legal troubles over the child support he owed for the son, Chase, he had had with his first wife. "I asked him why he hadn't paid," said Judge Donald Teeple. "He said he didn't have to pay, that the court didn't have any jurisdiction, that he wasn't a citizen. . . . I sentenced him to thirty days in jail for contempt of court and for not paying child support. Within a few days he paid." Nichols also wrote the Michigan Department of Natural Resources claiming he did "not need to obtain any of the state's privileges [e.g., licenses, since] I am no longer . . . a citizen of the corrupt political corporate State of Michigan and the United States of America. . . . I am a 'non-resident alien' . . . a natural born human being born in the area you call Michigan [and] not the corporate State of Michigan." He also wrote his township, explaining why he would no longer vote: "There is total corruption in the entire political system from the local government on up through and including the president of the United States of America, George Bush."

Nichols's anger at the government was so strong that he destroyed his driver's license, passport, and voter registration card. Like Posse Comitatus members who drove without license plates, Terry Nichols crafted his own plate for the front of his unregistered truck. He and his brother James also enjoyed staining currency with red ink, so that the bills would be removed from circulation. But being without a driver's license and other essential papers eventually caused him enough problems that he ordered a new license and new plates.

In the spring of 1993 his old Army friend, Timothy McVeigh, came to visit again. McVeigh had just been at the site of the Branch Davidian siege. He was no longer the relatively shy man Nichols remembered. He radiated confidence, was dressed in military attire, and kept a .45 in his pants. At McVeigh's prodding the Nichols brothers joined him not only in making bombs on the farm but also in paramilitary training in the woods. According to sources cited by *The Washington Post*'s Kovaleski, the Nichols brothers and McVeigh considered themselves a paramilitary cell. Calling themselves the Patriots, they disseminated literature calling for the assassination of law enforcement officers, attorneys, and judges, as part of a war on government.

✗ ✗ ✗

In Terry's older brother, James, the old Army buddies would find a kindred "patriot." Neighbors knew James as someone who not only had converted his land to organic farming, but also was extremely outspoken about his political views. He said—repeatedly—that President Clinton "is unfit to live, let alone be president."

In 1990 James Nichols tried to renounce his citizenship. Like Terry, he sent a document to the local county clerk declaring himself "a nonresident alien, nonforeigner, STRANGER!" He also gave up his driver's license and his Social Security card. He plastered his car with bumper stickers denouncing government and promoting the right to bear arms.

He talked to his neighbors about his ideas, his dislike for government, his refusal to pay taxes, his fury over Waco, his support for the "patriot" movement. "He told me it's nationwide," neighbor Randy Izydorek said, "they have plans to eliminate the government . . . and it's growing. They're into getting down deep into the law, and saying 'This law lets me drive down this road without a license,' and finding similar loopholes." James Nichols also told neighbors he knew what to do "to get yourself completely out of the system." Getting out of the system, also called "severation," is almost an initiation ritual for many white supremacists.

Another neighbor, Dan Stomber, said that James Nichols "claimed to be part of the Militia, he claimed to be part of the Patriots, but he claimed that aliens visited him too." Nichols also told Stomber, and others, that "we were all puppets and sheeple."

According to Elgie Zerod, head of a Michigan militia called For the People, James Nichols attended some of its functions. This was confirmed by state representative Kim Rhead, who spoke at a For the People meeting. Federal relief money was on its way to the region, because heavy rain had ruined some crops. Nichols asked Rhead whether, since he grew his crops organically, he was entitled to less money. Rhead promised to find out. "I was struck by how contradictory he was," Rhead said. "If the federal government has no role in anything, then why was he looking so hard for money like that?" Nichols, who had no use for government and refused to pay taxes, nonetheless accepted $89,950 in farm subsidies.

James Nichols also belonged to Zeno Budd's militia-linked Michigan Property Owners Association, was a follower of antitax extremist Karl Granse (Terry would call Granse from jail, seeking legal advice), avidly read the anti-Semitic, militia-promoting paper *Spotlight*, had a collection of pamphlets and other material about Waco, and owned videotapes such as *Secret Societies and the New World Order*. Christian Identity religion also interested Nichols. He flirted with it until a friend, a Methodist chaplain named Phil Morawski, talked him out of it.

Neighbor Paul Izydorek said, "It almost seemed like someone had control over Terry and James, like they were in a cult. It was as if their personalities completely changed when they kicked into this stuff."

✗ ✗ ✗

McVeigh and the Nichols brothers were seen together in Michigan, experimenting in bomb making, and sharing their venomous antigovernment philosophy. All three, witnesses say, went to meetings of the Michigan Militia (McVeigh told *Newsweek* that he did not go to these meetings). James spoke there of the "necessity" of going after judges, lawyers, and police officials. However, the militia didn't suit the Nicholses and McVeigh, nor did they suit it. Militia members did not appreciate the calls for illegal activity; the Nicholses and McVeigh thought the group insufficiently security-conscious. After the Oklahoma City bombing, Norman Olson of the Michigan Militia said: "These people had attempted to come to meetings and speak out, but they were silenced. In fact, they were told to leave." He said they spoke "anarchist rhetoric" and "of terrorism." According to the government, by the time McVeigh attended a Michigan Militia meeting in January 1995, he and Terry Nichols were well into their plot to blow up the Murrah Building.

PART SIX **Reverberations**

21 **Blaming the Victims**

[THIS WAS] OUR VERY OWN REICHSTAG FIRE.

A North Carolina woman interviewed by *The Washington Post*

Good evening, ladies and gentlemen," said Mark Koernke on April 19, 1995, over his *Intelligence Report* program on shortwave station WWCR.

> ... [W]e're one day closer to victory for all of our brothers and sisters behind the lines in occupied territory.... [O]ur enemy, the New World Order crowd, has a tendency to turn every event on its ear, and they have tried to do it once again. Of course, we all know that two years ago on the nineteenth of April there was the final destruction of the Waco church and home....
>
> [M]any of you are glued to your radios or are watching television to observe what happened in Oklahoma City today.... [This] is yet another foot-stomp on the part of the New World Order Crowd to manipulate the population.... We watched Bill Clinton make his public statement ... :

"We are going to hunt down these individuals who performed this bombing in Oklahoma City." What is Bill going to do then? Punish them the way he punished his murderers at Waco by putting letters of reprimand in their files? . . .

For those of you who are skeptical . . . [t]hese people have butchered our cities. They have killed whole population groups. They are greedy. They are power-mongers. And they EAT THEIR YOUNG! So, for those of you who don't think that there is a little bit of manipulation involved here—this is a propaganda campaign, and FEMA, as we expected, is right in the middle of it.

Most militia leaders condemned the terrorist attack on the Murrah Building. But in the next breath they tended to compare the bombing to Waco, viewing the tragedies as parallel, and to offer conspiratorial theories as to who the perpetrators were. Linda Thompson said, "I genuinely believe the government did this bombing. . . . I mean, who's got a track record of killing innocent children?"

Norman Olson and Ray Southwell were among the few in the militia movement who disagreed with Thompson and Koernke. They said that the bombing was the work of the Japanese government, in revenge for what they claimed was the American hand in the attack on Japan's subway with nerve gas. (Olson and Southwell resigned their leadership positions over this statement; Olson later quit the Michigan Militia and started another private army, saying the Michigan Militia had been "overrun by moderates.")

"Clinton Ordered Oklahoma Bombing," read a flyer circulated in North Dakota. "With the help of his two co-conspirators, Attorney General Janet Reno, the cigar-smoking 'butch' lesbian who owns 47 pet peacocks, ALL named 'Horace,' and the Communist-Jew FBI Director Louis Freeh (appointed the day BEFORE the suspicious death of Clinton crony, Vince Foster), Clinton used Jewish CIA agents who had infiltrated certain patriotic militia organizations to orchestrate and carry out this murderous crime."

Bo Gritz called the bombing a "Rembrandt—a masterpiece of science and art put together." He was explaining, with an odd choice of words, that he thought McVeigh could not have blown up the building with a fertilizer bomb, that there was a more sophisticated explosive—and explanation.

"Janet Reno is behind this," a posting on the Internet read; "the campaign will succeed because the media will persuade the public. Expect a crackdown. Bury your guns and use the codes."

The ability instantly to communicate via the Internet fueled the fires of conspiracy and created an immediate body of rumor and suspicion that rivaled in both size and complexity the plots that Kennedy assassination buffs had taken years to build. And that was only the beginning.

The tons of physical evidence gathered for the prosecution of McVeigh and Nichols; the uncertainty of eyewitness identifications; the complexities of scientific evidence; McVeigh's psychological quirks, aggravated after he returned from the Persian Gulf War; the various motives of witnesses; the underlying political agendas—all became webs that militia members could use to spin tales of ever more intricate conspiracies. The theories would become more involved after highly skilled defense lawyers, paid to blow smoke in order to create a reasonable doubt, were assigned to represent Nichols and McVeigh.

X X X

It was an article of faith among most of the militia movement that the government was directly or indirectly responsible for the Oklahoma City bombing. Given their belief that the government was spending its time plotting with the forces of One World Government to enslave Americans, government culpability for the bomb made "sense." What better excuse to bring in the U.N. (or Gurkhas, or Hong Kong, or Russia, or the Bloods and Crips) and take away Americans' freedoms than a state of emergency created by a well-orchestrated attack?

"Facts" backing up the government-did-it theory circulated through the Internet, by fax, over shortwave radio, and by other means. A "convoy" of black helicopters was supposedly seen near the Oklahoma City building—"proving" that the government was responsible. There was the "Manchurian Candidate" theory—that the people who set off the bomb were actually programmed by the government to do so. Through microchips, drugs, or other means, the government supposedly had scores of such drones, ready to release, zombielike, to commit similar acts. After all McVeigh, it was said, told people that while he was in the Army a chip was implanted in his body. And why, it was asked, after killing so many people, would he not have resisted arrest? Why had he just offered "name, rank, and serial number" as his answer to questions, even though it had been years since he had been in the military?

Then there was the Waco theory: The government was trying to blow up evidence of its illegal activity at Waco; this evidence was stored in the Oklahoma City building. Supposedly a fire in the storage area might have been too suspicious, but destroying the whole building was not.

The *Spotlight*, of course, had to find a way to blame the Oklahoma City bombing on someone Jewish. Beside a wild-eyed caricature of an Israeli intelligence agent holding a bomb labeled "Terrorism," the *Spot-*

light claimed it had "learned that Oklahoma City bombing suspect Timothy McVeigh was in close, and probably sustained long-time, contact with an agent of the Anti-Defamation League (ADL) of B'nai B'rith operating in McVeigh's immediate circle." How did the *Spotlight* learn this? The ADL had said that McVeigh had advertised a "rocket launcher" in the *Spotlight* under the alias "T. Tuttle." The *Spotlight* speculated that ADL's information came from an " 'inside source' in McVeigh's circle of acquaintances." It apparently never occurred to the writer that the ADL got its clue from press accounts that mentioned McVeigh's use of the aliases "Terry Tuttle" and "Tim Tuttle," and then found the name and the ad in its clippings files. The *Spotlight* even called on "law enforcement agencies to come clean and investigate the ADL's connection with McVeigh."

Lyndon LaRouche's organization, whose literature is a frequent feature of militia meetings, tried to put the bombing into historical perspective. Claiming that the British were behind the assassinations of Lincoln, Garfield, McKinley, and Kennedy, it claimed that "circumstantial evidence places the British at the top of the suspects' list."

Neo-Nazi William Pierce, author of *The Turner Diaries*, wrote that while he was "shocked" at the bombing, Clinton and Reno were "the real terrorists. When a government engages in terrorism against its own citizens, it should not be surprised when some of those citizens strike back and engage in terrorism against the government." There are "many, many Americans," he wrote, "who have come to consider the U.S. government their worst enemy [because it caters to] the politicians and the bureaucrats. And the homosexuals and the 'career' women. And the minorities. . . . They can't imagine why anyone would want to go back to the bad, old days when this was a White country, and men were men, and women were women, and the freaks stayed in the closet, and everyone worked for his living."

Eustace Mullins wrote an article entitled "J'ACCUSE!" blaming the Oklahoma City bombing, of course, on the government. "This," he wrote, "was a deliberate conspiracy by corrupt and treasonous elements in the federal agencies in Washington as part of a plan to provoke martial law, confiscate legal guns from American citizens, and to wipe out the citizens militia of the several states." Mullins claimed that the bombing was "a standard FBI operation. . . . The rented vehicle . . . [was] a very important factor in identifying FBI participation; professional terrorists would have stolen a vehicle which could not be traced to them. FBI rules demand the use of a rented vehicle, so that it can be traced for the all important Moscow show trial which is . . . crucial to their techniques."

Some in the militia movement also noticed that one of the people killed in the Murrah Building was Alan Whicher, a Secret Service agent who had once been a bodyguard for the President. "Can I point out how this bomb benefitted Bill Clinton?" an Idaho member of the United States Militia Association asked. "That makes four different bodyguards killed. Three in Waco, and this one."

Some said the bombing was the long-awaited U.N. offensive to take over America. "This is what the U.N. does when they go in and overthrow a country," one self-described researcher said. "They produce unrest in the country first."

Some claimed that McVeigh was not actually arrested shortly after the bombing, but two days later.

A "summary of Mark Boswell's [shortwave] radio talk show of 12AM EDT on April 29" appeared on alt.activism and other Internet news-groups. "Two government officials confess to Oklahoma Bombing," it read. "Boswell interviewed 25 year CIA veteran James Black and assistant Ron Jackson regarding sworn affidavits now in their possession, sworn by two Justice Department officials which state that they were part of a committee of ten who planned the Oklahoma bombing. The officials claim the bomb was supposed to be detonated at 6AM (with no one around) as a scare tactic to procure sympathy, money and power for government agencies, but that something went wrong and it was detonated later during business hours. This could explain why McVeigh was reported being so lost while driving the bomb-truck to the scene that he had to stop and ask a policeman for directions."

In that same posting it was asserted that the day before the bombing "BATF Agents underwent explosives training in the basement of the federal building [and that they] were told not to come to work at the office the next day, but to report elsewhere [because] the building was coming down"; that "a Secret Service agent overheard shrouded talk in the White House regarding the bombing the day before it occurred, but did not understand the significance of what he had heard until the details of the blast and the President's propaganda speeches which followed started matching what he had previously heard"; that "The government's records and evidence lockers related to Waco were evidently destroyed in the blast"; and that "Hillary Clinton was indicted on $50 million Bank Fraud (Whitewater) and Obstruction of Justice charges related to stealing Foster's files on the eve of his death. The indictments were due to be unsealed on the 19th. But were not due to fear of further chaos on the day of the bombing."

Soon the militias' paranoia turned on itself. Some in the movement even suggested that the private armies themselves were begun as a government plot to ferret out people who would be willing to conduct war against Americans. After all, they said, look at all the threatening statements made by people like Bo Gritz, Mark Koernke, Linda Thompson, John Trochmann, and Norman Olson. Yet none had been arrested. Maybe they were government agents. It was only "logical."

✗ ✗ ✗

The bomb. Why, the suspicious militia minds asked, did the government first say it used about twelve hundred pounds of fertilizer, then up the estimate to close to five thousand pounds? And why did early television broadcasts say searchers might have found an undetonated second bomb in the hours after the explosion?

Linda Thompson sent a fax claiming the bomb was an "A-Neutronic" bomb. She said it looked like "a propane tank with a zig zag shaped wedge surrounding the outside diameter of the tank," and that it made an ammonium nitrate bomb more potent.

And, just as there was a two-gunman theory of the Kennedy assassination, there was a two-bomb theory of Oklahoma City. The Oklahoma Geological Survey seismograph recorded two blips 11.6 seconds apart at the time of the bombing. Jim Lawson, OGS's chief geophysicist, originally said that there might have been two bombs and two explosions, but when he learned that witnesses only heard one blast, he said that the second event was probably the building crashing down. "A lot of them [conspiracy theorists] are anxious to explain to me," he said, "that our government committed mass murder. They are disappointed that I'm not saying it was two blasts. I don't think anybody's mind is changed by what I say." Despite OGS statements, MOM and many other militia groups began distributing copies of the seismographic chart.

The "it wasn't fertilizer" line was highlighted by the *Spotlight* as well. In the May 22, 1995, edition, a large headline spread over two pages: "Evidence Mounts That Bomb in Oklahoma Not Fertilizer—The FBI Knows the 'Official' Bomb Story Is Pure Fiction." The story quoted a former FBI agent as saying that the device was a secret military bomb "as small as a pineapple. It could have been delivered to the blast site in something as small as a lunch bag." Supposedly, the bomb "released a gaseous cloud of aqueous (liquid) ammonium nitrate and microencapsulated aluminum silicate, which caused a second explosion," explaining the two blips on the OGS chart.

"Ten seconds is a long time," said Charles Mankin of the OGS. "If you put up a cloud, it would dissipate in ten seconds." That, however, did not stop an endless discussion on the Internet of P-waves, S-waves, the geology of Oklahoma City, the placement of seismological equipment, surface waves, and the speed of sound in dry air. Some reporters discovered the controversy and investigated; they, too, concluded that the second "blip" was caused by the pancaking of the building. That, however, still did not stop the debate.

Meanwhile, some not connected to the militia movement were also interested in the bomb's components. In May 1995 Robert Brinson was charged in Halifax, Massachusetts, with attempting to assemble an Oklahoma City–type fertilizer bomb. He wanted to blow up his ex-girlfriend and her family, so he placed two bombs—one inside a bathroom, another in a doghouse. He had, however, had a fundamental misunderstanding about Oklahoma City. He used potting soil instead of fertilizer.

✗ ✗ ✗

The bombing affected militia groups in four different ways. First, some people, no doubt shocked by the carnage, stayed clear of the militias. Two groups disbanded after April 19. Doug Christiansen of the Utah-based Box Elder County Militia closed his organization. Mike Cross, a twenty-eight-year-old militia leader in Salem, Oregon, did likewise, even though he had been able to recruit three hundred members in his group's half-year existence.

Second, some groups decided to keep active, but no longer call themselves "militias." Jeffrey Goldberg, a reporter for *New York* magazine, told of a New York–area militia meeting he attended shortly after the Oklahoma City bombing. Aware of a reporter in their midst, and having decided that the word "militia" was now too unsavory to use, the militia members decided to call themselves a Committee of Correspondence. Except sometimes they forgot. "It was like that old Cheech and Chong skit," Goldberg said. " 'We're not a gang, we're a club.' "

Third, the militias' membership actually grew after April 19, as a result of the flood of publicity they received. Bob Starr said that his Military At Large of the Republic of Georgia had grown fourfold since the bombing. "It has done nothing but wake people up," he said. And when Bo Gritz, Mark Koernke, and Jack McLamb appeared at the June 11, 1995, Preparedness Expo, between two thousand and three thousand people attended. This was not surprising. Militias draw people because of concern about guns, the environment, federal regulations, and ideals of freedom. Those attractions remained constant, despite the bombing.

The fourth reaction was the most troubling: People near the narrow end of Ken Toole's funnel were plunged further down by the terrorist attack on the Murrah Building. Some of those who earnestly believed that the bombing was part of a government plot to crack down on the militias advised burying guns, going underground, and biding their time. Some, no doubt, have done just that.

22 Poster Children

EQUIVOCATION FROM ANY OF IDAHO'S POLITICAL
LEADERS OVER THE DEADLY BOMBING IN
OKLAHOMA CITY WON'T DO. . . . WHETHER SHE
REALIZES IT OR NOT, [REPRESENTATIVE HELEN]
CHENOWETH IS QUICKLY BECOMING THE POSTER
CHILD FOR [MILITIA] GROUPS.

Idaho Statesman

Libyan dictator Muammar el-Qaddafi had the most interesting reaction of any politician to the Oklahoma bombing. "Oklahoma was the beginning of the reaction of the masses living in America," he said on state-run radio. "It was a reaction against the nightmare and tyranny. . . . Thousands of militias [are] waging armed popular revolution in America." Fearing for the safety of Hillary and Bill Clinton, Qaddafi offered them sanctuary in Libya, "the only safe country in the world."

The record of American public officials, both before and after the Oklahoma bombing, was less bizarre, but still shameful. While only a handful cozied up to the militia groups before the bombing—some from naïveté, some from a desire to please angry constituents, some because their ideology overlapped the militias'—most (and especially conservative Republicans) continued to weigh political considerations rather than do something about the militia groups even after April 19, 1995. That the bombing should have produced immediate major congressional hearings into Waco and Ruby Ridge—but not, for months, into the militia movement—was astonishing. The Branch Davidian and Weaver sieges were, of course, worthy subjects of House and Senate investigation. But they paled in comparison to the importance and urgency of hearings into the armed militias. After all, not only was the ideology of these proviolence, antigovernment armies behind the carnage at the Murrah Building, the militia groups believed that the bombing itself was the first move in a war against them. Yet instead of concern over the danger of a heavily armed movement fueled by paranoia and hatred, Congress rushed to hold hearings about FBI actions at Waco and Ruby Ridge—a reaction that empowered the militia movement.

Pretend for a moment that the militias had been mostly black; now imagine how fast hearings into them would have been convened after April 19. Members of Congress would have left skid marks. If you don't think that the color of the alleged bombers' skin and of the groups to which they were linked was the key factor for many politicians, recall the first days after the bombing, when the media assumed that Islamic terrorists were guilty. Even those public officials who did not scapegoat Islam argued that the ideological system that gave license to "the bombers" should be condemned. Sheiks were blasted for saying such things as "Attend shooting practice. There is nothing greater than the shot." If the culprits *had* been Islamic terrorists, members of Congress would have been leaping over each other—correctly—to condemn such incendiary statements. If any member had received campaign contributions from such sheiks, the media would have exposed the fact in multicolumn headlines.

How different was that sheik's statement from the NRA's talk of "jackboots" and "Nazis"? Or from the statements of Larry Pratt of Gun Owners of America, who had attended Pete Peters's Estes Park meeting and called for the formation of armed militias? But both the NRA and Pratt remained welcome lobbyists on Capitol Hill. When terrorism comes from people associated with the "mainstream," it is at its most dangerous. But that is also when politicians prefer to ignore, diminish, or excuse it—and, history shows, at our peril.

The unescapable fact was that New York Democratic congressman Charles Schumer—despite death threats from people associated with the militia movement—for months begged House Speaker Newt Gingrich to hold hearings on America's private right-wing armies. To no avail. Schumer had to convene his own "unofficial" hearings on July 11, 1995, bringing public servants and others forward to tell their horror stories of intimidation, threats, and even beatings from people associated with mili-

tia groups. Karen Matthews, a California court clerk, was brutally assaulted, told she was going to be killed, and had a fake bomb planted
under her car. Martha Bethel, a Montana judge, whose story appears in
Chapter 7, was told her house would be riddled with bullets. Ellen
Gray, a Washington state Audubon Society official, was threatened with
a hangman's noose. Montana representative Deborah Kottel was told that
her children would be killed. Washington state assistant attorney general
Cynthia Sypolt was followed, threatened, and had "common law" charges
filed against her. Susan Schock, an environmentalist from New Mexico,
was menaced, surrounded, and told "Get out of our county." She was
threatened with hanging. She was stalked. Her house, where she lived
with her ten-year-old daughter, Katy, was targeted; a picture of it was even
printed in a local paper to intimidate her, she believed. "I've been advised
to leave the area by environmentalists . . . in the bigger cities," Schock
told Schumer's hearing, "and my response is no. You make it safe for me
to be here. If we start running away from these situations, then the people
that perpetrate the violence and the violent threats are going to take
over." When newspapers, reporting on Schumer's "renegade" hearing,
picked up these bone-chilling stories, the Republican leadership finally
agreed to schedule official hearings.

✗ ✗ ✗

Of the members of Congress identified with the militia movement, no
one has come under more public scrutiny than Representative Steve
Stockman (R–Texas). On the morning of April 19, his office received a
fax from Libby Molley, an associate of Mark Koernke. The fax appeared
to be a warning of the blast, but authorities believe that in fact it was sent
shortly thereafter and that the 8:59 A.M. transmission time stamped on it
resulted from a problem with the fax machine. The fax said: "First update.
Bldg 7 to 10 floors only. Military people on the scene—BATF/FBI. Bomb
threat received last week. Perpetrator unknown at this time. Oklahoma."

That this congressman should receive a fax from Koernke was not
accidental. By April 19, 1995, Stockman was known as a good friend to
the militias on Capitol Hill. In early 1995, Stockman had been contacted
by Neil Watt, regimental commander of a militia group called the Texas
Light Infantry, who was concerned about reports of a March ATF raid.
Stockman then wrote to Attorney General Reno, echoing the militia
rumors. (See Chapter 17 for a fuller discussion of this episode.)

Stockman also talked the militia line on Waco. He wrote that the
government staged the raid as a ploy to increase support for gun control,
and that if President Clinton had been genuinely disturbed by the outcome, he would have made sure Attorney General Reno was indicted
"for premeditated murder."

Militia leaders, who loathed the federal government as a whole, none-theless homed in on the few freshman Republicans who, like Stockman, shared their basic concerns and had positioned themselves at the fringes of their party. Not surprisingly, Stockman, a strong advocate of gun own-ership, was the largest recipient of campaign contributions from Larry Pratt's GOA. He also appeared as an honored guest on a Liberty Lobby radio show (through its radio programs, such as *Radio Free America*, the Liberty Lobby promoted the militia movement, much as it did through *Spotlight*). Even after April 19, 1995, Stockman continued to defend his appearance on that program.

✗ ✗ ✗

The May 22, 1995, *Spotlight* had a large article praising Congressman (the title she prefers) Helen Chenoweth of Idaho. Complete with public-ity photo, the article praised a new bill she was expected to introduce: "The Civil Rights Act of 1995." Prior civil rights acts had made it easier for Americans to fight discrimination. How would Chenoweth's bill help preserve civil rights? Federal authorities would have to seek and obtain permission from county sheriffs before making an arrest, conducting a search, or otherwise enforcing federal law. "They shouldn't be armed," she said, "unless they're deputized by the local sheriff." The *Spotlight* no doubt commended Chenoweth because her bill echoed the ideology of the Posse Comitatus, which held that the highest lawful authority rests in the county sheriff. Chenoweth's bill not only legitimized the Posse's political premise but pushed it closer to the political mainstream. Ac-cording to the *Spotlight*, Chenoweth's co-sponsors included Roscoe Bartlett (R–Maryland), Wes Cooley (R–Oregon), John Doolittle (R–California), John Hostettler (R–Indiana), Jack Metcalf (R–Wash-ington), Linda Smith (R–Washington), and Steve Stockman.

Whereas Stockman's relationship with the militia movement centered around his strong position on gun ownership and his willingness to quote the militias' spin on Waco, Chenoweth emphasized county-versus-federal issues, especially resource management. But she also indulged in militia-speak about One World Government and those pesky helicopters. Her indulgence in these conspiratorial icons was not surprising. Years before her election, she traveled the national circuit speaking to chapters of the John Birch Society.

On February 15, 1995, Chenoweth issued a press release about black helicopters. Complaining that "armed [Fish and Wildlife] agency offi-cials and helicopters" were being used to enforce the Endangered Species Act and other regulations, she said this violated Idaho's constitution. If the actions did not stop, said Chenoweth, she "guarantee[d]" that she would become Assistant Agriculture Secretary Jim Lyons's "worst nightmare for at least the next two years." Her ideology was so much in line with the militias' that MOM sold tapes of a 1993 Chenoweth speech (before she was elected) in which she said, "We are in a day and age now when we are facing an unlawful government from time to time." She said environmentalists were linked to the "Communist threat," and that protecting species such as the spotted owl was going to result in "breakdown in state sovereignty and possibly [lead] to One World Government."

Chenoweth, who believed there was only one endangered species—"the white Anglo-Saxon male"—also advocated turning federal lands over to state, local, and private ownership. This did not surprise her critics, since mining concerns gave her financial backing. Her rationale, however, could have come straight from Bob Fletcher: "They declared war on private ownership in the Communist Manifesto," Chenoweth explained. "If we are forced to place all the world's resources in the hands of a few who are controlling a world government, that is not what God planned for us, and it is certainly not in our best interests."

On March 17, 1995, Chenoweth held a hearing at Boise City Hall entitled "Excessive Force Used by Federal Law Enforcement." In her opening remarks she said, "We have democracy when the government is afraid of the people." Samuel Sherwood was a witness. This was two weeks *after* Sherwood's statement about shooting legislators, but he and Chenoweth apparently had a special relationship. Sherwood claimed that his USMA had produced a thousand volunteers to help elect her.

In what must have been a chilling moment, Sherwood said, "Melissa, come up here," to the young daughter of Lieutenant Governor Butch Otter, one of the Idaho officials who had broken with him. "Butch," Sherwood said, "what you told me has painted a bull's-eye on this little girl's back." The girl returned to her chair, and Sherwood resumed his testimony. When he finished Chenoweth said, "Thank you, Sam. We'll see what we can do." Criticized for maintaining her coziness with Sherwood even after April 19, 1995, Chenoweth replied, "I appreciate all people who worked for me and that includes Sam Sherwood."

Reacting to the Oklahoma City bombing, Chenoweth said, "I don't think violent acts like that can be condoned and must be punished. While we can never condone this, we still must begin to look at the public policies that may be pushing people too far. . . . I'm not opposed to the concept of a militia, because I think people ought to be able to protect themselves, and I think it was a concept embraced by our founding fathers."

According to the congressional publication *Roll Call*, "Chenoweth . . . is already taking hits from a Democratic opponent and the local press for suggesting that the bombing may have been the result of government actions. Her opponents say Chenoweth's criticism of federal law enforcement agencies helped breed an environment that fostered militia activity." And the *Idaho Statesman* editorialized: "Equivocation from any of Idaho's political leaders over the deadly bombing in Oklahoma City won't do. . . . With dozens of people, including children, lying dead, any suggestion that there is a thread of an excuse for such a horrific deed is shameless. Yet . . . Helen Chenoweth spun such a thread when she said the Oklahoma tragedy indicates possible problems among the federal bureaucracy, state government and individual rights. . . . Whether she realizes it or not, Chenoweth is quickly becoming the poster child for such groups."

George Miller, a Democrat from California, chastised Chenoweth and U.S. Senator Larry Craig, also of Idaho, for their statements (Craig had talked about disarming some federal law enforcement officials). Miller called on them "to end the casual demeaning of federal employees who risk their lives every day to defend public property and U.S. citizens. . . . Their words can legitimize and incite and there are already more than enough dangers facing rangers and other enforcement officials."

Some, however, found Chenoweth's statements to their liking. She was praised in an Aryan Nations newsletter.

✗ ✗ ✗

The contrast in politicians' post–Oklahoma City reaction to the militias was stark. Whereas some were repulsed by the image of armed groups expressing hate, others saw a constituency with which they felt at home. Kansas governor Bill Graves, for example, said that he had been approached about supporting a militia in his state. He rejected the idea forcefully. It "wasn't the type of group we needed here," he said. New Mexico governor Gary Johnson, however, met with militia leaders only days after the bombing. He rebuffed criticism that he was doing a disservice to the victims of the blast by meeting with apologists for violence. Defending the meeting, and asserting that he wanted to be an "intermediary" with the group, Johnson said they shared his view that "the federal government needs to stop mandating to the state through their agencies." And he called the militias "very patriotic."

Some politicians further down the political ladder were very close to the militias. These local leaders included county commissioners, state representatives, and sheriffs. Their views concerning their neighborhood paramilitary groups were crucial, just as their southern counterparts' views of the Ku Klux Klan had been in the 1960s. Local officials' statements and actions opposing or supporting the militias (silence was effectively support) helped set the community levels of bigotry, violence, and fear.

Of all the local leaders who aided the militia movement, none was more active than Charlie Duke, a Colorado state senator. In a July 30, 1994, speech to fellow "patriots," he said:

> We are dealing with something that's evil here. We're dealing with something that took over a nation led by Christ, created by Christ and put in place by Christians. If you listen real close, if you really turn up your sensitivity, you can hear the evil that flows through the [legislative] body. . . . You can hear cackling in the ceiling, you can hear the smiles of the beast as it's trying to force its puppets to do its bidding.

According to the Anti-Defamation League, Duke also said, "We need some ability to get some firepower to protect the citizens. I would like to see a militia . . . [of the type] that functions as a sheriff's posse and has sufficient training."

At the June 1994 Constitutionalist Networking Conference in Indianapolis, Charlie Duke asked the gathering why members of Congress "do not seem to understand what the [Tenth] Amendment is about?" "Bilderbergers! Bilderbergers!" shouted some in the audience. (The Bilderbergers are a group the Liberty Lobby claims is part of a Jewish plot to control the world's money.) Duke replied, "I think you're right."

Duke referred to himself as a "state representative and part-time revolutionary." Of the federal government, he said: "I'm tired of their lies. I'm tired of their money. I'm tired of their corruption." According to Duke, U.S. Senator Hank Brown of Colorado was "owned" by special interests. "I think [Brown] should be very careful when he comes back to the state," Duke said. "Most of Colorado is armed."

The *Colorado Statesman* reported that this remark referred "to citizen militias [which] Duke . . . advocates." "We're trying to find ways to convince sheriffs," said Duke, "whose side they ought to be on. If push comes to shove people are ready. . . . The militia is forming with or without [sheriffs]. It would be nice if they'd come along; if they don't, it's not required." The *Statesman* story continued, "The legislator said citizens are prepared to fight United Nations troops on Colorado soil—a scenario envisioned if the state were engulfed in a civil war against the federal government."

Duke adopted other militia conspiracy theories too, including the belief that identifying microchips were being implanted into babies. Supposedly, the chips would one day make credit cards unnecessary. Duke said the chips are "not fiction. I can tell you those microchips will do a lot more!"

Duke became best known for his nonbinding "Tenth Amendment

Resolution," passed in one form or another in fifteen states, which exalted states' rights over the laws of the federal government. But he had also introduced bills in Colorado that would have had the force of law if enacted. One would have allowed the state to ignore federal firearms laws; another would have put federal taxes into an escrow account. "The beast in Washington feeds on money," said Duke. "The way you control the beast is to get all of the money."

Duke had contingency plans, assuming his legislation to starve the beast foundered. He would call a "Second Constitutional Convention" in Denver, which would pass what the militia movement calls the Ultimatum Resolution. Rather than storm Congress, as Linda Thompson had suggested, this Ultimatum would supposedly make federal government self-destruct if one of three events occurred: the debt exceeded $6 trillion; the budget was not balanced after a ninety-day notice period; or the government acted beyond its constitutional authority. Of course, Duke believed that the government had already overstepped its boundaries and the debt limit.

After the Oklahoma bombing Duke said that "there are serious allegations of government involvement." He wrote a press release condemning the bombing, but defending the "militia, the patriots and the constitutionalists."

Even after April 19, 1995, Duke; Nye County Commissioner Dick Carver; Sheriff Richard Mack of Graham County, Arizona; California state senator Don Rogers; and a handful of other state and local officials have continued to travel the country promoting hatred of government and support for the militias' ideology. Some observers were most distressed when these elected officials spoke to overtly white supremacist audiences, such as Christian Identity groups. But the greatest threat these men posed lay in the courage they gave to like-minded but less well known county and state officials who might use the legitimacy of their offices to spread the militias' agenda.

✗ ✗ ✗

The Republican victories in 1994 brought with them people who were able to stake out the fringes of their party. That was inevitable; when the center shifts, the margins move too. And just as militias were able to attract hundreds of ordinary people to their meetings through issues such as gun control and the environment, many politicians tapped in to the same anxieties.

The organizing principle of the 1980s Posse Comitatus—that all white males eighteen and over belonged to the "posse," which would be commanded by the county sheriff, the highest legitimate elected official—was remarkably similar to that of the militias: that all white males eighteen and over belonged to the "unorganized militia" that would protect ordinary citizens from the federal government. These ideas about citizens organizing to fight the federal government were different in detail, but not in flavor, from the vitriolic antifederal sentiments of some of these newly elected officials.

This growing antifederal ideology implies a reshuffling of America's political identity that will likely affect elections as we begin the next century. The immigrants who came to America in the nineteenth and twentieth centuries saw their destination as America first; where in America their boat happened to land came second. And despite great forces challenging the ideal of "E pluribus unum"—the Civil War; the "states' rights" movement to preserve segregation—there has always been a coalescing ideal of the whole: the United States of America.

The premise of *Iron Mountain* was not entirely wrong. Wars, the space program, political assassinations, the Olympics—all intensify allegiances to America. Most Americans define their political associations from top to bottom: One is an American, a Texan, from Dallas. There has always been a countervailing tendency—which is experiencing an upsurge in the post-Soviet era—to reshape allegiances so that small comes first, and large last, if at all. Militia members and others who define themselves as "sovereign citizens" are the extreme of this trend, but it cuts across the American landscape. The indulgence in "group politics," for example, is partly responsible. This is reflected in the fallout from political programs —the Voting Rights Act, affirmative action—that, when enacted, were desperately needed for simple social justice, but were at the same time corrosive of an overarching national identity. Also pulling in the small-over-large direction was the Reaganite mantra that the federal government was too large, that it was out of touch, and that it impinged too much on the lives of ordinary Americans. This idea has become a commonplace in American politics, giving ammunition to those who, rather than reform from top to bottom, would empower from the bottom to get rid of the top and much in between.

This tension of identity can only be expected to intensify. As resources grow scarcer, mining, lumber, and ranching interests in the West will continue to fund Wise Use groups that will not only support candidates who agree with their agenda—such as Helen Chenoweth—but also help promote the ideology of county supremacy, one closely aligned with the militia movement. Helen Chenoweth spoke of giving national resources over to state, local, and private control, claiming this was in the best American tradition. In so doing she touched upon the identity issues that might drive American politics in the next century, and pull America apart not from north to south, but from east to west. "Our way of life out here is something that in the East they can't fathom," Helen Chenoweth said. Western politicians are increasingly comfortable telling their constituents that there is a "war on the West." America's private armies are ready, in fact itching, to take part in that war.

✗ ✗ ✗

When riots broke out in Crown Heights, Brooklyn, in the summer of 1991, some of the young black men who targeted Jews yelled "Whose streets? Our streets!" When the Lubavitcher street patrols insulted black people who, it turned out, lived on the block where they were challenged, the same sentiment was in play. Two self-identified communities shared the same living space, and tension and claims of superior rights to the whole were inevitable.

Who owns national land? It belongs to all Americans, but those who live near it have grown accustomed to using it for their livelihood, all the while downplaying the role of the federal government in subsidies, water control, and firefighting. These nationally owned natural resources are likely to become the subject of a major policy debate including ideological questions of sovereignty and political allegiance, especially as the resources diminish and the demands on them increase. In other words, the large end of Ken Toole's funnel will grow and more politicians will be pulled in, giving legitimacy to the ideas further in.

History has shown us at least four things relevant to the militias. First, that there is danger when a political movement is increasingly aligned with armed groups that would impose their political agenda through threat and violence. The S.A. in Germany between the world wars is only one example. The Ku Klux Klan in America is another. Somalia with its warlords is a third. The militia movement, in a worst-case scenario, has similar potential, or at least a similar agenda.

Second, whenever Americans have talked of "states' rights" or "county supremacy," that is a cover for bigotry. This was the argument George Wallace and others used to fight federal laws guaranteeing black Americans the right to vote and to enjoy equal protection of the laws. America is a large country, and people shape their daily lives pretty much as they will. When a political movement rejects the idea of common basic American values and says, "Let me do it my own way," it usually means it wants to do things that are objectionable, and yearns to do them undisturbed and unnoticed. Otherwise the issue wouldn't crop up. It is one thing to complain about federal intrusiveness, silly regulations, mounds of red tape. It is another to remake America into a weak whole comprising fifty herculean states that can do as they wish, without any guarantee that the rights of all Americans will be protected no matter in what part of the country they live. Militia members say they have a right to superior arms, to defeat the U.S. government. Proponents of "states' rights" want laws to make states superior, to defeat the U.S. government. If politicians like Charlie Duke succeed, the idea of America, and the attendant rights and freedoms of Americans, will be at stake.

Third, politicians such as Helen Chenoweth and Steve Stockman see in the militias only political allies, and avert their eyes from the hatred and potential violence of the movement. They do so at their own risk. Sooner or later there will be more militia-related poisonous rhetoric and violence. It will be harder for these elected officials to retain office as their grassroots constituents get fed up with the militias, either because of their thuggish impact on the local community or because political challengers—who may even agree with the militias on the issues of gun control and the environment—make use of the incumbents' moral blindness, their inability to see that the ends do not justify the means.

And, sooner or later, leading American conservatives will begin to understand that the militias and their ideology target them, too. House Speaker Newt Gingrich might have been reluctant to hold hearings concerning militias because he was afraid of alienating a key Republican core: gun owners, antienvironmentalists, those opposed to a strong federal government. But the militias do not see him as an ally; they call him "Newt World Order" Gingrich. Some Republicans, such as Congressman Peter King of Long Island, quickly understood that the militias were not "friends." King was a lone, courageous early Republican voice calling for congressional hearings into the movement.

Fourth, America has weathered far worse episodes of extremists' intrusion into the political process. In 1955, for example, two U.S. senators, six U.S. representatives, and five serving or former governors were on the advisory board of the so-called Federation for Constitutional Government, whose agenda Senator James Eastland of Mississippi described as "a great crusade [for the] untainted racial heritage, culture and institutions of the Anglo-Saxon race." The historical lesson is not that catastrophe is inevitable whenever elected officials advocate hatred and front for groups that promote it; rather, it is that the connection between hatemongers and politicians is a "miner's canary" for democracy. When politicians cozy up to hatemongers—especially armed ones—people of goodwill *must* speak out. Those politicians who are too timid to criticize colleagues must at least condemn the hateful ideology that underlies the militia movement. As too many historians have had the opportunity to observe, the greatest danger is in silence, and the worst hatred that to which we become accustomed.

23 The Technology of Bigotry

YOU GOT A BIG TARGET ON THERE . . . SAYS ATF.

DON'T SHOOT AT THEM BECAUSE THEY GOT A

VEST ON UNDERNEATH THAT. HEAD SHOTS.

HEAD SHOTS. . . . KILL THE SONS OF BITCHES!

G. GORDON LIDDY

In the weeks and months before the Oklahoma City bombing, there were hateful conversations going on in America, conversations heard by thousands but overlooked by most. The deaths at the Murrah Building forced Americans to look at what they were saying and at the instruments through which they were saying it.

Shortly after the bombing, President Clinton criticized the voices of hate on talk radio. The Clinton presidency had been bashed by conservatives of the "new media," and his statement was seen by many as a political response to an American disaster. After all, John Trochmann, Mark Koernke, Samuel Sherwood, and the others were not organizing their groups by means of guest appearances on the Rush Limbaugh show. I said as much to a staffer of the Democratic National Committee, who called because I had written a monograph called "Hate on Talk Radio" in 1991. Hate on talk radio *is* a problem, but to assign this slice of the media responsibility for the Oklahoma City bombing seemed to stretch the point too far. "Tell your bosses," I said to the staffer, "that going after talk radio is like wrestling a pig. You get dirty, and the pig likes it."

Clinton's criticisms of talk radio had some truth, however. AM and FM talk radio had been helpful to the militias because some of the issues that drove America's private armies also played well on talk shows. Mainstream media, for instance, forgot the Branch Davidians after their fiery end. Not so talk radio. Waco was a huge topic.

The talk-show host Rush Limbaugh—whom some think Clinton was targeting—also spoke about concerns that overlapped the militias' agenda. For example, Limbaugh supported the 1994 nationwide protests of United Nations Day, protests promoted in part by the militia movement. Before the Oklahoma bombing, Limbaugh also said: "The second violent American revolution is just about—I got my fingers about a quarter of an inch apart—is just about that far away. Because these people are sick and tired of a bunch of bureaucrats in Washington driving into town and telling them what they can and can't do with their land." But day in, day out, people who were bent on forming militias were not tuning in Limbaugh to find out how to do it. In fact, militia leaders thought Limbaugh was part of the "liberal establishment." John Schloser, commander of the Colorado Free Militia, said Limbaugh was "a Judas Priest."

The one mainstream talk-radio host to whom militia members may listen is G. Gordon Liddy, heard on over two hundred stations across America. Liddy said, "You got a big target on there . . . says ATF. Don't shoot at them because they got a vest on underneath that. Head shots. Head shots. . . . Kill the sons of bitches!"

Liddy also told his listeners:

> You have every right to fear your government. Look at what the brutal thugs of the Bureau of Alcohol, Tobacco and Firearms do, smashing into homes, shooting as they come in, killing people. When they don't do that, they *trash* the home, *steal* the money from the people who have *never* been accused of a crime, take their possessions, *stomp* the cat to death on the way out, then threaten the wife that if she talks about it, *that they'll be back*, that they're federal agents—they can do *anything they want to do*. That's the kind of people we're talking about here, the kind of people that take a pregnant woman and *smash* her against a concrete wall—that's the Bureau of Alcohol, Tobacco and Firearms—so she loses her *baby*. You'd better be afraid of 'em!

The Washington Post, reporting this tirade, wrote that "it excludes logic": "Liddy is merging three incidents [including Waco]" and getting the facts wrong besides. After documenting Liddy's fundamental errors, the *Post* lamented that "Liddy's mind is made up on these cases. Presenting the other side isn't an issue." But talk radio is not about fairness or evenhandedness. Talk radio is not journalism. It is a medium suited to strong opinion strongly stated. There is no pretense of fairness. There is only "entertainment." The danger is that entertainment can be taken seriously. Liddy has been quoted by militia leaders at militia meetings.

The talk-radio that has had the most impact on the militia movement is local programming and syndicated shows aired on small stations in small markets. For example, the Portland-based Coalition for Human Dignity reported that racists in rural Stevens County, Washington, have been emboldened by the weekly broadcast of Pete Peters's Christian Identity program on Colville station KCVL. KCVL also aired a show called *Love of Truth*, hosted by Mark Reynolds, a Christian Identity adherent and a leader of a militia group. "Laws to execute sodomites," said Reynolds, "would surely put a quick end to people dying from AIDS they got in a restaurant or the dentist's chair! So-called tolerance is anti-Christian and lukewarm." In March 1995, Reynolds warned that if government continued "pushing people the way they are doing, people like Reno will end up hanging from telephone poles or trees."

Bo Gritz had a morning radio program, which was suspended from WMKT in Charlevoix, Michigan, on Monday, April 24, 1995. "Our decision to suspend," said general manager Trish MacDonald Garber, ". . . was centered around the inflammatory language and message that he has and the proximity of the Michigan Militia to our radio station." Two days later, after a flood of calls, Gritz was back on. "We were convinced," Garber explained. "The listenership suggested, 'Let us interpret his message; don't censor it so we don't even have a chance to hear that side of the story.' "

On occasion you can find a caller on talk radio promoting the militia movement. In September 1994 (around the time of Thompson's "Ultimatum"), a caller to the Chuck Baker Show, on the Colorado Springs station KVOR, said: "The problem we have right now is who do we shoot? Other than Kennedy, Foley and Mitchell, the other [members of Congress] are borderline traitors. They're the kingpins right now, beside the Slick One [Clinton]. . . . You've got to get your ammo. . . . We cannot do it as individuals, we have got to do it as an orchestrated militia." According to the media watchdog organization Fairness and Accuracy in Reporting, Chuck Baker used to "mimic the sound of a firing pin—'kching-kching' —as he rave[d] against the government and talk[ed] to listeners about shooting members of Congress and forming guerrilla cells." Among Baker's guests have been Linda Thompson, Richard Mack, Larry Pratt,

Charlie Duke, and Pete Peters. "Am I advocating the overthrow of this government?" Baker has asked. "I'm advocating the cleansing. . . . Why are we sitting here?"

Such words may have consequences: In this President Clinton was correct. Francisco Martin Duran, who shot at the White House in October 1994, was one of Mr. Baker's listeners.

✗ ✗ ✗

The rapid formation and growth of the militia movement were due in part to new technologies that made communication quicker, easier, and cheaper. Least important of these was talk radio. Most important were the Internet and, to a lesser degree, fax networks. To the extent that radio played a part in militia communication, it was shortwave, a band designed for international programming but used by many targeting a domestic audience. While the rest of America got its broadcast news and analysis from CBS, NBC, ABC, Fox, or CNN, militia members tuned in to these "alternative" wavelengths. In addition to such stalwarts as Mark Koernke and Linda Thompson, Jack McLamb and "patriot" William Cooper aired shortwave programs five nights a week. And shortwave radio remains a key organizing tool of militias around the country.

The four main shortwave stations in the United States that carry racist or antigovernment conspiracy-theory programs are WWCR in Nashville, WRNO in New Orleans, WHRI in South Bend, Indiana, and WINB in Red Lion, Pennsylvania. Mark Koernke's shows were broadcast on WWCR ("World Wide Christian Radio"). For months he railed against government, wove conspiracy theories, and ended programs with a call for "death to the New World Order." Nine days after the Oklahoma City bombing, George McClintock, the station's general manager, suspended the program. "We've got to get the gasoline off the fires," McClintock said.

WWCR was an important source for the militia movement's fuel of hate and for information-sharing around the country and beyond. Not only did it host Koernke, it promoted William Cooper (whose conspiracy theories are described in Chapter 14). Broadcasting from Nashville, Cooper received calls from as far off as Long Island and Texas. And he claimed listeners in Canada, Russia, South Africa, Norway, and elsewhere. On November 21, 1994, Cooper said:

> Some in the militia will be receiving direction in the form of legal justification, training and action, and battle plans. Use these materials as they become available. The value of these items will be obvious when you receive them.

Militias in several states must be ready in all respects in training, spiritually and mentally, to fight the war to reinstate the Constitution of the United States of America to its legal and lawful place as the supreme law of the land within six months.

Six months away was April 21, 1995.

According to the human rights group Radio for Peace International, Kurt Saxon, another host on WWCR, "gave instructions for how to build a bomb with materials from a local store." You could also hear a caller on Mr. Saxon's show ask "what the best weapon was for picking off Martians at 300 feet." "Martians" is the shortwave term for "minorities."

Tom Valentine hosted *Radio Free America*, a long-running program associated with, and promoted by, the Liberty Lobby. For years, Valentine had a steady stream of Holocaust deniers, neo-Nazis, and similar characters on his program, which was heard on several small radio stations around the country, but also nationally on WWCR. "A bloody civil war is brewing, and I'm serious," Valentine said. He claimed that his audience had grown from nine thousand people in 1989 to two hundred thousand in 1995. "It is happening," he said, "because government has stopped listening to the people and become intrusive . . . and because the media is part of the conspiracy."

After the bombing, the Federal Communications Commission was reported to be investigating whether shortwave stations such as WWCR were violating federal regulations.

✗ ✗ ✗

When the veterinarian Donald Ellwanger was facing eviction in Washington state, militia members were called to his land by a faxed flyer. A copy of the notice made its way to the American Patriot Fax Network, run by Gary B. Hunt, who had had David Koresh's power of attorney at Waco. The APFN then forwarded it to another "reflector," relaying the message far and wide.

Fax machines are cheaper than computers, and they are simpler to use. To call out the troops they may be fine. But they are not interactive and do not allow research into a reservoir of information. The main communication system of the militias is the computer. Computers, after all, substitute for a fax machine with the installation of a fax board. But they can do so much more; they can hook you up with like-minded people around the globe through bulletin boards and newsgroups on the Internet.

Bulletin board services include Patriot Net, Liberty Net, and Paul Revere Net. There may be up to three hundred such systems serving the extreme right in America. Militia members can even sleep while their computers dial up and download the bulletin boards' news. In the morning, new information awaits.

Linda Thompson runs a bulletin board through which she claims to reach 36,000 people. "We're a news service," she says. "We use the computer as the end of the line, not the beginning. We get information in by Federal Express, faxes, and phone, then we put it on the bulletin boards for the widest distribution." Bulletin boards allow more privacy and security than do Internet newsgroups, because there is more control of access and because bulletin boards permit easier encryption of messages. Sometimes messages are encrypted (with a common system called PGP, for "Pretty Good Privacy") simply to befuddle people who may be "listening" in. "We send copies of the Constitution out encrypted," said Thompson, "just to keep 'em [the CIA, she claims] busy."

The Internet may be a recent invention to most Americans, but the far right has been using computer-based communications for more than a decade. Louis Beam operated a computer network for the Aryan Nations in the mid-1980s. He used it to issue a "hit list." According to the *Atlanta Journal*, Beam "proposed an assassination point system by which whites would earn the designation 'Aryan warrior.' It would take one full point to become an 'Aryan warrior.' The murder of a member of Congress would be worth one-fifth of a point, judges one-sixth, FBI agents and federal marshals one-tenth, journalists and local politicians one-twelfth. One full point would be given for assassinating the president."

By the birth of the militia movement in 1994, computers and computer services were cheaper, quicker, and more readily available. And while bulletin boards provided control and security, the Internet newsgroups allowed speed and a huge audience. Anyone with access to Usenet (obtainable through CompuServe, America Online, and other providers) could subscribe to these groups with the click of a button.

When John Trochmann was arrested in March 1995 at the courthouse in Montana, reports were aired on shortwave station WWCR. "I'm listening to WWCR," a CompuServe member posted in alt.conspiracy, describing details of the charges. "This appears to be a Waco style setup. Federal Officers involved."

In newsgroups such as alt.conspiracy and talk.politics.guns, militia members shared a wealth of information, advice, and paranoia. Whole treatises on the history of militias, and guides to their formation, were posted. Manuals and handbooks were shared. There were detailed instructions on "How to Activate the Constitutional Militia in Your Area," with advice about first finding "like minded persons in your area," then "form[ing] a safety committee" and "[p]icking a suitable date . . . for the first muster. . . . It should commemorate some historical event." The posted information could guide you through all the important steps: The muster should be publicized, mailing lists compiled, by-laws drafted, local officials and the press invited, documents distributed, training sessions conducted, alert systems established, "abusive officials" gotten "rid of." And, of course, the Internet accessed.

If you dialed up talk.politics.guns in March 1995 you might have found "Military Training: Operation WitWeb" which described itself as "a spider, spinning [a] web to catch some flies. In this case, the flies are corrupt or abusive officials. . . . Participants should remain mobile so that they do not themselves become easy targets for attack or apprehension. There should be preparations for any participant who learns 'too much' to go underground . . . with everything needed, such as money, ID, a cellular phone or ham radio, a vehicle with plates not linked to him, or disguises, to remain underground for an extended period of time, while preserving the ability to maintain necessary contact."

As the end of March 1995 approached, and the paranoid rumors of government attack were ricocheting across cyberspace, you could find militia postings that not only exacerbated the fear, but also discussed how to cope in the aftermath. One read:

> Up to now, we have been depending on making use of telephone communications for voice, fax and e-mail. However, many of us have been experiencing apparent interference with our transmissions lately, in ways that indicate that our adversaries are prepared to interrupt service for any or all of us on a call by call basis. That means we must develop an alternative means to communicate with one another nationwide that is not subject to interdiction. Shortwave can be jammed. Sirens and flares are too short range and depend on people being within range. We must think in terms of mobilization points, couriers, short-range two-way radio, pirate broadcasting to radio and TV channels, and lists of alternative contact points in each area that can be tried to re-establish broken communication links. . . . The model we must use for our comm network is the Internet: a dense store-and-forward system that can withstand major disruptions without losing its ability to get messages to their destination.

The next day someone posted instructions for making an ammonium nitrate bomb—the same type that would be used three weeks later in Oklahoma City—and offered to share the formula for C-4. In the newsgroup rec.pyrotechnics, someone else shared the recipe for Sarin, the poison used on the Tokyo subway. According to researcher Rick Eaton,

"The only outrage came from a user who complained the formula was posted in the wrong place."

The Internet was one of the major reasons the militia movement expanded faster than any hate group in history. The militias' lack of an organized center was more than made up for by the instant communication and rumor potential of this new medium. Any militia member in remote Montana who had a computer and a modem could be part of an entire worldwide network that shared his or her thoughts, aspirations, organizing strategies, and fears—a global family.

The anonymity of the Internet was also the perfect culture in which to grow the virus of conspiracy theory. Messages appeared on the screen with no easy way to separate junk from the credible. Even people trained to scrutinize sources of information were fooled. Immediately following Timothy McVeigh's arrest, news reports said that he had an account at America Online, where he went by the nickname "Mad Bomber." Someone had created that account as a hoax. For conspiracy enthusiasts like militia members, unverified statements from cyberspace reaffirmed their set conclusions by providing an endless stream of additional "evidence." They could join alt.conspiracy and live in a parallel universe where a Bob Fletcher or a Mark Koernke was a Walter Cronkite.

✗ ✗ ✗

Shortly after Timothy McVeigh was arrested, the Aryan News Agency posted the following advice: "EVERYONE either cease public Net activities, or restrict them exclusively to posting NEWS about 'the incident,' at least for the next few days until we can ascertain the program and plan of the Washington Criminals in the aftermath of what is on all our minds."

Internet activity slowed for a while after the bombing. One self-described "patriot" list, known as SAMSBEST, said it was closing on May 4, 1995. Asserting that the list was intended for "patriots and Constitutionalists," the owner lamented that "recent events have persuaded me that, in fact, SAMSBEST is being used as a resource for those who hate and fear us. . . . I believe this second group is getting more mileage out of the list, especially the archives, than the readership I wanted to serve."

On the other hand, shortly after the bombing, another posting in alt.conspiracy instructed how to make an Oklahoma-style fertilizer bomb. "The information specifically details the construction, deployment and detonation of high-powered explosives," the anonymous message read. "It also includes complete details of the bomb used in Oklahoma City, and how it was used and could have been better."

On July 8, 1995, three days before Congressman Schumer held his "renegade" hearing on the militia movement, Mike Chapman, identified as the moderator of the newsgroup misc.activism.militia, wrote:

> According to an AP story Rep. Charles "Cereal Killer" Schumer, D–NY, will hold an unofficial forum on private militias. He's been unable to get congressional support for full-blown congressional hearings on militias so he's going this route instead.
>
> I sure wouldn't cry if some militia fellows showed up at that meeting and gave Schumer a special high-energy present for his efforts.

Chapman's posting got a serious reply. "Then what?" his correspondent asked. "Yes the guy may be an ass. But what do you think would happen if tomorrow morning 260 million people were to pick up the morning paper or turn on the tube and see the headline of 'ARMED MILITIA MEMBERS GUN DOWN CONGRESSPERSON IN COLD BLOOD'? Do you not agree that the backlash would hinder, and not further, the cause of liberty?"

Chapman replied:

> Nope—it would force a conflict that only we can win. The government cannot win a civil war on Americans at this point. . . . Perhaps for a while, but once the American people understood what war was really about, they'd compromise. Or we can all die and build something up out of the rubble. What we have right now is just evil. . . .
>
> Nope, I wouldn't cry if someone MP5'd Schumer or Klinton [sic] or Reno or any of them. I wouldn't necessarily agree with the action, but once it's done, well, it's done and we're all better off.

In the aftermath of the Oklahoma City bombing, there have been calls for increased oversight of the Internet. But America is still not sure how to regulate the Net, if at all. What takes place there is, after all, a new form of an old, protected interest—speech. If I can say it on the phone, write it in a letter, scream it from a soapbox, or whisper it to my spouse, why shouldn't I be able to put it on the Internet? The Internet is to communications nothing more than the paperback was to the hard-cover—a technological advance that makes it easier and cheaper for more people to share ideas with mass audiences. The Internet is *everyone's* printing press. Government should not restrict what people want to say simply because it is said there. How could it do so anyway? With millions of messages posted all the time, how could such a huge enterprise be monitored for enforcement purposes?

There are, however, ways to control the information on the Internet.

Most users subscribe through private companies, which have the right to enforce rules of conduct and can discontinue accounts. And just as parents can block cable television shows they don't want their children to watch, improved technology will become available for blocking certain messages—for example, directions for making explosives at your kitchen table.

The far-right fringe has been a decade ahead in the use of this new technology, and as people ponder what to do, the right is ahead yet again. The magic word is "encryption." There have been reports, for example, that German neo-Nazis have used encrypted messages on bulletin boards as a secure means of communicating, organizing, and sharing bomb-making recipes. But the point is that even though people should have the same relative expectation of privacy when they send private messages through computers as they do when calling on the phone or sending a letter, they should not be able to use the Internet for illegal activities any more than they could the telephone or the mail.

Even before April 19, 1995, the militias' hatred and its boasts of heavy armaments and potential illegal acts were there for all to see in cyber-space. Yet the FBI, explaining why it had not been overly concerned with the militia movement before the bombing, said that it was not allowed to surf the Net. If that was true, the restriction on law enforcement should be debated. The Internet should not be censored any more than the daily newspaper should be. But if someone is posting statements in a news-group, or being quoted in the newspaper, or writing an article for either medium, he or she no longer has a reasonable expectation of privacy in that communication. *If* indications of criminal activity—rather than just distasteful speech—travel across the Internet, there is no reason that the government should not be able to observe that, just as it should be able to take cognizance of what is written in the morning newspaper or broadcast on radio or TV. Encrypted bulletin board messages, of course, have a greater expectation of privacy. But the newsgroups of the Internet are irresistible to militias precisely because they "publish" their message quickly and widely.

24 Law Enforcement and Private Armies

THE MORE THE FEDERAL AND LOCAL LAW
ENFORCEMENT AGENCIES BEHAVE WITH A
HANDS-OFF ATTITUDE, THE MORE BOLD AND
DARING THESE GROUPS BECOME.

JOHN BOHLMAN, a Montana county attorney

In early 1995, an official in a midwestern office of a human rights organization learned, from the Internet, that a local militia group was forming. She called the FBI. The agent told her that "people have a right to dress up funny and shoot in the woods. We're not going to pay any attention to the militia, until and unless it breaks the law."

This vision of the militia movement as overgrown boys playing with weapons pervaded all levels of law enforcement, local, state, and federal. Even the federal agency most vilified by the militias—the Bureau of Alcohol, Tobacco and Firearms—dismissed these groups. "We're not involved with [investigating] folks because of what they believe," an ATF official said. "You can have horrible beliefs in this country and make horrible statements and not be a matter for federal investigation." Only a month before the Oklahoma City bombing, Bill Wallace of the *San Francisco Chronicle* wrote that "Local law enforcement officials have shown little interest in the activities of the militias, and the FBI says it is precluded by law from scrutinizing them. 'That's what we call free speech,' said Rick Smith, a spokesman for the FBI's San Francisco field office.'" No one, however, was suggesting that militias be investigated because they had odious views. What law enforcement did not appreciate was that militias were doing much more than talking. These folk were arming themselves; some even bragged about their possession of illegal weaponry and other violations of the law (such as not paying taxes), while practicing for violent confrontation with public officials.

Nearly two months after the Oklahoma City bombing a former high-ranking FBI official tried to explain to me why the FBI was slow to monitor these groups. He said it was because lawsuits had opened agents to liability if they were overzealous. As former trial counsel for Dennis Banks of the American Indian Movement, I was aware of those decisions, as well as of the "overzealousness" of the FBI when it investigated political groups it did not like. "Do you mean to tell me," I said to the former FBI official, "that the FBI would have had the same reaction . . . if thousands of blacks were arming themselves to fight with the federal government? You mean to tell me the FBI wouldn't have opened a file last September if Linda Thompson were the adjutant general of the Black Liberation Army and proposed a march of these armed black men to arrest members of Congress at gunpoint, summarily try them for treason, and hang them from the nearest light pole or tree?" That, in the end, was the rub. The FBI was not overly concerned with the militias because they looked too much like mainstream America—and like the FBI.

Throughout its history the Federal Bureau of Investigation has had a mixed record of investigating political groups. The FBI broke the law in cases dealing with the Black Panthers and the American Indian Movement, and in many other cases involving minority groups and the political left. Its performance when federal agents have been killed—as in the Randy Weaver case—has been no better. On the other hand, it did an excellent job bringing the Order to justice after the group killed Alan Berg and robbed a number of armored cars. And it has also put together strong cases against skinhead groups and others who were white of skin and neo-Nazi in politics.

If the militias had been a "traditional" network of armed white supremacists, such as the Posse Comitatus or the Minutemen, the FBI would likely have reacted quicker. But the militia movement was more perplexing to the FBI. It was a mass phenomenon, attracting average people or, more correctly, average white conservative male people—the one group to whom the FBI would give the benefit of the doubt. This double standard arises from the racism and sexism that, unfortunately, still exist in the FBI. Minority and women agents continue to complain about (and file suits over) discrimination within the agency.

There are other possible explanations for the FBI's slowness, too. Perhaps the FBI feared that, since the militias' rhetoric heaped venom on it for Waco and Ruby Ridge (with some justification), any investigation would be seen as a petty vendetta. But the fact remained that the militias were issuing threats against public officials, threats backed up with a huge collection of guns, ammunition, and explosives. And MOM leaders, for example, boasted of their large mail-order business and their disdain for taxes.

There was, of course, little the FBI could do about all the small "Leaderless Resistance" cells that popped out of the small end of Ken Toole's funnel; it would have needed one agent for each person who attended a militia meeting to prevent the Oklahoma City tragedy. But there was plenty that it should have done, and did not.

✗ ✗ ✗

State and local law enforcement officials, with some exceptions—those in Idaho, for example, who spoke out against Sherwood's militia—were also slow to recognize the danger. Typical was Emmet County, Michigan, sheriff Jeffrey Bodznick who was quoted in the September 24, 1994, *Chicago Tribune* as saying: "They're not violating any Michigan or federal law at this point, and I don't expect them to." But militias were violating state law in many parts of the country.

In the early 1980s groups aligned with the Ku Klux Klan had created private armies in Florida, North Carolina, and Texas. The Texas group—which called itself the Texas Emergency Reserve—not only conducted armed military drills, it also terrorized Vietnamese fishermen. On February 14, 1981, Louis Beam, then Grand Dragon of the Texas Realm, Knights of the Ku Klux Klan, led three hundred people to Galveston, where he set a mock Vietnamese boat ablaze. He proclaimed that white people must "take back" the United States "by blood." In response the Anti-Defamation League of B'nai B'rith drafted a model state statute outlawing such paramilitary activity. Then Morris Dees, chief trial counsel of the Southern Poverty Law Center, brought successful suits against the Texas and North Carolina paramilitary groups. By 1995 twenty-four states had laws banning what we now call militias and twenty-four (including seven of the "antimilitia" states) had laws against paramilitary "training." But since the mid-1980s, there have been no prosecutions under these laws. Why?

Perhaps some of the states' attorneys general are worried about possible constitutional problems with the laws on their books. Perhaps prosecutors are not comfortable "trying out" a new law, especially one they know would be politically charged. And perhaps prosecutors simply lack will—after all, some people linked with militia groups in Montana were allowed to hide beyond the arm of the law after committing more "ordinary" crimes, such as attempted murder.

Before April 19, 1995, the American Jewish Committee, the Anti-Defamation League, the Southern Poverty Law Center, the Northwest Coalition Against Malicious Harassment, and many other civil rights groups urged police and prosecutors to enforce the antiparamilitary laws on their books (and encouraged legislatures to enact such laws in states that did not have them). After April 19, 1995, why would a prosecutor still be reluctant to bring a case if a militia group was violating an antiparamilitary statute? The uncertainty of conviction would be a logical concern. It is one thing for human rights organizations to yell about prosecuting the militias; it is another to put a case together that will convince a jury to convict.

Imagine the problems. There is a statute on your books, and it is patterned after the ADL model bill.* Fine. But the First Amendment lets people scream all they want about civil war with government, and they can gather with their guns. The human rights groups correctly state that no one has the right to create a private army, and these groups might be private armies. But in order to get a conviction against specific individuals a prosecutor would have to prove they were "teaching" or "demonstrating" how to use guns or explosives, with the knowledge, intent, or reason to know that this training would be used to create a "civil disorder." These are the "elements of the crime." To prove them requires witnesses and documents showing that on specific dates specific people did specific things with specific weapons with specific intent.

It is another thing to bring a case *after* some form of "civil disorder." Then witnesses would tell a jury who trained whom and when, showing the connection to the event. The prosecutor would be able to keep the focus on the "civil disorder," rather than on the "training." But without a civil disturbance around which to build the prosecution, the case would be difficult at best. The defense would call it a witch-hunt against people with unpopular ideas. "Hysteria!" they'd say, in the aftermath of the Oklahoma bombing. And even if a talented prosecutor could pull a cohesive case together, consider the difficulties in picking a jury. This might be a more difficult task than that in the O. J. Simpson case. Everyone knows something about militias since April 19, 1995. But whereas the Simpson jurors only knew of O.J., many potential jurors in a

* See Appendix.

militia case would have had direct contact with militia members. And that contact wouldn't just create possible bias; the fear level would be like that in a Mafia trial. What potential juror would not be afraid of the militia wanting revenge for a guilty verdict?

These are only some of the problems that would face a state prosecutor who *wanted* to bring a case against militia members for illegal paramilitary training, a prosecutor who was not frightened of the militias or worried about the personal political implications. What about prosecutors who are not sure where they stand?

Another aspect of the lackluster local law enforcement response to the militias was the willingness of many to write off militia activities as nuttiness or as "isolated incidents." For example, before the Oklahoma bombing, officials of some groups that monitored militias discussed what would be the best way to educate attorneys general about the danger militias posed and about the antiparamilitary-training laws and other statutes (e.g., harassment) they were violating. One idea was to highlight the relationship between the ideology of this movement and the flood of "common law" documents, especially "constitutional liens" against public officials. In a private conversation, an official in the Washington state attorney general's office acknowledged that the liens were a problem; there was no county in Washington state without at least one such lien filed against a public official. One man had filed twenty liens against legislators for their refusal to impeach Governor Mike Lowry. But the liens were seen as nuttiness, not as part of a larger pattern of tormenting and intimidating officials, who with liens filed against them would have problems getting credit and selling or buying homes. The legislative remedy that had been decided upon was a provision making their removal easier. This approach is somewhat akin to Indiana's decision to change its road signs because militia members and sympathizers believed that information on the back of the signs was designed to aid invading troops. When the Washington official began to understand, during the conversation, that the liens were not filed by individual "wackos" but by people who had a political agenda, many of whom were associated with armed militias, she begged that no one associate her publicly with the new legislation. Among her fears was that she would have hundreds of liens filed against her.

Others in local law enforcement might have been reluctant to investigate the militias because—as was often the case with police officials and the Klan in the 1960s—they belonged to or supported it. In January 1995 the *Denver Post* ran a story about a questionnaire some Colorado militia members had answered for the paper. One militia member noted that some federal and local law enforcement officers supported their cause. "This is one of the main reasons why our people stay as motivated as they are," he wrote. "They know what the federal police are up to. . . . [They provide] whatever [information] they can. To get into specifics would compromise their positions, but they have given us the names of undercover agents, status of current investigations."

Law enforcement personnel have been heavily recruited by Jack McLamb and others. Many officers acknowledge this effort. A Florida law enforcement officer, for example, was told by a militia member, "You've got to decide which side you're on." Not every small-town law enforcement agent has the fortitude to ignore such an appeal (perhaps from a lifelong friend), and the implicit threat behind it.

Ken Toole of the Montana Human Rights Network conducted a 1995 training session for law enforcement officers in Montana. He distributed a small number of informational packets to participants, and to no one else. Three days later he received a call from John Stadtmiller, Mark Koernke's former on-air radio partner, who read Toole parts of the material. He could only have gotten it—directly or indirectly—from a police officer Toole had trained.

One victim of militia death threats who testified before the Schumer panel told me that she believed someone in her local police force might be connected with the militia. She had been harassed by repeated death threats on her home phone. The threats stopped the day the police installed a trace.

A Snohomish County, Washington, private investigator, who claims to have infiltrated three militia groups, said: "Of course county sheriffs are going to downplay this. These guys are recruiting in the sheriff's departments. In a lot of cases, sheriff's deputies know all these guys by their first names."

The probability is that very few members of law enforcement are involved with militias. But it is unrealistic to expect local law officers to be enthusiastic about arresting armed and angry neighbors for violation of laws against paramilitary activity. Consider the effort it took to resolve two of the Montana cases, in which people were charged with more traditional crimes. After the Oklahoma bombing, Calvin Greenup finally surrendered after extensive negotiations. But authorities had to endure a shoot-out to arrest Gordon Sellner, who had not paid taxes in twenty years and who since 1992 had been a fugitive from charges of shooting a sheriff's deputy. Authorities found over thirty weapons, among them .50-caliber rifles, thousands of rounds of ammunition, and bomb-making materials at Sellner's place. Montana militia leaders quickly spoke out in his support. Imagine if the shoot-out had developed out of an attempt to arrest Sellner simply because he had belonged to an illegal militia. What sheriff would be enthusiastic about risking the lives of his few deputies to effect such an arrest?

America's militias are a federal problem, and there should be federal laws to proscribe them. After all, people have the First Amendment right to say what they will about government, and the right to own guns if they comply with applicable laws. But there is no federal right to take those guns, form a private army, and practice for war against the federal government. A federal antiparamilitary law would not infringe constitutionally protected conduct.* A militia such as Samuel Sherwood's, for instance, which does not train with arms, can meet and talk about war against Washington all it wants. But it cannot, for that purpose, or any other, create a private, armed, combat-ready group. In the final analysis, armies are for the people, who express their will through elected governments, not for vigilante groups.

One advantage of such a law is that there would be no need to debate "additional powers" for the FBI. The real restrictions on FBI activity (not the Bureau's excuses for inaction) *are* important to preserve liberty. The FBI has enough authority to infiltrate groups when there is a reasonable suspicion that the targets are violating or are about to violate federal law. Rather than try to justify investigations based on other federal law militias may be breaking, the Congress should give the FBI an easy federal predicate, without opening the Pandora's box of expanding the FBI's powers. If the FBI found that someone was starting a militia, and arming it in the manner proscribed by a new federal antiparamilitary law, it could open a file. Period. Because private armies would be against federal law.

What would happen if the federal government tried to enforce such a law? No doubt, in some places, tragedy. Militia groups see themselves as warring with an evil government, which they believe is coming to get them. If they faced arrest, some might live up to their images of Waco and Ruby Ridge and fire on the FBI. That, of course, would be a horrible scenario—as would be the less troublesome, but also problematic, matter of prosecuting resisting militia members. Such trials would become a rallying point for the movement. But to do nothing would be worse.

Some suggest that to enact federal antiparamilitary legislation will only ratify the militias' views and make them more paranoid. But the militias have demonstrated remarkable paranoia in the absence of any action. It doesn't matter if a new law is passed. These people, after all, think that the Oklahoma City blast was designed by government to create an excuse for their capture.

---

* Sam Rabinove, legal director of the American Jewish Committee, has proposed federal antiparamilitary legislation since 1986. His draft language is in the Appendix.

Not to enact federal legislation will only embolden the militias. Especially in grassroots America, these private armies are bullies who think they can intimidate officials and poison the political process using threats and vitriolic rhetoric backed up by a massive collection of arms. When government backs off, they become more, not less, venomous. Federal lawmakers owe an obligation to people like Judge Martha Bethel, Audubon Society member Ellen Gray, ten-year-old Katy Schock, and the thousands of other brave souls—many of them forest rangers and other federal employees and their families—who now live in fear because of death threats from America's armed militia groups. The government's obligation is not to silence the militia members' hate; it is to ensure that no American should find himself or herself living the nightmare of being threatened by an army.

25 Another American Export

VIRTUALLY ALL OUR PROPAGANDA AND TRAINING
MANUALS CAME FROM RIGHT-WING EXTREMIST
GROUPS IN [AMERICA].

INGO HASSELBACH, former German neo-Nazi leader

Because conspiracy theories are international; because the political issues driving militias are not limited to guns and the environment; and because of the ease of global communication, the militia movement may affect other issues, here and abroad.

Abortion is one such issue. Although to a much lesser extent than gun control or the environment, it has played a role in parts of the American militia movement. In many places it is a low-intensity issue, more of a concern or an afterthought than an organizing magnet. But in others—for example, Wisconsin—abortion is one of the key militia issues. It makes sense that some people, with a foot in both the militia and anti-abortion camps, would want to combine the two.

All militia groups, regardless of focus, strategy, or white supremacist direction, share conspiratorial notions and a belief that the federal government is "the enemy," picking off Americans' freedoms one by one. For those who see abortion as simple baby-killing, the federal government is the foe. The United States Supreme Court, in *Roe v. Wade*, not only made abortion legal, it gave the practice constitutional protection. Federal funds pay for some abortions for poor people. Federal laws restrict protest activities around clinics.

If a person's religious or other values define abortion as no different from taking a child out of his backyard swing set and dismembering him while alive, animus toward a government that protects the practice so understood would be fathomable. That is why, on the fringes of the anti-abortion movement, there are people willing to kill people to stop what they define as killing people. Simple murder is then "defensive action." Such "logic," of course, cannot excuse murder, but it is internally consistent. If I kill that doctor, or burn that clinic, some "children" who might have "died" may now be born. Killing, in this version of anti-abortion newspeak, saves lives. But if the evil is not the individual abortion provider but the system that allows him or her to operate, then government becomes the "scapegoat," as much as it does for people primarily concerned with environmental issues or gun control.

Reverend Matthew Trewhella is probably the best known anti-abortion/ militia leader. He is a member of the U.S. Taxpayers Party, a co-founder of Missionaries to the Preborn, and a signatory to a document approving "defensive action." In May of 1994, at a U.S. Taxpayers Party meeting exposed by Planned Parenthood, Trewhella said that we "need to teach [young people] to be responsible Freemen." He said "the most loving thing" you could do for a child is to buy him or her "an SKS rifle and 500 rounds of ammunition." He bragged that his sixteen-month-old son could show off his "trigger finger" and that he played with the child in militialike manner. "We need to quit playing these stupid little games of blindfolding them and playing pin the tail on the donkey," Trewhella told his audience. "We need to start blindfolding them, sitting them down on the living room floor, and saying, 'Now, put some weapons together.'" Claiming that "plans of resistance are being made," Trewhella urged members of Missionaries to the Preborn to get paramilitary training. The material for sale at that meeting included "Principles Justifying the Arming and Organizing of a Militia," which advocated "assault teams to protect the unborn."

Frederick Clarkson, a researcher at Planned Parenthood, says that "abortion clinics have an average of fifteen bombings or arsons every year for a decade. If that had happened at churches or newspapers or federal office buildings, we would have called it terrorism." That is undoubtedly true. But Planned Parenthood must also admit that it can cite no attack on an abortion clinic conducted by a militia group.

On the other hand, John Salvi, who killed two women in a Boston-area abortion clinic on December 30, 1994, may have associated with a militia. Salvi's former employer Mark Roberts said that Salvi had showed off his gun and said that he had trained with an Everglades militia group. Chip Berlet, an expert with the Cambridge, Massachusetts–based think tank Political Research Associates, said that several anti-abortion militia groups met in November 1994 only a few miles from the Brookline, Massachusetts, clinic that Salvi attacked. They met under the name "Patriot Pro Family Movement." According to Berlet, Salvi went to one, if not more, of these meetings.

There are other connections, too. Larry Pratt of Gun Owners of America also runs the Committee to Protect the Family Foundation, which *New York Times* columnist Frank Rich calls "a fund-raiser for Operation Rescue." And Jeff Baker, co-chair of the Florida U.S. Taxpayers Party, said he is also associated with the Tenth Amendment Militia. His videotapes were found for sale at a Snohomish County, Washington, militia meeting.

Asked about the connection between militias and anti-abortionists, Jack McLamb said, "I've never heard, at any of our groups that our officers or soldiers have been at, the word abortion come up. It's always been the Constitution, the Bill of Rights." Pressed by a *Phoenix Gazette* reporter, McLamb admitted that he is a friend of Jeff Baker. "Jeff's a good guy," McLamb said. "I didn't know he was involved in the anti-abortion movement. But he is a Christian man, so I would assume he's against abortion."

Most Americans who are in the anti-abortion camp will, of course, see no need to join private armies in order to assert their views. But some at the extreme, who already believe that shooting and arson are legitimate options, may want to advance their agendas by joining or forming private armies.

✗ ✗ ✗

The international connections of the militia movement are undeniable, and growing. Ingo Hasselbach is a former leader of a neo-Nazi political group in Germany who has renounced his past. A week after the Oklahoma City bombing he wrote about his experience with "an international network of neo-Nazis and racist movements" and his efforts to build up "caches of weapons" and open "paramilitary camps." He wrote that, as is the case in American militia groups,

> the common attitude we shared was a hatred for Government, especially federal Government agents, a belief that our freedoms and traditions as

white men (or as we said, Aryans) were being infringed by a multicultural society, and a general anti-Semitism that held that the Jews ran a conspiracy that emanated from New York and Washington. . . . Virtually all of our propaganda and training manuals came from right-wing extremist groups in Nebraska and California. . . . We also received . . . a U.S. Army training manual called "Explosives and Demolitions," which has since been copied and circulated (still with the top-secret stamp across the title page) to thousands of right-wing extremists all over Europe.

Not only is militia material making its way to Europe, it has also found promoters in Canada and, most prominently, in Australia. The Militia of Montana wrote that it "has had contact (twice we believe) with an Australian militia organization. The Militia of Montana has appeared on the Sidney [sic], Australia Today Show by satellite link-up to discuss the purpose of the Militia of Montana and what type of movement (if any) was taking place in Australia."

Only weeks after the Oklahoma bombing, Australians would find out how active their militia movement was. "The Department of Defence faced a potential security crisis last night," reported the May 4, 1995, *Canberra Times*, "after revelations that a . . . right-wing extremist group had penetrated its ranks, with members facing prosecution over a cache of illegal weapons. . . . It has been reported that the group possessed up to 20,000 rounds of ammunition." An Australian Defence Force spokesperson described the paramilitary group, known as the "Loyal Regiment of Australian Guardians," as "anti-democracy, anti-Government, anti–new world order, anti–United Nations, and in the middle of that they're for no taxes as well." According to news stories, the group, whose members were described as "Christian fundamentalists," supposedly had "military training camps" and "was willing to defend itself to the death against what it described as 'illegal' government forces. It also intended to defend Australia from invasion by Indonesia." One of those associated with the group, Darren Couchman, "allegedly told police . . . that the Magna Carta, the [Australian] Constitution and the common law entitled all Australians to bear arms."

Another paramilitary group, Australians United for Survival and Individual Freedom, was nicknamed the AUSI Scouts, but most knew it as Murphy's Militia. Murphy was Ian Murphy, a wealthy cattleman. According to the *Sydney Morning Herald*, Murphy's group had "strong links to radical right-wing groups in America." And just as America's militias were legitimized by Bo Gritz of *Rambo* fame, Murphy's group was trained by Australian brigadier Ted Serong, who was a leading soldier in counter-insurgency and unconventional warfare in Vietnam.

Murphy and Serong's literature, distributed to three thousand supporters, said that "the armed citizen is now needed to support our professional defence," and that they must "prepare physically for the world crisis." Murphy claimed that politicians were "guilty of treason" by "betraying Australia's sovereignty." He said a "ruling elite of international bankers are dominating the world economy [and that Australians] are losing our freedom. . . . Our national survival is threatened."

Murphy was also associated with Ross Provis, leader of the far-right-linked Australian Community Movement. Provis claimed: "We have had truckfuls of ex-military weapons shipped into the Inverell area [of New South Wales]. We have heavy and light machine-guns, mortars and artillery pieces. We have much better equipment than the Australian Army."

✗ ✗ ✗

The antigovernment ideology of the American militia groups has become another American export. Change some of the ideological props—substitute the Magna Carta for the Second Amendment—and the same mania can take root in foreign soil.

The Internet is one way that militia information has been and will be shared internationally, but there are other, more traditional means as well. The Australian magazine *Nexus* runs its share of stories on UFOs and crystals, but even before the Oklahoma City bombing it had reprints from American "conspiratorial" and right-wing anti-Semitic groups (such as the LaRouche organization and *Spotlight*). In 1994 it ran a six-page article entitled "Toward a New World Order" which contained extracts from a speech by Mark Koernke. *Nexus* also sported articles by Linda Thompson and Bo Gritz, a reprint of Jack McLamb's "Operation Vampire Killer 2000," and advertisements for *Waco: The Big Lie* and the *Protocols of the Elders of Zion*.

Also circulating in Australia were flyers for McLamb's group Police Against the New World Order. And, far away from home, the need to keep one's distance from overt white supremacists was diminished. To order McLamb's "Operation Vampire Killer 2000" in Australia, send a donation to "Christian Identity Ministries" at a post office box in Cardwell, Australia. You can, at the same time, order other militia-related information, including tapes of Identity minister Pete Peters.

Antidemocratic and anti-Semitic right-wing groups around the world have shared strategies and ideology for decades. Since 1979, for example, neo-Nazis from far and wide have traveled to America for conferences of the California-based Institute for Historical Review, the world's premier Holocaust-denying organization. In less than two decades Holocaust denial has become an article of faith and an ideological glue for many far-right groups around the globe. It would be unreasonable to believe that the far right's international perspective and networks will not affect the formation of paramilitary groups—especially since, for militias, the "evil force" that threatens national governments is One World Government.

White supremacists in other parts of the globe may well model themselves after John Trochmann and others who have had a great impact on the American militia movement. Through the *Spotlight* and by other means American racists encourage their cohorts in other countries to create private armies. These "militias" will help promote a common international aim—not "patriotism," but white supremacy.

The Australian model shows how easily militia paranoia can be adapted to a different country. Vulnerability to a New World Order driven by "international bankers" is a common theme, but in Australia the rallying point seemed not so much the individual's "right to bear arms," which does not have the same mythological power as in America, but vulnerability to invasion. The AUSI propaganda repeatedly focused on the downscaling of the Australian military, and drew a scenario of invasion from the north. If American militia members can believe in Hong Kong troops, why shouldn't Australians be paranoid about invading Indonesians?

Most European and English-speaking countries have some far-right, anti-Semitic conspiracy-believing groups on their soil. Just as Americans now know that terrorism is not uniquely Middle Eastern in origin, other countries must become cognizant that the ideological ingredients for an Oklahoma City bomb may be brewing on their shores.

26 A Degree in Hate

THE BODY WORK IS PAINTED WITH RELIGION,
PATRIOTISM, AND THE U.S. CONSTITUTION; BUT
THE MOTOR IS ANTI-SEMITISM AND RACISM AND
THE DRIVERS ARE WHITE SUPREMACISTS.

LEONARD ZESKIND

From the start of the militia movement until well after the Oklahoma City bombing, there was a friendly but heated debate among those who watched it closely: How much of the movement was driven by white supremacism? On one extreme were respected researchers like Leonard Zeskind, former research director of the Center for Democratic Renewal, who saw white supremacism and anti-Semitism as the base of the movement. Others, who pointed to the abortion-linked militia groups, tended to be at the other extreme, downplaying, or at least questioning, the role of anti-Semitism and racism in the movement. The answer, I think, is somewhere in the middle. More importantly, the question is really many questions that need to be asked in different ways.

Senator Arlen Specter of Pennsylvania has said there were 224 armed militia groups in thirty-nine states shortly after the bombing, with forty-five of those having ties to neo-Nazi and white supremacist groups. How one defines "ties" is another question, but Specter's statement is reasonable. And it misses the point.

The militia movement is a mass social movement. People who have never given a thought to blacks or Jews were attracted to these groups because they cared about other things—guns, the environment, abortion. People were not joining militias, as they would the Ku Klux Klan, to beat up on minorities or give vent to racist ideas. The organizing principle of the militias was that the government had been taken over by evil forces and could not be reformed, that it had to be combated—with arms.

That being said, racism, especially anti-Semitism, was essential to the movement in four ways. If America is to deal effectively with the militias, beyond passing and enforcing antiparamilitary laws, it must understand the different layers and types of bigotry within these private armies.

First, many of the movers and shakers of the militia movement are anti-Semites. Consider John Trochmann, the founder of the first active American militia, and his connections to the Aryan Nations and Christian Identity beliefs; Bo Gritz and his anti-Semitism; the Estes Park meeting called by Christian Identity leader Pete Peters; the national role of *Spotlight* and other white supremacist organs, all promoting the movement. These professional haters were, and continue to be, crucial to the growth of the militias.

Second, it would be nearly impossible to attend any militia meeting in the United States, even one run by a group without an anti-Semitic history or agenda, and not encounter literature from anti-Semitic and white supremacist individuals and groups: Bo Gritz; the *Spotlight*; Christian Identity; Lyndon LaRouche. To use, once again, Ken Toole's metaphor of the funnel: Once you enter the large side, having been sucked in by gun control, you are exposed to the other ideas swirling about, promoted by your new "friends." What with speakers at meetings, literature on tables, computer forums, and shortwave programs, your universe now includes people who promote racism and anti-Semitism. Such ideas become safer, less remarkable, no longer subject to taboo, believable, part of "the explanation."

Third, as discussed before, the ideas of "states' rights" and "county supremacy" that fuel so much of the militia movement are covers for bigotry. The former has always been used to shield local governments from criticism over discriminatory practices. The latter is the idea of the Posse Comitatus, that the white, Christian males who make up the Posse (or, now, predominate in the militia) have special rights and protections beyond those of other American citizens. Most militia literature regarding county supremacy won't come out and say this in so many words, but the Posse ideology is undeniably central to much of the militia movement. You don't want to make the county sheriff the highest legitimate government official if you are concerned about building an egalitarian society.

Fourth, the conspiracy theories that underlie the movement are rooted in the *Protocols of the Elders of Zion*. The militia folk believe that an "unseen hand" is pulling the strings of government, forcing Americans into a One World Government that will serve foreign interests. The *Protocols* posits that Jews are secretly plotting to run the world. The idea is identical, although militia leaders are careful to talk about "international bankers" or the "Federal Reserve" or the "Trilateral Commission" or "eastern elites." But these are code phrases, carefully picked by the leadership, to pull people into their movement without greeting them with overt anti-Semitism.

Historically, Jews have not fared well around conspiracy theories. Such ideas fuel anti-Semitism. The myths that Jews killed Christ, or poisoned wells, or killed Christian children to bake matzo, or "made up" the Holocaust, or plot to control the world, do not succeed each other; rather, the list of anti-Semitic canards gets longer. The militia movement today believes in the conspiracy theory of the *Protocols*, even if some call it something else and never mention Jews. From the perspective of history, we know that this is just the type of climate in which anti-Semitism can grow. It is not a difficult leap—and many have already made it—from the "unseen hand" to the Jewish people. Mass movements that dabble in anti-Semitism in whatever form are dangerous, not only to Jews but to the fabric of democracy.

Something else is going on, too. Coupled with the hatred of the federal government that the militias preach is malice toward the government employee—especially the federal employee. And that hatred is couched in old-fashioned terms of bigotry. Who in America today would tolerate a sign that refused service to blacks or Jews? But in Burns, Oregon, you can find stores that refuse service to federal employees. Some public servants living in areas where there are militia or militia-linked "patriotic" or Wise Use groups are being shunned at church. Their children are avoided by classmates and some have even been threatened with death.

Part of what is new in the militia movement is that it has come in the post-Soviet world. We no longer have an "evil empire" on which to focus, so the search for evil has turned within. This new form of prejudice has co-opted the dehumanizing and stereotyping attributes of gutter bigotry and turned them on our public servants, who are seen not as doing the work of America—delivering the mail, clearing Forest Service roads, protecting the environment and wildlife, maintaining the interstate highway system, helping lost campers—but as doing the work of "the beast." The extreme of that dehumanizing bigotry was displayed on April 19, 1995, in Oklahoma City.

There are things we can and should do about the militias. One is to prosecute those who are breaking laws banning private armies, and to pass and enforce such laws in jurisdictions that do not have them. But that is only the start.

The social issues the militias use as a "funnel" are real, and it is incumbent upon local groups, elected officials, and others to get to the people hovering at the wide end and steer them away from the hate of militias, show them that the American political process, for all its flaws, really does work.

Local elected officials and ordinary citizens who are threatened must be defended and the intimidation of the militias opposed by the community, the press, politicians, and law enforcement. When groups preaching hate are allowed to act like bullies, the community as a whole must make such behavior unacceptable. Otherwise the bullies become bolder. Newspaper editors, business leaders, sheriffs, elected officials, sports figures, and others have to lend their voices, to speak out against the hatred and the implicit and explicit threats of violence from these private armies.

In Billings, Montana, shortly before the militia movement began, a hate group shattered the bedroom window of a young Jewish boy. Wayne Inman, the local police chief, galvanized the community. With the help of Wayne Schile, the *Billings Gazette*'s publisher, paper menorahs were printed. People were encouraged to display them in their windows as a sign of solidarity and a rejection of bigotry. I asked Inman, "What do you tell people who want to help, but are afraid that displaying the menorah will make them and their children targets, too?" He said, "I tell them the more people that put them up, the less chance that anything will happen to any particular family."

To make such statements against bigotry is, or should be, the easy thing. More difficult is to have a comprehensive theoretical understanding of what to do about hate. The sad fact is that no one knows. Throughout history, people have found ways to divide, call people "other," and kill them. Regardless of epoch, region, geography, economic system, religion, and political structure, people have always managed to indulge in hate. Sometimes hatred becomes state ideology, and genocide results. In the 1800s, in America, Colonel John M. Chivington explained at public forums why Indian babies had to be killed: "Nits make lice," he said. During the Armenian genocide of the early 1900s, Taalat Pasha, a Turkish leader, was asked why innocents had to be killed; he explained: "Those who are innocent today might be guilty tomorrow." During the Nazi era Jewish and Gypsy babies were killed. In the 1990s you could listen to Khalid Muhammad of the Nation of Islam explaining why not only white adults but also white babies in South Africa might have to be killed. Watch the news about Bosnia, where babies are killed. Listen to the death threats against public officials by some linked to the militias; the officials' babies are targeted, too. Look at the pictures of the day care center in Oklahoma City. The babies were killed, too.

Whenever an ideology justifies baby-killing—even at the fringes of the fringes—that is an especially strong danger signal. That much we know. It is astonishing to think that here we sit at the approach of a new millennium—the first to be entered with weapons of mass destruction and immediate global communication—and yet we still know precious little about human hate, something that has harmed more people throughout history than any other cause. Hatred is the one basic component of existence about which we are essentially ignorant.

People need housing, so we have schools of architecture. People get sick, so we have schools of medicine. But there is no comprehensive field of study devoted to the most serious of human conditions, hate. Yes, there are bits and pieces of learning in political science, literature, sociology, history, anthropology, psychology, philosophy, religion. But there is no overarching intellectual framework, no vocabulary to discuss the subject. There is no college from which you can graduate today with a degree in hate. But there should be.

We tend to define people as being bigots or not, as if there were a switch that could be turned on and off. Gary E. Rubin, executive director of Americans for Peace Now and one of the brightest thinkers in America today, challenged that notion. He complained about polls that defined a particular percentage of Americans as racist or anti-Semitic. The fact is, Mr. Rubin said, that while few people are one hundred percent racist or anti-Semitic, most harbor some prejudice, and rather than measuring just those who are "prejudiced" and those who are "not," we should be measuring the *relative* level of bigotry throughout society.

That observation applies to militias, too. It makes sense to be concerned about the militias' leaders and those who are at the small end of Ken Toole's funnel. But those who are hovering near the large end are important, too, if we are to understand how the movement has grown, and what its growth says about our society and about the dangers of hatred turned inward, against ourselves.

If we had a theory about how hate works, we could make reasonable estimates, not only about what to do, but about the prognosis. Sometimes, in history, when the fringes threaten the mainstream, the mainstream absorbs the fringe issues, trying to co-opt the danger. That happened recently in Germany: When neo-Nazis began assaulting and killing immigrants, the government curbed immigration. But neo-Nazis remain a force in Germany. What will happen in America? If there are "retreats" on environmental protection and gun control—even if the retreats are based on the merits of these issues without regard to the reaction of the militias—will that co-opt the private armies, or make them stronger?

How important is the movement's identification with the Branch Davidians and Randy Weaver, both of whom began their sieges with shoot-outs involving government officials? The heated rhetoric, the heavy arming, the preparation for a showdown with government suggest that many militia members want to refight Waco and Ruby Ridge. Is this comparable to a street gang accepting the myth of some perceived injustice to a long-ago member, and plotting revenge by reenactment? What do we really know about the mass psychology of groups that have violent tragedies as their icons?

How do competing ideas of political allegiance play in the world of conspiracy and hate? For instance, Jack McLamb claims:

> No person can be loyal to the Constitution for [sic] the United States AND uphold the Charter of the United Nations. They are as opposite as light and dark, good and evil, freedom and slavery, God and Satan. *No man can serve two masters.* Support of the United Nations by government officials and employees is a violation of their Oath. Wittingly or unwittingly, it is treasonous.

What about allegiances to country versus state, state versus county, or county versus municipality, to say nothing of concepts of group and religion—how do these variables affect hate? Add to these questions a new phenomenon with militias. Their ideology defines our government's public servants (and their children) from whichever group as being outside the social compact, while defining militia members as the "true" members of society, with the "patriotic" right and duty to impose their vision on America with guns. What are the implications of this twist in identity, that victimizes people on the basis of their jobs?

While grassroots groups, civil rights organizations, ordinary citizens, and our government are countering the impact of militias in America by doing what we know how to do—speaking out against hate remains the most important thing that we know *does* work—some university or think tank or foundation should convene the leading minds in the related fields, and give them a task: What would a field of study of hate look like? The answer to that question, with theories and a vocabulary and case studies to show what increases or diminishes hate inside and outside of politics, and why, is long overdue. A greater understanding of human hate would be the best memorial for Chase and Colton Smith, Baylee Almon, and the others who died of that human disease on April 19, 1995, in Oklahoma City, Oklahoma, the United States of America.

Postscript

THIS IS A FREEDOM-LOVING DEMOCRACY
BECAUSE THE RULE OF LAW HAS REIGNED
FOR OVER TWO HUNDRED YEARS NOW—NOT
BECAUSE VIGILANTES TOOK THE LAW INTO
THEIR OWN HANDS.

PRESIDENT BILL CLINTON

On May 2, 1995, Charles Harrison Barbee and Robert Sherman Berry were arrested in Kelso, Washington, with a 9mm Cobray M-11 pistol, ammunition, and a silencer, as well as "chunks of C-4 plastic explosive and two 32-ounce beer bottles that appeared to be homemade bombs, other guns, survival gear, police scanners, marijuana and more than 100 silver bars and coins," according to the *Bonner County* (Idaho) *Daily Bee*. Both men were reported to be members of the Idaho Citizens Awareness Network (ICAN), a group associated with Christian Identity leaders and neo-Nazis. According to the *Longview* (Washington) *Daily News*, Barbee's landlord said that Barbee was part of a local militia group, "a leaderless cell of four to seven men who would get together once in a while and strategize about what would happen should something happen."

On May 13, 1995, a little-noticed news story appeared in the *Columbus*

(Ohio) *Dispatch*. The dateline was Lancaster, Ohio. Larry Wayne Harris, a reported member of the Aryan Nations, had been arrested. Blasting caps, primer cord, and fuses were found in his house. In the glove compartment of Harris's car were three vials of bubonic plague bacteria.

On June 28, 1995, fifty-year-old Michael H. Hill was driving in Frazeysburg, Ohio, where Sergeant Matt May of the Muskingum County Sheriff's Office stopped him. Hill's car had no official license plate, just a homemade one reading, "Militia." May asked Hill to get back into his car, which he did. Then Hill sped off. May followed. Hill stopped, got out of his car, and reportedly pointed a gun at May, holding it in a shooting stance, with two hands. May fired, killing Hill.

On July 5, 1995, twenty-seven-year-old Darwin Michael Gray was arrested in Spokane, Washington, on suspicion of plotting to blow up a government building. Gray was reportedly a "visible and vocal opponent of the Federal agents at Ruby Ridge" and had ties to the Aryan Nations. He knew Randy Weaver and was Kevin Harris's stepbrother. Gray allegedly stole blueprints to the U.S. courthouse in Spokane from his employer, a company that had installed the building's insulation. According to court papers, "Gray and another individual were involved in the manufacture and testing of destructive devices, more specifically, fertilizer bombs."

On July 30, 1995, five hundred pounds of explosives were stolen from the Lucky Friday mine in the Idaho panhandle. Kent Allen Johnson, thirty-one, a reported member of an Idaho militia group, was charged with the theft. Sources said Johnson and his compatriots intended to sell the explosives to a Canadian group that planned to blow up a dam.

On September 12, 1995, Charles Ray Polk was charged with planning to blow up an Internal Revenue Service regional center office in Tyler, Texas. At peak times nearly four thousand people worked in that building. Described as "outspoken" about his belief that the government should be attacked, Polk had been trying to buy more than a thousand pounds of C-4 explosives. The local U.S. Attorney said Polk had links to militia groups.

On October 9, 1995, an Amtrak train with 268 people aboard was sabotaged in the Arizona desert, near Hyder. Spikes were removed, an alarm system bypassed, and the train derailed, killing one and injuring scores. A note was found at the scene, supposedly from the "Sons of Gestapo," complaining about Ruby Ridge and Waco. Because of the militialike references and the possibility that "Sons of Gestapo" was a play on "Satanic Occupational Government," a Christian Identity version of "Zionist Occupational Government," some speculated that militia members might be involved. Not so, said Jack McLamb. According to the Mesa, Arizona, *Tribune*, "McLamb . . . said the derailment . . . could be part of an organized terror campaign meant to . . . heighten fears and make the public more receptive to a repressive government crackdown."

✗ ✗ ✗

It wasn't in *The New York Times*, or even on page one of the May 7, 1995, *Daily Inter Lake*, a northwestern Montana newspaper. On page D-4, surrounded by ads for tree pruning, mountainside developers, and high-pressure cleaning services, was the headline "Townsfolk Tired of Militia," dateline Noxon.

The town was still being overrun by media back then. Japanese TV. Danish TV. French TV. CBS. ABC. *The Washington Post. The London Independent. The Calgary Sun.* They had all come to interview John Trochmann. The townsfolk were not tired of the press, but of the militia leader.

An unsigned flyer appeared under the windshield wipers of cars parked at the town's only motel:

> The reason we say "WE WANT OUR TOWN BACK" is because once all the stories hit your papers across the nation, you will be gone. We will be here having to live with the aftershock of all the publicity being given to the militia. We fear the type of people this coverage may draw to our community. Many locals avoid speaking out because they are intimidated by the militia. But before you leave, try to uncover what makes the heart of the community tick. There is [sic] two sides to every story. Just remember that.

Joyce Coupal, a retired nurse, had to do more. Trochmann was having a press conference. She walked across Noxon's park and stood near the reporters. She called out to Trochmann. She told him he was irrational, saying things without any proof. There was the time he said the Thompson Falls jail was irradiated because, after he spent time there, some of his hair fell out. And there were the comments he made while square-dancing—saying, for example, that only white male landowners should be able to vote.

Coupal looked away from Trochmann, toward the reporters. "John makes a good neighbor," she said. "He's a good person, but the kind of stuff I hear going out is very dangerous. Belgian police wandering around in the woods, Hong Kong police training in New Orleans . . . it's paranoia."

The press conference ended. Another neighbor, Jill Davies, hugged Coupal. Reporters spoke to them both. Davies said: "I think our whole country should be afraid of what they are creating. They're creating a situation where the federal government has to get tougher. . . . It's madness. We need to be afraid of our own apathy in this situation."

"He told me there's a basement full of gold brick in New York City," Coupal said, "and the Jews control money all over the world. Oh, I think [he's anti-Semitic], but he'll deny it. He'll deny being a racist."

"When he first came here," Rod Gallaway, Davies's husband, added, "he was preaching white supremacy. I think this is just the same thing in a different form."

"These madmen," Davies said, imploring the reporters to listen, "do not represent us."

Acknowledgments

A Force upon the Plain could not have been written without the support of many extraordinary people, each of whom I owe a tremendous debt. Any mistakes, of course, are my own.

First, an enormous thanks to Margie, Daniel, and Emily, who put up with a husband and father who not only had to write a book quickly, but also had to keep his day job. I'm blessed to have such a wonderful and supportive family. Margie only grumbled every five days or so—this makes her a model of patience, given the load that fell on her. Daniel made a wish in a wishing well that "Daddy didn't have to work." For a three-year-old to express his feelings like that made me proud, but did nothing for my sense of guilt. Emily, at one, I hope, didn't notice much of a difference.

Thanks also to my mother, Dr. Gertrude Stern, and her sister, Terry Frank, who let me invade their house with computers and thousands of scattered pieces of paper—and who came by and helped the kids feel less of a loss. My mother also helped by reading the manuscript. I owe a special debt to my sister, Alice, who not only was thrilled by the prospect of this book, but who also came up with the title. "I don't know what it means," she said, "but I like it."

A singular thanks to my agent, Suzanne Gluck, who immediately understood the importance of this book and made the match with Simon & Schuster in less than a week; to Susan Jensen and Marsinay Smith, Suzanne's able assistants; and to Bob Mecoy, my editor, who not only greatly improved the text, but with whom it was a pleasure to work and to trade e-mail. And thanks to his helpful and friendly assistant, Brian McSharry, and to Simon & Schuster's Victoria Meyer, Leslie Ellen, Jolanta Benal, Sarah Eaton, and Joseph Jerome. Every author should be so lucky to work with such a team.

This book would have been markedly inferior without the assistance of one person whom I have yet to meet: Dan Yurman. Through the miracle of e-mail he kept me informed of key events in the militia movement.

Dan is also a model of what one person can accomplish—a man with a computer, in Idaho Falls, collecting and sending important information to people all over the world.

Many of my colleagues at the American Jewish Committee were excited by and supportive of this project. Special thanks go to Sandy Gandelman and Sondra Beaulieu, who not only gave me encouragement but also ran interference. Sondra also read part of the manuscript and provided excellent suggestions. Thanks also to Harriet Abrahm, Joyce Ackerman, Mimi Alperin, Michele Anish, Shula Bahat, Andy Baker, Arthur Berger, Rosalyn Borg, Carol Buglio, Joan Canner, Joel Cohen, Renae Cohen, Steven Derfler, Gene DuBow, Lisa Eisen, Nikki Fish, Richard Foltin, Sherry Frank, Frederick Frank, Anita Fricklas, Murray Friedman, Fran McDermott Fox, Allyson Gall, Rebecca Galler, Marlene Glickman, Barbara Glueck, Doris Goldman, David Goldstein, Jenny Golub, Bob Goodkind, Bill Gralnick, Gary Greenebaum, Larry Grossman, David Harris, Judy Hellman, Cyma Horowitz, Barbara Hurst, Janice Hyman-Wolpo, Jason Isaacson, Nancy Israel, Marc Ittelson, Judith Kahn, Rachel Kalikow, Minto Keaton, Andrea Klausner, Miriam Kleiman, Shirley Kohn, Bob Kravitz, Linda Krieg, Linda Lansky, Larry Lebow, Jon Levine, Larry Lowenthal, Aryeh Meir, Martin Plax, Sam Rabinove, Lucy Ramsay, Andrea Rifkind, Helen Ritter, Lois Rosenfield, Geri Rozanski, Jim Rudin, Suzanne Sachnowitz, Micky Sadoff, Neil Sandberg, Ann Schaffer, Elinor Schuman, Sharona Shapiro, Joan Silverman, David Singer, Stephen Steinlight, Diane Steinman, Sunny Stern, Darrel Strelitz, Ellen Vendeland, Nancy Vineberg, Ernie Weiner, Jeff Weintraub, Barbara Wohlander, Dotty Woodland, Herb Zuckerman; and to my former AJC colleagues Milton Ellerin, Lori Forman, Wendy Lecker, Karen Paul, Gary Rubin, David Saltman; and to David Roth, who passed away while this book was being written.

Chip Berlet of Political Research Associates is also owed a special thanks. He helped me ferret out important information from around the country.

I was also fortunate to have the critical help, penetrating analysis, and friendship of Lenny Zeskind and Danny Levitas; Tom Halperin and Marvin Stern of the Anti-Defamation League; Bill Wassmuth, Eric Ward, and Gretchen Henry of the Northwest Coalition Against Malicious Harassment; Loretta Ross of the Center for Democratic Renewal; Al Ross and Sandi Dubowski of Planned Parenthood; Jonathan Mozzochi, Steve Gardner, and Robert Crawford of the Coalition for Human Dignity; Ken Toole, Marlene Hines, Christine Kaufmann, and Mark Nagasawa of the Montana Human Rights Network; Jay Tcath of the Minneapolis Federation's Community Relations Council; and Bernie Farber of the Canadian Jewish Congress.

In the days following Timothy McVeigh's arrest, I was deluged with phone calls from reporters because of my April 10 report on the militia movement. I was impressed, as were my fellow "experts," at how quickly the press picked up the essence of the militia movement. This was American journalism at its best, and I was gratified, as were other militia-watchers, to find our story ideas and analytical suggestions followed—in fact, vastly improved upon—by the media. When it came time for me to write this book, the roles were reversed. I relied heavily on the best investigative journalists for insights, feedback, and information. Their contributions to A Force upon the Plain are self-evident and are reflected in the source notes. I thank them all—four especially. Bill Morlin of the Spokane Spokesman Review got me up to speed quickly on the intricacies of the Weaver case. Jim Redden of PDXS shared his excellent material and insights about Linda Thompson. Serge Kovaleski of The Washington Post was a good sounding board and his writing was the best I saw on the militia movement—particularly his profile of Terry Nichols. And most especially, thanks to my good friend Larry Cohler of New York Jewish Week. He wanted to know whom to speak to about militias in Idaho and Montana. I gave him phone numbers; he brought back a treasure trove of primary materials.

Thanks also to Kathy McKay; without her enthusiasm and organizing, my May 1994 trip to Montana, my resulting interest in militias, and thus this book would not have happened. Thanks also to Jeremy Jones in Australia, Doug Heiken of the Association of Forest Service Employees for Environmental Ethics, Bernadette Baker, David Bellel, Joe Berger, Erin Berger, Stephanie Berger, Dan Berry, Esta Bigler, Matthew Bigler-McCorkell, Nathan Bigler-McCorkell, Tom Burghardt, Devin Burghart, Joan Clark, Tad Cook, Mary Daley, Allison Daly, Paul deArmond, Jeff DeBonis, Jon Ellenbogen, Natalie Fisher and her family, Pat Foster, Wendy Friedman, Susan Garvin, Bill Guis, Michael Harrison, Dennis Henigan, Muriel Hogan, Dan Junas, Kathleen Lane, Jack Lang y Marquez, Bob Lerch, Rachel Lerch, Mary Lerner and her family, Paul Lindholdt, John Lunsford, Betsy Malloy, Ralph Maughan, Charlie McCorkell, Sybil Milton, V. Annette Murphy, Thomas Ortner, Gerald Post, Emma Queener, Lorraine Queener, Madeline Queener, Steven Queener, Tarso Ramos, Judge James A. Redden, Jim Redden, Mike Reynolds, Bob Rowe, Brian Schnitzer and his family, Shelly Shapiro, Nancy Slome, Alfred Wallace, and Marcy Westerling.

And, finally, a special thanks to the Alpine Motel in North Creek, New York. Many remarked on the timing of my AJC militia report, released less than two weeks before the Oklahoma City tragedy. Few heard about my sojourn into the Adirondack Mountains to finish the first draft of this book. The morning of my arrival a severe storm struck, killing six campers and leaving random swatches of the Adirondacks looking like clear-cuts. My rented house would have been a perfect writer's setting—but without electricity for four days, it was useless. The Alpine Motel came to my rescue.

Appendix

The ADL Model Statute reads:

Paramilitary Training

A. (1) Whoever teaches or demonstrates to any other person the use, application, or making of any firearm, explosive, or incendiary device, or technique capable of causing injury or death to persons, knowing, or having reason to know or intending that same will be unlawfully employed for use in, or in furtherance of, a civil disorder; or

(2) Whoever assembles with one or more persons for the purpose of training with, practicing with, or being instructed in the use of any firearm, explosive or incendiary device, or technique capable of causing injury or death to persons, intending to employ unlawfully the same for use in, or in furtherance of, a civil disorder—

Shall be fined not more than $——— or imprisoned not more than ——— years, or both.

B. Nothing in this section shall make unlawful any act of any law enforcement officer which is performed in the lawful performance of his official duties.

C. As used in this section:

(1) The term "civil disorder" means any public disturbance involving acts of violence by assemblages of three or more persons, which causes an immediate danger of or results in damage or injury to the property or person of any other individual.

(2) The term "firearm" means any weapon which is designed to or may readily be converted to expel any projectile by the action of an explosive; or the frame or receiver of any such weapon.

(3) The term "explosive or incendiary device" means (a) dynamite and all other forms of high explosives, (b) any explosive bomb, grenade, missile, or similar device, and (c) any incendiary bomb or grenade, fire bomb, or similar device, including any device which (i) consists of or includes a breakable container including a flammable liquid or compound, and a wick composed of any material which, when ignited, is capable of igniting such flammable liquid or compound, and (ii) can be carried or thrown by one individual acting alone.

(4) The term "law enforcement officer" means any officer or employee of the United States, any state, any political subdivision of a state, or the District of Columbia, and such term shall specifically include, but shall not be limited to,

members of the National Guard, as defined in section 101(9) of title 10, United States Code, members of the organized militia of any state or territory of the United States, the Commonwealth of Puerto Rico, or the District of Columbia, not included within the definition of National Guard as defined by such section 101(9), and members of the Armed Forces of the United States.

Proposed Federal Anti-Paramilitary-Training Statute

A. No body of men and/or women, other than the regularly organized military forces of a state or of the United States, shall associate themselves together as a military or paramilitary company or organization, or conduct training as a military or paramilitary company or organization in the use, application, or construction of any firearm, explosive, or incendiary device, capable of causing injury or death to persons, or parade in public with firearms in any village, city or town; provided that students in educational institutions where military science is a prescribed part of the course of instruction, and veterans honorably discharged from the military forces of the United States may, with the consent of a state, drill and parade with firearms in public. Nothing herein shall be construed to prevent parades by the active militia of any state.

B. Any person or persons violating this section shall be fined not more than ten thousand dollars ($10,000), or imprisoned for not more than five years, or both. For purposes of this section:

(1) The term "firearm" means any weapon which is designed to or may readily be converted to expel any projectile by the action of an explosive; or the frame or receiver of any such weapon.

(2) The term "explosive or incendiary device" means (A) dynamite and all other forms of high explosives, (B) any explosive bomb, grenade, missile, or similar device, including any device which (i) consists of or includes a breakable container including a flammable liquid or compound, and a wick composed of any material which, when ignited, is capable of igniting such flammable liquid or compound, and (ii) can be carried or thrown by one individual acting alone.

(3) The term "military company or organization" means an organized group of persons who are trained and armed for the purpose of engaging in combat, warfare, or sabotage.

(4) The term "paramilitary company or organization" means an organized group of persons, resembling or akin to a military organization, formed on a military pattern as an auxiliary or diversionary group, and trained and armed for the purpose of engaging in combat, warfare, or sabotage.

Sources

Sources for A *Force upon the Plain* included both primary and secondary material. Rather than burden the text with hundreds of footnotes per chapter, I have listed my major sources here. They are arranged by chapter in alphabetical order by author — or, where no author is given, by source. The sources listed for Chapters 1 and 2 are combined, since most of the material regarding the Weaver siege was used in both chapters.

Much of the primary source material regarding the Minutemen, the Posse Comitatus, the Militia of Montana, and so on, is archived at the American Jewish Committee. All Internet postings are also archived at the AJC, in the file "Militias 94–95."

Sources for Introduction

Associated Press. "Blast Rips Fed Office Site," April 19, 1995.
————. "36 Dead in Oklahoma Bombing," April 20, 1995.
Belluck, Pam. "Terror in Oklahoma: The Victims; Identifying Injured Loved Ones by Clues of Hair and Birthmarks," *The New York Times*, April 21, 1995.
Bragg, Rick. "Terror in Oklahoma City: At Ground Zero," *The New York Times*, April 20, 1995.
Dees, Morris. "Emergency Update on Militia Terrorists," letter of Militia Task Force of the Southern Poverty Law Center, undated (circa August 1995).
Foster, J. Todd, and Bill Morlin. "Weaver Discusses Surrender," *Spokane Spokesman-Review*, August 30, 1992.
Herbert, Bob. "In America: The Terrorists Failed," *The New York Times*, April 22, 1995.
Jackson, Derrick Z. "The Heartbeat of Hate," *The Baltimore Sun*, May 15, 1995.
Johnston, David. "Terror in Oklahoma City: The Investigation; At Least 31 Are Dead, Scores Are Missing After Car Bomb Attack in Oklahoma City," *The New York Times*, April 20, 1995.
Kenworthy, Tom, and George Lardner, Jr. "The Militias: Guns and Bitter; Federal Push to Rein in Arms Sparked Fire of Resentment Among Owners," *The Washington Post*, May 4, 1995.
Kifner, John. "Terror in Oklahoma City: The Overview—At Least 31 Are Dead, Scores Are Missing After Car Bomb Attack in Oklahoma City Wrecks 9-Story Office Building," *The New York Times*, April 20, 1995.
Levitas, Daniel. "Antisemitism and the Far Right: 'Hate' Groups, White Supremacy, and the Neo-Nazi Movement," in Jerome Chanes, ed., *Antisemitism in America Today: Outspoken Experts Explode the Myths*. New York: Birch Lane Press, 1995.

Newsweek. "The Dead," May 8, 1995.

Stern, Kenneth S. *Militias: A Growing Danger.* New York: American Jewish Committee, 1995.

Vick, Karl. "Quiet Descends as Recovery Efforts Cease; Final Oklahoma City Death Toll Stands at 167 as Rescuers Struggle with Emotions," *The Washington Post,* May 6, 1995.

Walsh, Edward. "One Arraigned, Two Undergo Questioning," *The Washington Post,* April 22, 1995.

Sources for Chapters 1 and 2

Abrams, Joan. "Can Bo Gritz Save America?" *Lewiston* (Idaho) *Morning Tribune,* September 17, 1992.

Ashton, Linda. "Weaver Wounded in Shootout Last Week," Associated Press, August 30, 1992.

―――. "North Idaho Standoff Continues as Wounded Friend of Fugitive Surrenders," Associated Press, August 31, 1992.

―――. "Bo Gritz, Ex–Green Beret, Negotiated an End to Standoff," Associated Press, September 2, 1992.

Associated Press. "Feds Wary of Fugitive in Mountaintop Hideout," March 10, 1992; "Mountaintop Fugitive Says He Will Not Give Up," May 4, 1992; "Standoff with Fugitive Racist Enters Third Day," August 24, 1992; "Standoff Continues Between Fugitive, Feds," August 25, 1992; "Authorities Seek Peaceful Resolution to Tense Standoff," August 26, 1992; "Chronology in Standoff with Fugitive," September 1, 1992.

Atlanta Journal and Constitution. "Marshals Bide Their Time in Capturing Fugitive White Supremacist in Idaho," March 13, 1992.

Bovard, James. "Overkill: When Government Abuses Power, Is It an Accident or Murder?" *Playboy,* June 3, 1995.

Center for Action Newsletter, vol. 3, no. 6 (January 1994).

Center for Democratic Renewal. *The Monitor,* December 1991.

Chicago Tribune. "Man Wounded in Idaho Siege Surrenders," August 31, 1992.

Coakley, Tom. "Colleague Recalls Battle That Took Life," *The Boston Globe,* August 27, 1992.

―――. "Marshal Recalls Day Friend Died and Standoff Began," *Spokane Spokesman-Review,* August 31, 1992.

Coalition for Human Dignity. *Northwest Imperative,* November 1994.

Coates, James. "Idaho Siege Might Fuel Neo-Nazis," *Chicago Tribune,* August 30, 1992.

Columbus (Ohio) *Dispatch.* "Gritz's Pal Says U.S. Is Meddling," October 12, 1992.

Dawson, Diane. "Slain Marshal Specialized in Dangerous Missions," *Spokane Spokesman-Review,* August 23, 1992.

Drumheller, Susan. "Local Businesses Thrive During Time of Trouble," *Spokane Spokesman-Review,* August 26, 1992.

―――. "Supremacists' Wives Recall Another Standoff," *Spokane Spokesman-Review,* August 31, 1992.

―――. "Towns Try to Return to Normal," *Spokane Spokesman-Review,* September 1, 1992.

Dunn, Ashley. "Mountain Standoff Rallies Idaho Cradle of the Fringe," *Los Angeles Times,* August 28, 1992.

The Economist. "Persecution Complex," September 5, 1992.

Egan, Timothy. "Fugitive in Idaho Cabin Plays Role of Folk Hero," *The New York Times*, August 26, 1992.

————. "Hate Groups Hanging On in Idaho Haven," *The New York Times*, August 30, 1992.

————. "White Supremacist Surrenders After 11-Day Siege," *The New York Times*, September 1, 1992.

Fisher, Jim. "Idaho's Lure to Randy Weaver, Home Schooler," *Lewiston* (Idaho) *Morning Tribune*, September 1, 1992.

Foster, J. Todd. " 'He Told Me He Wasn't Coming Down,' Says Counselor Who Met with Weaver," *Spokane Spokesman-Review*, August 22, 1992.

————. "Concerned Father Admits Crossing Police Line," *Spokane Spokesman-Review*, August 25, 1992.

————. "Letters Show Family Would Die for Beliefs," *Spokane Spokesman-Review*, August 26, 1992.

————. "Neighbor Taunted for Hosting Feds," *Spokane Spokesman-Review*, August 27, 1992.

————. "Document Predicted Deadly Confrontation," *Spokane Spokesman-Review*, August 28, 1992.

————. "Ex-Judge Scared of Weaver," *Spokane Spokesman-Review*, August 29, 1992.

————. "Shed Where Boy's Body Found Was Birthplace of Sister Last Fall," *Spokane Spokesman-Review*, August 29, 1992.

————, and Kevin Keating. "Harris' Parents Say Son's Been Framed," *Spokane Spokesman-Review*, August 24, 1992.

Freeland, Jonathan. "Adolf's U.S. Army," *The Guardian*, December 15, 1994.

Fusion, Ken. "Survivor of Mountain Shootout Can Neither Forgive nor Forget," Gannett News Service, September 22, 1992.

Gleick, Elizabeth. "Fighting to the Death," *People*, September 14, 1992.

Gritz, Bo. *Called to Serve*. Sandy Valley, Nev.: Lazarus Publishing Co., 1991.

Guthrey, Molly. "Judge Defends Decision to Free Weaver," *Spokane Spokesman-Review*, August 29, 1992.

————. "Northern Idaho's Image Casualty of Standoff," *Spokane Spokesman-Review*, August 30, 1992.

Hall, Bill. "It's Reason vs. Violence on an Idaho Mountain," *Lewiston* (Idaho) *Morning Tribune*, August 27, 1992.

Junas, Dan. "Rise of the Citizen Militias—Angry White Guys with Guns," *Covert Action Quarterly*, Spring 1995.

Keating, Kevin. "Parents Fear for Life of Son Who Lives in Fugitive's Cabin," *Spokane Spokesman-Review*, August 23, 1992.

————. "Ruby Creek Evacuees Say Red Cross Not Helping," *Spokane Spokesman-Review*, August 24, 1992.

————. "Agents Not Sure Who Killed Boy," *Spokane Spokesman-Review*, August 26, 1992.

————. "Boundary County Schools to Open Today After Delay," *Spokane Spokesman-Review*, August 31, 1992.

————. "Die-Hard Protesters Keep Roadblock Vigil," *Spokane Spokesman-Review*, September 1, 1992.

————, and J. Todd Foster. "Rural Peace Shattered—and Some Blame Feds," *Spokane Spokesman-Review*, August 22, 1992.

————, J. Todd Foster, and Jess Walter. "Weaver Makes Contact," *Spokane Spokesman-Review*, August 27, 1992.

Kelly, Michael. "The Road to Paranoia," *The New Yorker*, June 19, 1995.

McBride, Kelly. "Weaver Was Target of Arms Sting," *Spokane Spokesman-Review*, August 26, 1992.

————. "Federal Firearms Laws Labeled Valuable Tool," *Spokane Spokesman-Review*, August 28, 1992.

McGrory, Brian. "Slain Hub U.S. Marshal Recalled as Among Best," *The Boston Globe*, August 23, 1992.

————. "Friend of Idaho Fugitive Is Accused of Killing Marshal," *The Boston Globe*, August 24, 1992.

————. "In Idaho, a Wider Standoff: Many in Hills See Fugitive as Victim," *The Boston Globe*, August 24, 1992.

————. "Using a Robot, FBI Establishes Phone Link with Idaho Fugitive," *The Boston Globe*, August 27, 1992.

Miller, Dean. "No Winners in Siege, Says Marshal," *Spokane Spokesman-Review*, September 1, 1992.

Morlin, Bill. "Agents Arrest Ex-Candidate," *Spokane Spokesman-Review*, January 19, 1992.

————. "Feds Have Fugitive 'Under Our Nose,'" *Spokane Spokesman-Review*, March 8, 1992.

————. "Copter Crew Claims Shots Fired as It Flew Over Fugitive's Cabin," *Spokane Spokesman-Review*, April 23, 1992.

————. "Authorities Brace for Long Wait," *Spokane Spokesman-Review*, August 23, 1992.

————. "Charges Filed in Marshal's Killing," *Spokane Spokesman-Review*, August 24, 1992.

————. "Roadblock Scene Gets Ugly After Bars Close," *Spokane Spokesman-Review*, August 24, 1992.

————. "Agents Find Body of Fugitive's Son," *Spokane Spokesman-Review*, August 25, 1992.

————. "Weaver Wanted to Arm Gangs, Informer Claims," *Spokane Spokesman-Review*, August 28, 1992.

————. "FBI Turned to Right Man for Unorthodox Job," *Spokane Spokesman-Review*, September 1, 1992.

————, and Kevin Keating. "Five Skinheads Arrested with Arsenal of Weapons," *Spokane Spokesman-Review*, August 26, 1992.

————, Kevin Keating, and J. Todd Foster. "Two Other Lawmen Rescued; Fugitive's Cabin Surrounded," *Spokane Spokesman-Review*, August 22, 1992.

————, and Jesse Walter. "Weaver-Harris Letter Tells Their Version of Gunfights," *Spokane Spokesman-Review*, August 31, 1992.

National Public Radio. "White Supremacist Barricaded in Idaho," *All Things Considered*, August 28, 1992; *Morning Edition*, August 26, 1992; "Barricaded Supremacist Weaver Gives Up," *All Things Considered*, August 31, 1992.

The New York Times. "Marshals Know He's There but Leave Fugitive Alone," March 13, 1992; "Federal Marshal Is Slain in Idaho Near Mountain Home of Fugitive," August 22, 1992; "1 Marshal Dead, Others Confront Fugitive in Idaho," August 23, 1992; "Negotiator Arouses Hope in Idaho Standoff," August 30, 1992; "Fugitive's Friend Gives Up in Idaho," August 31, 1992.

Norton, Dee. "Weaver Backed, 'Feds' Ripped—Area Residents React to Standoff," *Seattle Times*, August 24, 1992.

————. "Fugitive Guards Family, Beliefs Atop Sheer Cliff," *Seattle Times*, August 25, 1992.

————. "Weaver's Son May Be Victim of 'Friendly Fire,'" *Seattle Times*, August 26, 1992.

————. "Parents of Harris Keep Vigil on Road to Weaver's Cabin," *Seattle Times*, August 27, 1992.

————. "Fugitive's Wife Died in Siege—Federal Officials Reveal Vicki Weaver's Death," *Seattle Times*, August 29, 1992.

————. "Weaver Says He Was Shot by Sniper—Fugitive in Idaho Cabin Talks Through Mediator," *Seattle Times*, August 30, 1992.

————. "Weaver, Girls Still in Cabin; Harris Gives Up," *Seattle Times*, August 31, 1992.

————. "Forged Letter Helps Open Door to Weaver's Surrender," *Seattle Times*, September 1, 1992.

————. "How to Get Away from It All at Preparedness Expo," *Seattle Times*, October 3, 1992.

Oliveria, D. F. "Public Calls Out to Congressmen About Standoff," *Spokane Spokesman-Review*, August 25, 1992.

Real, David. "Divide and Conquer; White Supremacists See Idaho Cabin Standoff as First Salvo in Race War," *Dallas Morning News*, November 2, 1992.

Reuters. "Fugitive Holding Off 200 Lawmen in Idaho Hills," August 24, 1992; "Idaho Outlaw May Surrender Monday, Mediator Says," August 31, 1992; "Idaho Outlaw Surrenders, Ending 11-Day Standoff," August 31, 1992.

Seper, Jerry. "Idaho Mountain Standoff Ends," *Washington Times*, September 1, 1992.

————. "The Shootout on Ruby Ridge," *Washington Times*, September 22, 1993.

Shatzkin, Kate. "Officers Wait Out Fugitive in Idaho," *Seattle Times*, August 23, 1992.

Sorensen, Eric. "Friends and Family Mourn Fallen Marshal," *Spokane Spokesman-Review*, August 27, 1992.

Sowa, Tom. "Christian Identity Believers Ready to Take Up Sword," *Spokane Spokesman-Review*, August 28, 1992.

Spokane Spokesman-Review. "Director Details Events of Friday Weaver Shootout," August 26, 1992; "Lawmen Have Duty to Carry Out Justice," August 26, 1992; "The Long Wait for Weaver," *Spokane Spokesman-Review*, September 1, 1992; "Weaver Surrenders," *Spokane Spokesman-Review*, September 1, 1992.

Stern, Kenneth S. "David Duke: A Nazi in Politics." New York: American Jewish Committee, 1991.

————. Telephone interview with Bill Morlin, June 14, 1995.

Sullivan, Julie. "Paul Harvey Makes Plea to Weaver," *Spokane Spokesman-Review*, August 28, 1992.

Threlked, Melanie. "Agent Says He Killed Dog Before Deputy Was Fatally Shot," Gannett News Service, September 11, 1992.

United Press International. "Tensions High as Idaho Standoff Continues," August 24, 1992; "Gritz Wants United States Out of United Nations," September 29, 1992.

Walker, Adrian. "Idaho Fugitive's Sister Talks with Him," *The Boston Globe*, August 28, 1992.

Walter, Jess. "Feds Spent a Year and a Half Studying Mountain Enclave," *Spokane Spokesman-Review*, August 22, 1992.

————. "Weaver Tried to Be Alone with His Ideas," *Spokane Spokesman-Review*, August 24, 1992.

————. "Army Made Weaver a Warrior," *Spokane Spokesman-Review*, August 26, 1992.

————. "They're Only Little Girls, Relatives Say of Weaver Children," *Spokane Spokesman-Review*, August 26, 1992.

————. "Separatist Has Talk with Sister," *Spokane Spokesman-Review*, August 28, 1992.

————. "Skinheads Get Mixed Reception," *Spokane Spokesman-Review*, August 28, 1992.

————. "Bo Gritz Plays Major Role by Getting Weaver to Talk," *Spokane Spokesman-Review*, August 29, 1992.

————. "Parents' Visit Has Become Wait for Body," *Spokane Spokesman-Review*, August 30, 1992.

————. "Sara Feared for Father," *Spokane Spokesman-Review*, September 1, 1992.

————. *Every Knee Shall Bow: The Truth and Tragedy of Ruby Ridge and the Randy Weaver Family*. New York: ReganBooks, 1995.

————, and J. Todd Foster. "Vicki Weaver Dead," *Spokane Spokesman-Review*, August 29, 1992.

———— and Bill Morlin. "Kevin Harris Gives Himself Up," *Spokane Spokesman-Review*, August 31, 1992.

Wiley, John K. "Officers Encircle Mountain Cabin After Marshal Killed," Associated Press, August 22, 1992.

————. "Fugitive's Battle Moves from Cabin to Courtroom," Associated Press, September 1, 1992.

Williams, Marla. "Gritz Backers Say Americans Being Sold Out," *Seattle Times*, September 1, 1992.

Yang, John E. "Idaho Siege Ends as Fugitive Gives Up in Killing of Marshal," *The Washington Post*, September 1, 1992.

Sources for Chapter 3

Anti-Defamation League of B'nai B'rith. "Special Report: Paranoia as Patriotism—Far-Right Influences on the Militia Movement." New York, 1995.

Burghardt, Tom. "Leaderless Resistance and the Oklahoma City Bombing." San Francisco: Bay Area Coalition for Our Reproductive Rights, April 23, 1995.

Coalition for Human Dignity. *The Northwest Imperative*, 1994.

DeArmond, Paul. "Draft Chronology of the Militias," May 11, 1995 (unpublished).

Erickson, Denise. "Idaho Standoff—Federal Officials to Blame," *Seattle Times*, September 7, 1992.

Johnson, Paul B. "Gritz Brings Doomsday Message Back to IF," *Idaho Falls Register*, August 1, 1993.

Johnston, David. "FBI Shaken by Inquiry into Idaho Siege," *The New York Times*, November 25, 1993.

————. "FBI Leader at 1992 Standoff in Idaho Says Review Shielded Top Officials," *The New York Times*, May 19, 1995.

————. "Senior FBI Agent Suspended in Probe of a Deadly Siege," *The New York Times*, July 13, 1995.

Junas, Daniel. "Rise of Citizen Militias—Angry White Guys with Guns," *Covert Action Quarterly*, spring 1995.

Kelly, Michael. "The Road to Paranoia," *The New Yorker*, June 19, 1995.

Klanwatch, *Intelligence Report*, August 1995.

Labaton, Stephen. "Separatist Family Given $3.1 Million From Government," *The New York Times*, August 16, 1995.

Lee, Jessica. "NAACP's Chavis Targets Economics," *USA Today*, July 12, 1993.

McBride, Kelly. "Weaver Was Target of Arms Sting," *Spokane Spokesman-Review*, August 26, 1992.

Modie, Neil. "Jury in Slaying Case Put Feds on Trial," *Seattle Post-Intelligencer*, July 11, 1993.

Morlin, Bill. "Weaver Wanted to Arm Gangs, Claims Informer," *Spokane Spokesman-Review*, August 28, 1992.

National Public Radio. *Morning Edition*, June 24, 1993.

The New York Times. "Another Federal Fiasco," July 12, 1993.

Peters, Pete. "Special Report on the Meeting of Christian Men Held in Estes Park, Colorado, October 23, 24, 25, 1992, During the Killing of Vicki and Samuel Weaver by the United States Government." LaPorte, Col.: Scriptures for America, n.d. (circa 1992).

Popkey, Dan. "When a Jury's Focus Is on the Government," *The Arizona Republic*, October 10, 1993.

Real, David. "Divide and Conquer; White Supremacists See Idaho Cabin Standoff as First Salvo in Race War," *Dallas Morning News*, November 2, 1992.

Ridgeway, Jim, and Leonard Zeskind. "Revolution U.S.A.: The Far Right Militias Prepare for Battle," *The Village Voice*, May 2, 1995.

St. Louis Post-Dispatch. "From Boise to Waco," July 13, 1993.

Seattle Times. "Weaver Verdict Clearly Indicts Siege Mentality," July 10, 1993.

Seper, Jerry. "White Separatist Sentenced to 18 Months," *Washington Times*, October 19, 1993.

Shagun, Louis. "Pair Acquitted of Murder in Idaho Mountain Shootout," *The Washington Post*, July 9, 1993.

Sources for Chapter 4

The American. "Posse Comitatus: Citizens' Arrests?" July 1974.

American Jewish Committee. "The Minutemen." November 1961.

Anti-Defamation League of B'nai B'rith. "The KKK and the Neo-Nazis: A 1984 Status Report." New York, 1984.

————. "Special Report: Paranoia as Patriotism—Far-Right Influences on the Militia Movement." New York, 1995.

Applebome, Peter. "Terror in Oklahoma: Weapons; Increasingly, Extremism Is Heavily Armed," *The New York Times*, April 30, 1995.

Butler, Richard. "The Christian Posse Comitatus," *National Chronicle*, October 2, 1975.

California Attorney General's Office. "Minutemen—Excerpt from Para-Military Organizations in California Attorney General Report," April 1965. AJC, file "Minutemen, 1965."

Carrier, Jim. "Ticking of Dangerous Time Bomb Heard Before It Exploded," *Denver Post*, April 24, 1995.

Chicago Sun-Times. "G-Men Seize 2, Huge Arms Cache," May 20, 1964.

Chicago Tribune. "'True Believer' Dead, but His Belief Isn't," June 12, 1983.

CLERC. "The Posse Comitatus." Portland, Ore., 1975.

Dinnerstein, Leonard. *Anti-Semitism in America*. New York: Oxford University Press, 1994.

Ellerin, Milton. "The Minutemen—An Appraisal." New York: American Jewish Committee, February 1, 1967.

"Extremist Groups Subsidized by Government." *Congressional Record* (1964), pp. 11681 ff.

Fauber, John. "Posse Ready for Catastrophe," *Milwaukee Sentinel*, February 25, 1982.

Footlick, Jerrold K., and William J. Cook. "Return of the Posse?" *Newsweek*, May 26, 1975.

George, John, and Laird Wilcox. *Nazis, Communists, Klansmen, and Others on the Fringe.* Buffalo, N.Y.: Prometheus Books, 1992.

Group Research Report, vol. 3, no. 10, May 29, 1964.

Herald Traveler (Boston). "Guns, Mines Found in W. Bridgewater," November 7, 1969.

Janson, Donald. "Minutemen Help Spur the Growth of Gun Clubs," *The New York Times*, August 6, 1964.

Jorgensen, Leslie. "Patriots," *The Colorado Statesman*, August 5, 1994.

Kansas City Star. "Reports Talk of Minutemen," June 18, 1968; "Leaflet Plan by Minutemen," February 24, 1969.

Klanwatch Project of the Southern Poverty Law Center. *Hate, Violence, and White Supremacy: A Decade in Review, 1980–1990*, December 1989.

Minutemen. "Principles of Guerrilla Warfare." Norborne, Mo.: n.d. (circa 1963).

————. *Know Your Enemies Tactics*, Vol. 1. n.d. (circa 1964).

————. *On Target*, November 1, 1963.

Long Island Press. "Police, Prosecutor Joined Minutemen," January 8, 1967.

The New York Times. "DePugh Rejoins Minutemen, Citing Internal Dissension," May 2, 1967; "Rightists Seized in Robbery Plot," January 27, 1968.

Norden, Eric. "The Paramilitary Right: Those Paranoid Patriots—the Minutemen—Plot to Save America by Assassinating Their Enemies and Taking Over the Country Themselves," *Playboy*, June 1969.

Oaks, Terrence D. "Posse Comitatus," *Tax Strike News*, October 1965.

O'Shaughnessay, Lynn. "Radical Group's Rumblings Unsettling West Kansas," *The Kansas City* (Kansas) *Times*, February 4, 1983.

The People. "Armed Right Building Terrorist Network," July 9, 1983.

Perlmutter, Emanuel. "Lefkowitz Urges Law to Curb Activities of Minutemen in State," *The New York Times*, October 27, 1967.

Posse Comitatus. "This Is the Internal Capture of the U.S." (undated). AJC, file "Posse Comitatus, 1981 to date."

Prochnau, Bill. "For the Posse, Its Weapons Hold Hostile World at Bay," *The Washington Post*, June 21, 1983.

Ridgeway, James. *Blood in the Face*. New York: Thunder's Mouth Press, 1990.

Seattle Post-Intelligencer. "Bizarre Redmond Plot: Bomb Gang vs. FBI—No Contest," January 27, 1968.

Suall, Irwin. "The Vigilantes Are Comin' if You Don't Watch Out," *ADL Bulletin*, November 1975.

Sward, Susan. "Those 'Stepped On by Big Brother' Are Joining Posse," *Houston Chronicle*, August 27, 1976.

Tatarian, Roger. "Rationale for Citizen Militias Is Frightening," *San Francisco Bee*, November 20, 1994.

Thomas, Jo, and Ronald Smothers. "Oklahoma City Building Was Target of Plot as Early as '83, Official Says," *The New York Times*, May 20, 1995.

Wade, Wyn Craig. *The Fiery Cross: The Ku Klux Klan in America*. New York: Simon & Schuster, 1987.

Ward, Robert. "Police Probe Arms Cache, Check Link to Rightist Unit," *The Boston Globe*, November 7, 1969.

Western Front, vol. 11, no. 121 (1976). AJC, file "Posse Comitatus, 1976."

Whearley, Bob. "Rabid Rightists Infest Colorado," *Denver Post*, September 24, 1967.

Wickstrom, James P. "Posse Noose Report," November–December 1981. AJC, file "Posse Comitatus, 1981 to date."

Wistrich, Robert S. *Antisemitism: The Longest Hatred.* New York: Schocken Books, 1991.

Zeskind, Leonard. "The Christian Identity Movement: A Theological Justification for Racist and Anti-Semitic Violence." Center for Democratic Renewal, Atlanta, Ga., 1986.

Sources for Chapter 5

Anti-Defamation League. "Armed and Dangerous." New York, 1994.

Broadway, Bill. "An Eye for an Eye?" *The Washington Post*, April 29, 1995.

DeArmond, Paul. "Draft Chronology of the Militias," May 11, 1995 (unpublished).

James, Meg. "Distrust Fuels Support for Pensacola Chapter," *The Palm Beach* (Florida) *Post*, April 30, 1995.

Kelley, Dean M. "Waco: A Massacre and Its Aftermath," *First Things*, May 1995.

Kenworthy, Tom. "Two Brothers Face Explosives Charges," *The Washington Post*, April 26, 1995.

Leiby, Richard. "Paranoia: Fear on the Left. Fear on the Right. Whoever They Are, THEY'RE CLOSING IN," *The Washington Post*, May 8, 1995.

Maraniss, David, and Thomas Heath. "T. Nichols Says McVeigh Vowed 'Something Big'; Witness Places Suspect in Oklahoma April 16," *The Washington Post*, April 27, 1995.

Mullins, Eustace. "J'ACCUSE!" Posted on the Internet and forwarded to author, May 19, 1995.

Niederpruem, Kyle. *Indianapolis Star*, May 12, 1995.

Parfrey, Adam, and Jim Redden. "Patriot Games: Linda Thompson, a Gun-Toting Broad from Indianapolis, Wants to Know 'Are You Ready for the Next American Revolution?' " *The Village Voice*, October 11, 1994.

Redden, Jim. "Nuts to You! Linda Thompson and the New World Order Conspiracy," *PDXS*, May 5, 1993.

Reuters report on Waco tapes. Posted on the Internet July 7, 1995.

Saul, Stephanie. "Armed, Angry: Militants in America's Heartland: Who Are They?" *Newsday* (Nassau and Suffolk, New York, edition), April 30, 1995.

Schmidt, Susan. "FBI's Point Man at Waco Leads Probe," *The Washington Post*, April 28, 1995.

USA Today. "Hundreds of Militias in USA," April 24, 1995.

Vest, Jason. "The Spooky World of Linda Thompson: Her Videos Inflame the Militias," *The Washington Post*, May 11, 1995.

Vobejda, Barbara. "Incident Revives Memories of Waco, Idaho Showdowns," *The Washington Post*, April 24, 1995.

Worthington, Rogers. "Private Militias March to Beat of Deep Discontent," *Chicago Tribune*, September 25, 1994.

Sources for Chapter 6

Anti-Defamation League. "Armed and Dangerous." New York, 1994.

Aryan Nations. Press release, April 5, 1995, "In regards [sic] to John Trochmann's comments about the Aryan Nations." AJC, file "Militias—Militia of Montana."

Cochran, Floyd. "OPINION: Racism Takes on a New Face," *Ravalli* (Montana) *Republic*, August 25, 1994.

Cohler, Lawrence. "Rocky Mountain High Anxiety: On the Trail of Paranoid, Pro-gun Renegades in Big Sky Country. How Anti-Semitic Are the Militias?" *Jewish Week*, June 2, 1995.

Erickson, Steve. "S.D. Militia: Bombing Made Us Sick," *Daily Republic* (Mitchell, S.D.), May 5, 1995.

Executive Order 12919, June 3, 1994, "National Defense Industrial Resources Preparedness," *Federal Register*, vol. 59, no. 108, Tuesday, June 7, 1994.

Freedland, Jonathan. "Adolf's U.S. Army," *The Guardian* (U.K.), December 15, 1994.

Junas, Daniel. "Rise of Citizen Militias—Angry White Guys with Guns," *Covert Action Quarterly*, spring 1995.

Macintyre, Ben. "Rambo Gets Religion," *The Times of London Sunday Magazine*, December 10, 1994.

Militia of Montana. "Executive Orders for the New World Order," n.d. (circa 1994). AJC, file "Militias—Militia of Montana."

————. "Information Booklet," n.d. (circa 1994). AJC, file "Militias—Militia of Montana."

————. *Taking Aim*, various issues, 1994–95. AJC, file "Militias—Militia of Montana."

————. "New Materials Update," n.d. (circa 1995). AJC file "Militias—Militia of Montana."

Missoulian (Missoula, Montana). "Perot Group Decries Hate Tract Inference," March 9, 1995; "Baer Says He Isn't Anti-Semitic—He's Jewish," March 10, 1995.

Montana Human Rights Coalition. "A Season of Discontent: Militias, Constitutionalists, and the Far Right in Montana—January through May, 1994." Helena, Mont., 1994.

Roddy, Dennis. "Patriot Zealots Arm to Repel Unseen Foes," *Pittsburgh Post-Gazette*, February 12, 1995.

Ross, Loretta. "The Militia Movement—in Their Own Words and Deeds." Center for Democratic Renewal, Atlanta, Ga., July 11, 1995.

Sahagan, Louis. "A Wave of Distrust in the West: A Protest Movement Is Rising Among People Who Resent or Fear the Government," *Los Angeles Times*, February 3, 1995.

Senate Judiciary Committee, Terrorism, Technology and Government Information Subcommittee, *Hearings on Militia Movement in U.S.* Testimony of Senator Max Baucus, 104th Cong., 1st Sess., June 15, 1995.

Simons, Jay. "Large Crowd Attends Meeting Staged by Militia Promoters," *Sanders County* (Montana) *Ledger*, December 15, 1994.

Smith, Christopher. "D.C. Politics Fueling a New Wave of Militias," *Salt Lake Tribune*, September 5, 1994.

Sullivan, Patricia. "Aryan Nations Leader Mocks Montana Militia Spokesman," *Missoulian* (Missoula, Montana), April 7, 1995.

Trochmann, John. "Affidavit of Facts Opposing Venue," January 26, 1992, Sanders County, Montana. AJC, file "Militias—Militia of Montana."

Vanek, Mona. Letter, "To the Senate Judiciary Committee on Terrorism," May 24, 1995. AJC, file "Militias—Legislation."

Voll, Daniel. "The Right to Bear Sorrow," *Esquire*, March 1995.

————. "At Home with MOM," *Esquire*, July 1995.

Sources for Chapter 7

Anti-Defamation League. "Armed and Dangerous." New York, 1994.

————. "Beyond the Bombing: The Militia Menace Grows." New York, 1995.

Baca, Stacey. "War Just Around the Corner," *Denver Post*, January 22, 1995.

Baucus, Max. "Montana Mean Time," *The New York Times*, May 1, 1995.

Coalition for Human Dignity. *Northwest Imperative*, 1994.

————. *Dignity Report*, winter 1995.

————. *The Northwest Update*, various issues, 1994–95.

Colville (Washington) *Statesman-Examiner*, various issues.

DeArmond, Paul. "Militia of Montana Meeting at the Maltby Community Center," February 11, 1995. Distributed via e-mail. AJC, file "Militias—Militia of Montana."

Farley, Christopher John. "The West Is Wild Again," *Time*, March 20, 1995.

Foster, David. "Confrontations Spread as Gun-Packing Militias Flourish in Montana," Associated Press, March 24, 1995.

Holland, F. Joe. Letter, December 30, 1994, to Judge Jeff Langton. Appendix 26 in Stern, Kenneth, "Militias: A Growing Danger." New York: American Jewish Committee, April 1995.

Militia of Montana. "Militia of Montana Catalog," November 21, 1994.

————. "Militia of Montana Information and Networking Manual," n.d. (circa 1994).

————. *Taking Aim*, vol. 1, no. 5 (1994).

————. Press release, n.d. (circa January 1995), concerning Holland letter to Langton. AJC, file "Militias—Militia of Montana."

————. Flyer, dated February 17, 1995.

Ravalli (Montana) *Republic*. "Proclamation," January 20, 1995.

Schneider, Keith. "Manual for Terrorists Extols 'Great Coldbloodedness': Tactics Include Bombing Federal Buildings," *The New York Times*, April 29, 1995.

Shapiro, Joseph P. "An Epidemic of Fear and Loathing," *U.S. News & World Report*, May 8, 1995.

Simons, Jay. "Large Crowd Attends Meeting Staged by Militia Promoters," *Sanders County* (Montana) *Ledger*, December 15, 1994.

Stern, Kenneth S. *Militias: A Growing Danger*. New York: American Jewish Committee, 1995.

Tharp, Mike. "Days of Frontier Justice May Not Be Dead," *U.S. News & World Report*, August 15, 1994; reprinted in *Rocky Mountain News*, August 22, 1994.

Sources for Chapter 8

Associated Press. "Garfield County Freeman Gets Maximum Sentence," March 3, 1995.

Babcock, Michael. "Cascade Council Wants Mayor Out," *Great Falls* (Montana) *Tribune*, March 3, 1995.

Baucus, Max. "Montana Mean Time," *The New York Times*, May 1, 1995.

Bender, Matt. " 'Freemen' Packed Firepower," *The Billings* (Montana) *Gazette*, March 5, 1995.

Blair, Mike. "Militiamen Arrested in Montana: Is the Federal Government Making Its Long Anticipated Move Against Citizen Militias, or Has One Local Law Enforcement Agency 'Jumped the Gun?' " *Spotlight*, March 20, 1995.

————. "Situation Tense in Montana: This Is a Trial for All Americans," *Spotlight*, March 27, 1995.

Brandon, Karen. "Scary Times for Officials Out West: In Wake of Bombing, Armed Citizens Seen as Threat," *Chicago Tribune*, June 5, 1995.

Carrier, Jim. "Ticking of Dangerous Time Bomb Heard Before It Exploded," *Denver Post*, April 24, 1995.

Cohler, Lawrence. "Rocky Mountain High Anxiety: On the Trail of Paranoid, Pro-Gun Renegades in Big Sky Country," *Jewish Week*, June 2, 1995.

The Columbian (Vancouver, Washington). "Sheriff Not Ready to Go After Fugitives," March 9, 1995.

Downs, Michael. "Angry Callers Threaten Commissioner's Pet Burro," *Missoulian* (Missoula, Montana), April 27, 1995.

Egan, Timothy. "Agents Weigh Move; Holed-up Fugitives Get Respite," *The New York Times*, May 17, 1995.

Fadness, Gene. "Militia Movement, Founded in Idaho, Cause for Concern," *Idaho Falls Post Register*, March 8, 1995.

Foster, David. "Confrontations Spread as Gun-Packing Militias Flourish in Montana," Associated Press, March 24, 1995.

Junas, Daniel. "Armed Militias on the Rise in the United States," Inter Press Service, April 21, 1995.

Maughan, Ralph. "Update to 'A Night on Bald Mountain,' " April 17, 1995. AJC, file "Militias."

McLaughlin, Kathleen. "Too High a Price?: Officials Describe Death Threats," *Missoulian* (Missoula, Montana), March 9, 1995.

Militia of Montana. Press release. Posted on the Internet in alt.politics.usa.constitution March 29, 1995.

Missoulian (Missoula, Montana). "Militia/Law Confrontation in Darby, MT," April 3, 1995.

Montana Human Rights Network (Helena, Montana). "At the Legislature," 1995. AJC, file "Militias — Militia of Montana."

Montana Standard (Butte, Montana). "Not Quite Funny: 'Militia' vs. Helicopter Incident Could Have Led to Killing," February 9, 1995.

Morlin, Bill. "Gun-Toting Radicals Busted in Montana," *The Idaho Spokesman-Review*, March 8, 1995.

————. "Militia Gains Strength; Officials Fear for Safety," *The Spokane Spokesman-Review*, March 12, 1995.

Murphy, Kim. "Fugitive with Militia Ties Put the Law on the Defensive: A Montana Man Is Seized After 3-Year Standoff," *Los Angeles Times*, July 20, 1995.

Saasek, Grant. "Freeman Beliefs," *Independent Record* (Helena, Montana), April 2, 1995.

Sahagan, Louis. "A Wave of Distrust in the West: A Protest Movement Is Rising Among People Who Resent or Fear the Government," *Los Angeles Times*, February 3, 1995.

Schwennesen, Don. "Fear and Loathing in the Flathead: Death Threats Reported in Planning Fight," *Missoulian* (Missoula, Montana), September 21, 1994.

Senate Judiciary Committee, Terrorism, Technology and Government Information Subcommittee, *Hearings on Militia Movement in U.S.*, written statement of John Bohlman, 104th Cong., 1st sess., 1995.

Shapiro, Joseph P. "An Epidemic of Fear and Loathing," *U.S. News & World Report*, May 8, 1995.

Spokane Spokesman-Review. "Militia Movement Not a Patriotic One," March 12, 1995.

Sullivan, Patricia. "Guard Chopper Stirs up Bitterroot 'Militia,' " *Missoulian* (Missoula, Montana), February 7, 1995.

————, and Greg Lakes. "Threats," *Missoulian* (Missoula, Montana), March 3, 1995.

Thorning, Ruth. " 'Copter Not a Threat," *Ravalli* (Montana) *Republic*, February 7, 1995.

Toole, Ken. "Why Even Tolerate Violent Threats?" *Missoulian* (Missoula, Montana), March 3, 1995.

Yurman, Dan. "Militia of Montana Update—March 10, 1995," Western Lands Gopher Service.

————. "Montana Manhunt on for Militia Fugitives," Western Lands Gopher Service, March 11, 1995.

————. "Militia of Montana Felony Charges Dropped," Western Lands Gopher Service, March 31, 1995.

————. "5/6/95 Militia Update from Idaho," Western Lands Gopher Service, May 6, 1995.

Sources for Chapter 9

Anti-Defamation League. "Armed and Dangerous," 1994.

Associated Press. "Militia Leader Claims Fax," May 24, 1995.

Carrier, Jim. "Ticking of Dangerous Time Bomb Heard Before It Exploded," *Denver Post*, April 24, 1995.

Center for Democratic Renewal. "Activist Update for March, 1995."

CNN News. " 'Michigan Militia' One of Several Paramilitary Groups," 5:09 P.M., October 24, 1994.

Corum, Michelle. "Militia Group Aims to Protect Citizens' Rights," National Public Radio, *All Things Considered*, February 5, 1995.

De Lama, George. "For Militias, Invaders of U.S. Are Everywhere," *Chicago Tribune*, October 31, 1994.

Farley, Christopher John. "Patriot Games," *Time*, December 19, 1994.

Flesher, John. "Hard-Core Gun Activists Ready for Day When Arms Are Needed," *Los Angeles Times*, November 13, 1994.

————. "Fearful of Government, 'Patriots' Organize to Defend Freedoms," Associated Press, April 21, 1995.

Greensboro (N.C.) *News and Record*. "Gun Activists Form Independent Militia," October 10, 1994.

Harrison, Michael. Telephone interview with author, September 11, 1995.

Hawkins, Beth. "Patriot Games," *Detroit Metro Times*, October 12–18, 1994.

Henderson, Nell. "Another View on 'Truth Radio,' " *The Washington Post*, April 25, 1995.

Kenworthy, Tom. "Two Brothers Face Explosives Charges; McVeigh Won't Talk, Claiming He's a POW," *The Washington Post*, April 26, 1995.

————, and George Lardner, Jr. "The Militias: Guns and Bitter; Federal Push to Rein in Arms Sparked Fire of Resentment Among Owners," *The Washington Post*, May 4, 1995.

Koernke, Mark. "Toward the New World Order: America's Secret Police," *Nexus*, February–March 1994.

Laurence, Charles. "Militia Leaders Hide Behind TV Crews at Secluded Stronghold," *The Daily Telegraph* (London), April 24, 1995.

Leiby, Richard. "Paranoia: Fear on the Left, Fear on the Right. Whoever They Are, THEY'RE CLOSING IN," *The Washington Post*, May 8, 1995.

McCarthy, Ryan. "Revolution, Federal Tyranny Topics at Militia Meeting," *Sacramento Bee*, October 23, 1994.

McHugh, David. "Far Right Figure Takes on Many Threats," *Detroit Free Press*, February 24, 1995.

Militia of Montana. Flyer, "New Material from the Militia of Montana," 1995.

Potok, Mark. " 'American Movement' of Arms and Ideology: Militias Stepping Out From Shadows," *USA Today*, January 30, 1995.

Richardson, Valerie. "Groups Nationwide Plan to Protest U.N. Influence," *Washington Times*, October 22, 1994.

Roddy, Dennis. "Patriot Zealots Arm to Repel Unseen Forces," *Pittsburgh Post-Gazette*, February 12, 1995.

————. "Ears to the Ground," *The* (Memphis, Tennessee) *Commercial Appeal*, February 21, 1995.

Saul, Stephanie. "Armed, Angry: Militants in America's Heartland," *Newsday* (Nassau and Suffolk edition), April 30, 1995.

Schmidt, Susan, and Tom Kenworthy. "Michigan Fringe Group's Leader Has National Reputation," *The Washington Post*, April 25, 1995.

Schneider, Keith. "Fearing a Conspiracy, Some Heed a Call to Arms," *The New York Times*, November 14, 1994.

Senate Judiciary Committee, Terrorism, Technology and Government Information Subcommittee, *Hearings on Militia Movement in U.S.* Statement of Robert M. Bryant, Assistant Director, National Security Division, Federal Bureau of Investigation 104th Cong., 1st sess., June 15, 1995.

Stanton, Sam. "Conference on Conspiracy," *Sacramento Bee*, May 8, 1995.

USA Today. "Sketch of Militia Groups," January 30, 1995.

Walker, Sam. " 'Militias' Forming Across U.S. to Protest Gun Control Laws," *Christian Science Monitor*, October 17, 1994.

Worthington, Rogers. "Private Militias March to Beat of Deep Distrust," *Chicago Tribune*, September 25, 1994.

Sources for Chapter 10

Anti-Defamation League. "Armed and Dangerous." New York, 1994.

Bridge, Catherine. "War Predicted at Militia Rally," *Sacramento Bee*, January 19, 1995.

Butterfield, Fox. "Terror in Oklahoma: Echoes of the N.R.A.," *The New York Times*, May 8, 1995.

CNN News. " 'Michigan Militia' One of Several Paramilitary Groups," 5:09 P.M., October 24, 1994.

Coalition for Human Dignity. "Patriot Games: Jack McLamb and the Citizen Militias," October 1994.

————. *Northwest Imperative*, 1994.

Cohler, Lawrence. "Rocky Mountain High Anxiety: On the Trail of Paranoid, Pro-gun Renegades in Big Sky Country," *Jewish Week*, June 2, 1995.

Dionne, E. J., Jr. "A Time for Politicians to Look Within," *The Washington Post*, April 24, 1995.

Face the Nation, with Senator Dianne Feinstein, Sunday, May 21, 1995.

Gladwell, Malcolm. "At Root of Modern Militias: An American Legacy of Rebellion," *The Washington Post*, May 9, 1995.

Henigan, Dennis A. "Arms, Anarchy and the Second Amendment," *Valparaiso University Law Review*, vol. 26, no. 1 (fall 1991).

Jones, Steven T. "Arms and the Men: Placer County Duo Readies for the Revolution," *Sacramento News and Review*, August 25, 1994.

Jorgensen, Leslie. "Patriots," *The Colorado Statesman*, August 5, 1994.

Kenworthy, Tom, and George Lardner, Jr. "The Militias: Guns and Bitter," *The Washington Post*, May 4, 1995.

LaPierre, Wayne. Fund-raising letter for National Rifle Association, 1995. AJC, file "Militias—NRA."

Leiby, Richard. "Paranoia: Fear on the Left. Fear on the Right. Whoever They Are, THEY'RE CLOSING IN," *The Washington Post*, May 8, 1995.

Leusner, Jim, and Jay Hamburg. "Anti-Government Militias Are Strong in Florida," *The Orlando Sentinel*, April 26, 1995.

Levinson, Sanford. "The Embarrassing Second Amendment," *Yale Law Journal*, vol. 99 (1989).

Macintyre, Ben. "Who Is Calling the Shots?" *The New York Times*, August 17, 1994.

Militia of Montana. Letter, May 12, 1995, to Governor Marc Racicot, et al. AJC, file "Militias—Militia of Montana."

————. Copy of Purchase Order 40-03J1-3-0241, dated September 25, 1993. AJC, file "Militias—Militia of Montana."

————. "Militia of Montana Information and Networking Manual," n.d. (circa 1994). AJC, file "Militias—Militia of Montana."

Navarro, Mireya. "At Fair for Survivalists, Fallout from Oklahoma," *The New York Times*, June 12, 1995.

Parfrey, Adam, and Jim Redden. "Patriot Games: Linda Thompson, a Gun-Toting Broad from Indianapolis, Wants to Know, 'Are You Ready for the Next American Revolution?'" *The Village Voice*, October 11, 1994.

Powers, William F. "Dressed to Kill?: Federal Agents' Militaristic Uniforms Enter the Fray," *The Washington Post*, May 4, 1995.

Ridgeway, James. "The Posse Goes to Washington," *The Village Voice*, May 23, 1995.

Sherwood, M. Samuel. *The Guarantee of the Second Amendment*. Blackfoot, Idaho: Founders Press Publications, 1992.

Spotlight. "RFAers Suggest Lots of Reforms," January 23, 1995.

Tatarian, Roger. "Rationale for Citizen Militias Is Frightening," *Fresno Bee*, November 20, 1994.

United States v. Miller, 307 U.S. 174 (1939).

Sources for Chapter 11

Associated Press. "Idaho Poll Eyes Armed Rangers," May 4, 1995; "Lawmakers Debate Species Act," May 10, 1995; "Federal Workers Say They Are Leery of Work in Forests," May 30, 1995.

Association of Forest Service Employees for Environmental Ethics. *Law Enforcement and Investigations Weekly Report,* U.S. Forest Service, 1995.

Brandon, Karen. "Scary Times for Officials Out West: In Wake of Bombing, Armed Citizens Seen as Threat," *Chicago Tribune,* June 5, 1995.

Carrier, Jim. "Ticking of Dangerous Time Bomb Heard Before It Exploded," *Denver Post,* April 24, 1995.

Clearinghouse on Environmental Advocacy and Research (CLEAR). "Ron Arnold on Militias." Posted on the Internet June 12, 1995. "Rep. Miller Calls for Violence Hearings." Posted on Internet, May 9, 1995. Internet posting May 9, 1995, on Miller press conference.

Craig, John. " 'Sagebrush' Revolt Will Be Won Without Bloodshed," *Spokane Spokesman-Review,* March 29, 1995.

DeArmond, Paul. "County Supremacist Tours Washington State," March 30, 1995. AJC, file "Militia — Wise Use."

DeBonis, Jeff. "Statement of Jeff DeBonis, Executive Director, Public Employees for Environmental Responsibility, Before the Public Forum 'America Under the Gun: The Militia Movement and Hate Groups in America,' " *PEER* press release, July 11, 1995.

De Lama, George. "West Chomping at the Bit over Federal Control," *Chicago Tribune,* October 27, 1994.

Egan, Timothy. "Federal Officials Under Attack in Several Western States," *The New York Times,* April 25, 1995.

————. "Unlikely Alliances Attack Property Rights Measures: Oppose Bills to Pay Owners for State Action," *The New York Times,* May 15, 1995.

Evan-Pritchard, Ambrose. "West Driven Wild by 'Meddling' Congress," *Sunday Telegraph* (London), February 19, 1995.

Farley, Christopher John. "The West Is Wild Again," *Time,* March 20, 1995.

Garton, Jane Dwyre. " 'Posse' Won't Be Stopped," *Post Crescent* (Appleton, Wisconsin), January 25, 1981.

Gorton, Steve. "Will People Give Way to Ecosystems? Proposed Actions Would Limit Property Rights and Population," *The Montanian,* n.d. (circa 1994). AJC, file "Militia—Wise Use."

Innerst, Carol. "Campus Stifling of Free Speech Has Stirred Backlash," *Washington Times,* November 2, 1994.

Jewish Telegraphic Agency. News release, April 1, 1981. AJC, file "Posse Comitatus—1981."

Jones, Steven T. "Arms and the Men: Placer County Duo Readies for the Revolution," *Sacramento News and Review,* August 25, 1994.

Junas, Daniel. "Militias are No Laughing Matter," February 14, 1995, published (with minor changes) in *Seattle Post-Intelligencer,* March 14, 1995.

————. "Rise of Citizen Militias: Angry White Guys with Guns," *Covert Action Quarterly,* spring 1995.

Kenworthy, Tom. "Angry Ranchers Across the West See Grounds for an Insurrection," *The Washington Post,* February 21, 1995.

————. "Dueling with the Forest Service," *The Washington Post National Weekly Edition,* February 27–March 5, 1995.

————. "U.S. Enters Range War, Suing Nevada County," *The Washington Post,* March 9, 1995.

Lavelle, Marianne. " 'Wise-Use' Movement Grows," *The National Law Journal,* June 5, 1995.

Lindhold, Paul. Posting on the Internet, April 1, 1995.

Lowe, John E. March 22, 1995, letter from Regional Forester to "All R-6 Employees," posted by Dan Yurman in Western Lands Gopher Service, March 23, 1995.

National Public Radio. *All Things Considered*, February 5, 1995, Transcript no. 1749-6.

Pryne, Eric. "The Property Rights Movement," *Seattle Times*, March 19, 1995.

Public Employees for Environmental Responsibility, *PEEReview*, spring 1995.

Ramos, Tarso. Posting on the Internet March 9, 1995.

Reuters. "Yellowstone Wolves Ready to Be Released," March 16, 1995; "Bomb Explodes at Forest Service Office in Nevada," March 31, 1995; "Witness in Blast Case Member of Property Rights Group," May 2, 1995.

Ridgeway, James, and Jeffrey St. Clair. "This Land Is Our Land," *The Village Voice*, June 20, 1995.

Rodrigue, George. "U.S. House Member Proud of Intense Anti-Government Views," *Dallas Morning News*, June 14, 1995.

Sahagan, Louis. "A Wave of Distrust in the West: A Protest Movement Is Rising Among People Who Resent or Fear the Government," *Los Angeles Times*, February 3, 1995.

Saul, Stephanie. "Armed, Angry: Militants in America's Heartland," *Newsday* (Nassau and Suffolk, New York, edition), April 30, 1995.

Schmidt, Susan, and Tom Kenworthy, "Michigan Fringe Group's Leader Has National Reputation," *The Washington Post*, April 25, 1995.

Schneider, Keith. "U.S. Seeks to Stop a County from Seizing Federal Land," *The New York Times*, March 9, 1995.

Schodolski, Vincent J. "Crusaders Battle Government; Ranchers, Miners Fight to Gain Local Control of Land," *Chicago Tribune*, May 14, 1995.

Sebelius, Steve. "NYE Commissioner to Attend Event with Ties to Hate Groups." *Las Vegas Sun*, August 26, 1994.

Senate Judiciary Committee, Terrorism, Technology and Government Information Subcommittee, *Hearings on Militia Movement in U.S.*, Testimony of Senator Max Baucus, 104th Cong., 1st sess., June 15, 1995.

Silver, Robin. Telephone interview with author, September 13, 1995.

Smith, Lang. "Protest Endangered Species and Their Habitats—Stop Anti-Forest Legislation." Posted on the Internet March 27, 1995.

Wickstrom, Jack. "The Planned 'Limited Nuclear War,'" *Shoppers Newsletter* (Evansville, Wisc.), February 4, 1981.

Witters, John. "Spider Meadows in Glacier Peak Wilderness to Be Logged." Posted on the Internet, May 5, 1995.

Wolfe, Warren. "Wisconsin Posses: Patriots or Scofflaws?" *Minneapolis Tribune*, December 15, 1974.

World Media Foundation. "Living on the Earth," January 11, 1995. AJC, file "Militias—Wise Use."

Yurman, Dan. "Update on Militia in Idaho," Western Lands Gopher Service, March 1995.

————. "Wolves and Guns in Idaho Forests," Western Lands Gopher Service, March 8, 1995.

————. "Wise Use to Feds, We're Not Wacky, Er, Waco," Western Lands Gopher Service, n.d. (circa mid-March, 1995).

————. "Civil War Predicted in Idaho," Western Lands Gopher Service, March 12, 1995.

————. "5/6/95 Militia Update from Idaho," Western Lands Gopher Service, May 6, 1995.

————. Telephone interviews with author, 1995.

Sources for Chapter 12

Anti-Defamation League of B'nai B'rith. "Special Report: Paranoia as Patriotism—Far-Right Influences on the Militia Movement." New York, 1995.

Applebome, Peter. "Terror in Oklahoma: Weapons; Increasingly, Extremism Is Heavily Armed," *The New York Times*, April 30, 1995.

Coalition for Human Dignity. *Northwest Update*, May 15, 1995.

Cornwell, Tim. "Back at the Ranch, the Militia Tools Up for a New Armageddon," *The Scotsman* (Cambridge, Minnesota), December 26, 1994.

Jones, Steven T. "Arms and the Men," *Sacramento News and Review*, August 25, 1994.

Leiby, Richard. "Paranoia: Fear on the Left. Fear on the Right. Whoever They Are, THEY'RE CLOSING IN," *The Washington Post*, May 8, 1995.

Parfrey, Adam, and Jim Redden. "Patriot Games: Linda Thompson, a Gun-Toting Broad from Indianapolis, Wants to Know, 'Are You Ready for the Next American Revolution?' " *The Village Voice*, October 11, 1994.

Rowland, Darrel. "Couple Expect Armed Showdown on Rights," *The Columbus* (Ohio) *Dispatch*, October 16, 1994.

USA Today. "Sketches of Militia Groups," January 30, 1995.

Worthington, Rogers. "Private Militias March to Beat of Deep Distrust," *Chicago Tribune*, September 25, 1994.

Sources for Chapter 13

Anti-Defamation League. "Armed and Dangerous," 1994.

————. "Special Report: Paranoia as Patriotism—Far-Right Influences on the Militia Movement," 1995.

Banks, Holly. "Peaceful Surrender Relieves Parents," *Oregonian*, February 27, 1995.

Bridge, Catherine. "War Predicted at Militia Rally," *Sacramento Bee*, January 19, 1995.

Clover, Charles. "The Girls, the Guns, the Globe: The Earth Summit Starts Today," *The Daily Telegraph* (London), June 3, 1992.

Cohler, Lawrence. "Rocky Mountain High Anxiety: On the Trail of Paranoid, Pro-gun Renegades in Big Sky Country," *Jewish Week*, June 2, 1995.

Congressional Record. 82nd Cong., 1st sess. (June 4, 1951).

Congressional Research Service Report for Congress. *Violent Crime Control and Enforcement Act: Summary of S.1607 (H.R. 3355)*, Congressional Research Service, December 23, 1993.

Cornwell, Tim. "Back at the Ranch, the Militia Tools Up for a New Armageddon," *The Scotsman* (Cambridge, Minnesota), December 26, 1994.

DeArmond, Paul. "Draft Chronology of the Militias," May 11, 1995 (unpublished).

Department of the Army. "Civil Affairs Operations," publication FM 41-10, cover with attached p. 13-2 of "Figure 13-1. Phases of Insurgency," n.d. (after Feb. 6, 1989). AJC, file "Militias—Militia of Montana."

Forster, Arnold, and Benjamin Epstein. *Danger on the Right*. New York: Random House, 1964.

————. *The Radical Right*. New York: Random House, 1966.

Fritze, David. "Patriots Vow to Fight Off 'One World Government': Militias See Threat in Arizona," *The Arizona Republic*, February 5, 1995.

Hernandez, Angel. "Lakewood Couple Yearns to Save World," *Rocky Mountain News* (Colorado), December 14, 1994.

Hofstadter, Richard. *The Paranoid Style in American Politics.* New York: Alfred A. Knopf, 1965.

JBS [John Birch Society] *Bulletin,* May 1965.

Militia of Montana. Sheet with pictures of trucks distributed by Militia of Montana, n.d. (circa 1994). AJC, file "Militias — Militia of Montana."

———. "Weather Modification," n.d. (circa 1994). AJC, file "Militias — Militia of Montana."

———. "Intel. Report April 19, 1994, Louisiana-Mississippi," n.d. (April 1994). AJC, file "Militias — Militia of Montana."

———. "Observation Report," dated June 12, 1994. AJC, file "Militias — Militia of Montana."

———. "Militia of Montana Catalog," November 21, 1994, Texas Constitutional Militia. "Texas Militia Statement," posted on Internet February 11, 1995, in misc:survival.

Potok, Mark. " 'American Movement' of Arms and Ideology: Militias Stepping Out from Shadows," *USA Today,* January 30, 1995.

Rich, Frank. "New World Terror," *The New York Times,* April 27, 1995.

Saul, Stephanie. "Armed, Angry: Militants in America's Heartland," *Newsday* (Nassau and Suffolk, New York, edition), April 30, 1995.

Senate Judiciary Committee, Subcommittee on Terrorism, Technology and Government Information, Hearings on Militia Movement in U.S., Summary Statement of James L. Brown, Deputy Associate Director for Criminal Enforcement, Bureau of Alcohol, Tobacco and Firearms, 104th Cong., 1st sess., June 15, 1995.

USA Today. "Hundreds of Militias in USA," April 24, 1995.

Welch, Robert. *The Blue Book.* Belmont, Mass.: John Birch Society, 1959.

———. *The Politician.* Belmont, Mass.: John Birch Society, 1963.

World Constitution and Parliament Association. "A Constitution for the Federation of Earth," 1977. AJC, file "Militias — Militia of Montana."

Sources for Chapter 14

Blair, Mike. "Arizona Desert May Hold Secret of Foreign Military Equipment. For Use Against Americans?" *Spotlight,* January 23, 1995.

———. "Citizen-Soldiers Diverted from Original Plan," *Spotlight,* January 23, 1995.

———. "Spesnax Troops in Pennsylvania: Russian or American?" *Spotlight,* March 20, 1995.

Cohler, Lawrence. "Rocky Mountain High Anxiety: On the Trail of Paranoid, Pro-gun Renegades in Big Sky Country," *Jewish Week,* June 2, 1995.

Cornwell, Tim. "Back at the Ranch, the Militia Tools Up for Armageddon," *The Scotsman* (Cambridge, Minnesota), December 26, 1994.

David, Tony. "Militia Members Scatter as FBI, Guard Turn Up in Catron," *Albuquerque Tribune,* September 14, 1994.

De Lama, George. "For Militias, Invaders of U.S. Are Everywhere," *Chicago Tribune,* October 31, 1994.

Egan, Timothy. "Men at War: Inside the World of the Paranoid," *The New York Times,* April 30, 1995.

Gladwell, Malcolm. "At Root of Modern Militias: An American Legacy of Rebellion," *The Washington Post,* May 9, 1995.

Hasselbach, Ingo. "Extremism: A Global Network," *The New York Times,* April 26, 1995.

Horwitz, Tony. "Rebel Voices: The Face of Extremism Wears Many Guises—Most of Them Ordinary," *The Wall Street Journal*, April 28, 1995.

Jones, Steven T. "Arms and the Men," *Sacramento News and Review*, August 25, 1994.

Kossoy, Donna. "A Guide to the Outer Limits of Human Belief." Posted on the Internet May 9, 1995.

Leiby, Richard. "Paranoia: Fear on the Left. Fear on the Right. Whoever They Are, THEY'RE CLOSING IN," *The Washington Post*, May 8, 1995.

Leusner, Jim, and Jay Hamburg. "Anti-Government Militias Are Strong in Florida," *The Orlando Sentinel*, April 26, 1995.

Rowland, Darrel. "Couple Expect Armed Showdown on Rights," *The Columbus* (Ohio) *Dispatch*, October 16, 1994.

Russakoff, Dale. "Grass Roots Rage: Below the Surface, Mid-America Simmers with Sense of Alienation," *The Washington Post*, May 5, 1995.

Saul, Stephanie. "Armed, Angry: Militants in America's Heartland," *Newsday* (Nassau and Suffolk, New York, edition), April 30, 1995.

Stanton, Sam. "On Guard," *Sacramento Bee*, January 29, 1995.

Tiffany, John. "What's the Government Doing Anyway?" *Spotlight*, May 1, 1995.

Tomsho, Robert. "A Cause for Fear: Though Called a Hoax, 'Iron Mountain' Report Guides Some Militias," *The Wall Street Journal*, May 9, 1995.

Tucker, James P., Jr. "Bilderberg to Meet in Switzerland," *Spotlight*, May 22, 1995.

Sources for Chapter 15

Applebome, Peter. "Terror in Oklahoma: Weapons; Increasingly, Extremism Is Heavily Armed," *The New York Times*, April 30, 1995.

"Bombs and Videotapes on Explosives and Demolitions." Forwarded on Internet to author, May 2, 1995.

Bonners Ferry (Idaho) *Herald*, January 23, 1993.

The Clackamas (Oregon) *Review*, May 28, 1992.

Coalition for Human Dignity. "Patriot Games: Jack McLamb and Citizens Militias," October 1994.

Davidson, J. F. A. "Open Letters to Our Readers: On Militia," *The Resister*, no. 4 (spring 1995).

Delta Press Limited (El Dorado, Arkansas), vol. 35 (spring 1995).

Evans-Pritchard, Ambrose. "Patriot Games Turn Deadly Illegal: U.S. Militias Threaten Rule of Washington," *Sunday Telegraph* (London), December 4, 1994.

Jorgensen, Leslie. "Patriots," *The Colorado Statesman*, August 5, 1994.

Laurence, Charles. "Militia Leaders Hide Behind TV Crews at Secluded Stronghold," *The Daily Telegraph* (London), April 24, 1995.

Loompanics Unlimited. "Online Catalog," forwarded to author.

McLamb, Jack. "Winning the Battle to Preserve Liberty." Lecture given at Seattle Preparedness Expo '94, September 10, 1994; quoted in "Patriot Games: Jack McLamb and Citizen Militias." Coalition for Human Dignity, Portland, Ore., October 1994.

Parfrey, Adam, and Jim Redden. "Patriot Games: Linda Thompson, a Gun-Toting Broad from Indianapolis, Wants to Know, 'Are You Ready for the Next American Revolution?'" *The Village Voice*, October 11, 1994.

Police Against the New World Order. *Aid and Abet Newsletter*, various issues.

————. "Operation Vampire Killer 2000," n.d. (circa 1986).

Priest, Dana. "Pentagon Reissues Extremist Group Ban," *The Washington Post*, April 26, 1995.

Sheppard, William. "Joint Task Force—6: Subversion of the Third Amendment," *The Resister*, vol. 1 (spring 1994), part 4, forwarded on Internet. AJC, file "Militias—Military."

Sources for Chapter 16

Associated Press. "States Conference in Jeopardy," April 16, 1995.

Coalition for Human Dignity. "Patriot Games: Jack McLamb and Citizens Militias," October 1994.

Fadness, Gene. "Militia Movement, Founded in Idaho, Cause for Concern," *Idaho Falls Post Register*, March 8, 1995.

————. Editorial, *Idaho Falls Post Register*, March 8, 1995.

Harrie, Dan. "Citizen-Militia Literature Distributed Among Utah Senators," *Salt Lake Tribune*, February 28, 1995.

Idaho Falls Post Register. "Eastern Idaho Digest: Sheriffs Do Not Want Help," August 15, 1994; editorial, March 8, 1995.

Idaho Liberty Network Public Lands Conference. April 23, 1994. Cited in Coalition for Human Dignity, "Patriot Games: Jack McLamb and Citizens Militias," October 1994.

Jews for the Preservation of Firearms Ownership. *The Firearms Sentinel*, April 1995.

Johnson, Dirk. "Conspiracy Theories' Impact Reverberates in Legislatures: Extreme Right's Outcry Scuttles Conference," *The New York Times*, July 6, 1995.

Kamen, Al. "His Own Private Idaho," *The Washington Post*, March 15, 1995.

Lockwood, Frank E. "Militiaman Writes Armageddon Recovery Plan," *Times-News* (Twin Falls, Idaho), May 16, 1995.

————. "Sherwood: Militiaman of Many Names," *Times-News* (Twin Falls, Idaho) May 17, 1995.

————. "Militiaman Resumes Talk of War," *Times-News* (Twin Falls, Idaho), May 1995.

Middlewood, Erin. "Racist Relations in Clark County," *The Columbian* (Vancouver, Washington) April 23, 1995.

The New American. "Citizen Militias," February 6, 1995.

Schouten, Fredreka. "Militias Deny Link to Bombing, Use of Violence," *Idaho Statesman* (Boise, Idaho), April 22, 1995.

Sherwood, M. Samuel. *The Guarantee of the Second Amendment*. Blackfoot, Idaho: Founder Press Publications, 1992.

————. *Establishing Independent Militia in the United States*. Blackfoot, Idaho: United States Militia Association, 1994.

Smith, Christopher. "D.C. Politics Fueling a New Wave of Militias," *Salt Lake Tribune*, September 5, 1994.

Spokane Spokesman-Review, July 30, 1994. Cited in "Patriot Games: Jack McLamb and Citizens Militias," Coalition for Human Dignity, October 1994; "Militia: Politicians May Need to be Shot," March 12, 1995.

State of Idaho. Senate Concurrent Resolution No. 125, Legislature of the State of Idaho, 53rd Legislature, March 13, 1995.

Trillhaase, Marty. "Militia Group Hopes to Grow in Idaho," *Idaho Falls Post Register*, July 27, 1994.

————. "Law Enforcement Officials Debunk Militia Man's Claims," *Idaho Falls Post Register,* August 3, 1994.

United States Militia Association. *Aide-de-Camp,* various issues, 1995.

Yurman, Dan. "Militia News From Idaho, 3/04/95," Western Lands Gopher Service, March 4, 1995.

————. "Idaho Leader Predicts Civil War in the West," Western Lands Gopher Service, March 12, 1995.

————. "Human Rights in Eastern Idaho #9," Western Lands Gopher Service, April 30, 1995.

————. "Update on Militia in Eastern Idaho 4/30/95," Western Lands Gopher Service, April 30, 1995.

Sources for Chapter 17

Aide-de-Camp (publication of the United States Militia Association), "Butch Otter; Idaho Lt. Governor Speakes [*sic*] to Idaho District II Gathering in Boise," vol. 3, no. 1 (March 1995).

Banks, Holly. "Peaceful Surrender Relieves Parents," *Oregonian* (Portland), February 27, 1995.

Bender, Matt. " 'Freeman' Packed Firepower," *Billings Gazette,* March 5, 1995.

Blair, Mike. "Militiamen Arrested in Montana," *Spotlight,* March 20, 1995.

Egan, Timothy. "Terror in Oklahoma: In Congress, Trying to Explain Contacts With Paramilitary Groups," *The New York Times,* May 2, 1995.

Gingrich, Newt. "Progress Report with Newt Gingrich," Journal Graphics Transcripts, transcript no. 6, March 7, 1995.

"Patriot Warning." Posted on the Internet in alt.conspiracy, 12:37 A.M., March 22, 1995.

Rapid City (South Dakota) *Journal.* " 'Patriot' Threat Put S.D. Power Plants on Alert," April 27, 1995.

Roland, Jon. "To All Militia Units, Other Patriots, and Selected Media Persons," posted in talk.politics.guns, March 22, 1995.

Saul, Stephanie. "Armed, Angry: Militants in America's Heartland," *Newsday,* April 30, 1995.

Sullivan, Patricia. "Guard Chopper Stirs Up Bitterroot 'Militia,' " *Missoulian* (Missoula, Montana), February 7, 1995.

Wheeler, Jack. "Behind the Lines," *Strategic Investment.* Forwarded on the Internet to alt.conspiracy March 21, 1995. AJC, file "Militias — 95."

White Mountain Militia Information Service. "Trochman's [*sic*] Gang in Jail." Posted on the Internet in alt.conspiracy, March 4, 1995.

Sources for Chapter 18

Associated Press. "36 Dead in Oklahoma Bombing," April 20, 1995; "Okla. Bomb Indictments Loom," August 7, 1995.

Belluck, Pam. "Terror in Oklahoma: The Victims; Identifying Injured Loved Ones by Clues of Hair and Birthmarks," *The New York Times,* April 21, 1995.

Bernstein, Emily M. "Terror in Oklahoma: The Overview; Evidence Linking Suspect to Blast Offered in Court," *The New York Times,* April 28, 1995.

Bragg, Rick. "Terror in Oklahoma: The Rescue; Decision at Bomb Site: Don't Risk the Lives of the Living to Free the Dead," *The New York Times*, May 1, 1995.

————. "Terror in Oklahoma: The Children," *The New York Times*, May 3, 1995.

Browne, Malcolm W. "Terror in Oklahoma: The Science," *The New York Times*, April 21, 1995.

CNN News. 8:29 A.M., May 23, 1995. Transcript in author's possession.

Conlon, Michael. "Militia Movement Widespread in United States," Reuters, April 21, 1995.

Duggan, Paul. "Fairfax Firefighters Close Blast-Site Duty With Salute," *The Washington Post*, April 30, 1995.

————, and Pierre Thomas. "Bail Denied for Suspect in Bombing; Federal Magistrate Cites an 'Indelible Trail of Evidence,' " *The Washington Post*, April 28, 1995.

Gonzalez, David. "Terror in Oklahoma: The Site," *The New York Times*, April 23, 1995.

Goshko, John M., and Anne Swardson. "Militias, an Angry Mix Hostile to Government; Waco, Idaho Confrontations Aid Recruiting," *The Washington Post*, April 23, 1995.

Heath, Thomas, and Walter Pincus. "Residents Remember 'John Does' in Junction City," *The Washington Post*, April 22, 1995.

Henneberger, Melina. "Terror in Oklahoma: The Trooper," *The New York Times*, April 23, 1995.

Herbert, Bob. "In America: The Terrorists Failed," *The New York Times*, April 22, 1995.

Johnston, David. "Terror in Oklahoma City: The Investigation; At Least 31 Are Dead, Scores Are Missing After Car Bomb Attack in Oklahoma City," *The New York Times*, April 20, 1995.

————. "Terror in Oklahoma: The Investigation," *The New York Times*, April 22, 1995.

————. "Terror in Oklahoma: The Overview; Oklahoma Bombing Plotted for Months, Officials Say," *The New York Times*, April 25, 1995.

Kifner, John. "Terror in Oklahoma City: The Suspect," *The New York Times*, April 22, 1995.

————. "Terror in Oklahoma: The Suspect," *The New York Times*, April 24, 1995.

Kovaleski, Serge. "In a Mirror, Nichols Saw a Victim," *The Washington Post*, July 3, 1995.

Leland, John. "I Think About It All the Time," *Newsweek*, May 8, 1995.

Manegold, Catherine S. "Terror in Oklahoma: At Ground Zero," *The New York Times*, April 22, 1995.

Maraniss, David. "Man Arrested Angered by Assault on Waco Cult," *The Washington Post*, April 22, 1995.

————. "Two Brothers May Face Explosives, Gun Charges," *The Washington Post*, April 24, 1995.

————, and Thomas Heath. "T. Nichols Says McVeigh Vowed 'Something Big'; Witness Places Suspect in Oklahoma April 16," *The Washington Post*, April 27, 1995.

————, and Walter Pincus. "Putting the Pieces Together," *The Washington Post*, April 30, 1995.

————, and Pierre Thomas. "Officials See Conspiracy of at Least Four in Blast," *The Washington Post*, April 23, 1995.

McAllister, Bill, and Stephen Barr. "Workers in Washington Express Fear, Concern:

Agencies Adjust to Higher Security After Attack," *The Washington Post*, April 20, 1995.

McKinley, James C. "Terror in Oklahoma City: Around the Nation," *The New York Times*, April 20, 1995.

Newsweek. "The Dead," May 8, 1995.

Purdum, Todd S. "Terror in Oklahoma: The Overview; Bomb Suspect is Held, Another Identified; Toll Hits 65 as Hope for Survivors Fades," *The New York Times*, April 22, 1995.

Quinn-Judge, Paul. "Luggage Said to Yield Items for Bombs," *The Boston Globe*, April 21, 1995.

Reuters, April 20, 1995. AJC file, Militias.

Russakoff, Dale, and Serge F. Kovaleski. "An Ordinary Boy's Extraordinary Rage," *The Washington Post*, July 2, 1995.

Thomas, Pierre. "How Detectives Cracked Oklahoma Bombing Case; Computers Aid Chase for Clues," *The Washington Post*, June 3, 1995.

Treaster, Joseph B. "Terror in Oklahoma City: The Bomb," *The New York Times*, April 20, 1995.

Verhovek, Sam Howe. "Terror in Oklahoma: At Ground Zero; Death Count Rises to 110 at Blast Site," *The New York Times*, April 28, 1995.

Vick, Karl. "Quiet Descends as Recovery Efforts Cease," *The Washington Post*, May 6, 1995.

Wald, Matthew L. "Terror in Oklahoma: The Building; Design Could Have Been Another Enemy," *The New York Times*, April 28, 1995.

Walsh, Edward. "One Arraigned, Two Undergo Questioning," *The Washington Post*, April 22, 1995.

Weiner, Tim. "Terror in Oklahoma: The Overview," *The New York Times*, April 23, 1995.

Sources for Chapter 19

Anti-Defamation League. "Special Report: Paranoia as Patriotism—Far-Right Influences on the Militia Movement." New York, 1995.

Duggan, Paul, and Pierre Thomas. "Bail Denied for Suspect in Bombing: Federal Magistrate Cites an 'Indelible Trail of Evidence,' " *The Washington Post*, April 28, 1995.

James, Meg. "Distrust Fuels Support for Pensacola Chapter," *The Palm Beach* (Florida) *Post*, April 30, 1995.

Janofsky, Michael. " 'Militia' Man Tells of Plot to Attack Military Base," *The New York Times*, June 25, 1995.

Johnston, David. "Terror in Oklahoma: The Overview; Oklahoma Bombing Plotted for Months, Officials Say," *The New York Times*, April 25, 1995.

———. "Terror in Oklahoma: The Investigation; As Hopes for Quick Answers Fade, Bombing Inquiry Enters Slower-Moving Phase," *The New York Times*, May 5, 1995.

Kenworthy, Tom, and George Lardner, Jr. "The Militias: Guns and Bitter; Federal Push to Rein in Arms Sparked Fire of Resentment Among Owners," *The Washington Post*, May 4, 1995.

Kifner, John. "Terror in Oklahoma: The Suspect," *The New York Times*, April 24, 1995.

——————. "Terror in Oklahoma: The Hunt: Agents Fan Out in a Town in Arizona. Retracing the Trail of the Jailed Suspect," *The New York Times*, April 29, 1995.

——————. "Terror in Oklahoma: In Arizona, a Town Where Gun-Toting Individualists Can Blend Right In," *The New York Times*, May 1, 1995.

——————. "The Gun Network: McVeigh's World—A Special Report," *The New York Times*, July 5, 1995.

——————. "Despite Oklahoma Charges, the Case Is Far from Closed," *The New York Times*, August 13, 1995.

Maraniss, David, and Thomas Heath. "T. Nichols Says McVeigh Vowed 'Something Big'; Witness Places Suspect in Oklahoma April 16," *The Washington Post*, April 27, 1995.

——————, and Walter Pincus. "Putting the Pieces Together," *The Washington Post*, April 30, 1995.

——————, and Pierre Thomas. "Officials See Conspiracy of at Least Four in Blast," *The Washington Post*, April 23, 1995.

McFadden, Robert D. "Terror in Oklahoma: The Suspect," *The New York Times*, April 23, 1995.

——————. "Terror in Oklahoma: John Doe No. 1—A Special Report; A Life of Solitude and Obsessions," *The New York Times*, May 4, 1995.

Purdum, Todd S. "Terror in Oklahoma: The Overview; Bomb Suspect Is Held, Another Identified; Toll Hits 65 as Hope for Survivors Fades," *The New York Times*, April 22, 1995.

Russakoff, Dale, and Serge F. Kovaleski. "An Ordinary Boy's Extraordinary Rage; After a Long Search for Order, Timothy McVeigh Finally Found a World He Could Fit Into," part 1, *The Washington Post*, July 2, 1995.

Schneider, Keith. "Terror in Oklahoma: The Internet; Talk on Bombs Surges on Computer Network," *The New York Times*, April 27, 1995.

Vobejda, Barbara. "Incident Revives Memories of Waco, Idaho Showdowns," *The Washington Post*, April 24, 1995.

The Washington Post. "Army Reports McVeigh Injury," May 6, 1995.

Sources for Chapter 20

ABC News Nightline #3632. "Trouble in the Heartland," April 25, 1995.

Belluck, Pam. "Terror in Oklahoma: The Evidence; Affidavit Offers Clues About Suspect's Activities in the Days Before the Bombing," *The Washington Post*, April 27, 1995.

——————. "Terror in Oklahoma: In Kansas; Agents Find Possible Link to Bombers at Lake Site," *The New York Times*, May 2, 1995.

Bennet, James. "Terror in Oklahoma: The Chase," *The New York Times*, April 22, 1995.

Goshko, John M., and Anne Swardson. "Militias, an Angry Mix Hostile to Government; Waco, Idaho Confrontations Aid Recruiting," *The Washington Post*, April 23, 1995.

In the Matter of the Search of All Buildings and Vehicles and Farm Equipment on Premises or Any Other Conveyances, 3616 North Van Dyke Road, Decker, Michigan, U.S. District Court for the Eastern District of Michigan, Case no. 95X71665-C, Receipt for Seized Property, April 21, 1995.

Jackson, Derrick Z. "The Heartbeat of Hate," *The Baltimore Sun*, May 15, 1995.

Johnston, David. "Terror in Oklahoma: The Overview," *The New York Times*, May 2, 1995.

————. "A Man Charged in the Oklahoma Bombing Talks About His Co-Defendant," *The New York Times*, June 24, 1995.

Kifner, John. "Terror in Oklahoma: The Suspect," *The New York Times*, April 24, 1995.

————. "Oklahoma Bombing Linked to Arkansas Robbery," *The New York Times*, June 15, 1995.

————. "Stolen Guns Linked to Oklahoma Bombing," *The New York Times*, July 3, 1995.

————. "Despite Oklahoma Charges, the Case Is Far from Closed," *The New York Times*, August 13, 1995.

Kovaleski, Serge. "In a Mirror, Nichols Saw a Victim," *The Washington Post*, July 3, 1995.

Lardner, George Jr. "Prosecutors Strongly Oppose Attempt to Free Bomb Suspect; Nichols Has Disclaimed Citizenship, Court Is Told," *The Washington Post*, June 2, 1995.

McFadden, Robert D. "Terror in Oklahoma: The Far Right," *The New York Times*, April 22, 1995.

Maraniss, David, and Thomas Heath. "T. Nichols Says McVeigh Vowed 'Something Big'; Witness Places Suspect in Oklahoma April 16," *The Washington Post*, April 27, 1995.

Maraniss, David, and Walter Pincus. "Putting the Pieces Together," *The Washington Post*, April 30, 1995.

Maraniss, David, and Pierre Thomas. "Man Arrested Angered by Assault on Waco Cult," *The Washington Post*, April 22, 1995.

————. "Two Brothers May Face Explosives, Gun Charges," *The Washington Post*, April 24, 1995.

Reuters. "Witness in Blast Case Member of Property Rights Group," May 2, 1995.

Rimer, Sara, and James Bennet. "Terror in Oklahoma: The Brothers," *The New York Times*, April 24, 1995.

Russakoff, Dale, and Serge F. Kovaleski. "An Extraordinary Rage: After a Long Search for Order, Timothy McVeigh Finally Found a World He Could Fit Into," *The Washington Post*, July 2, 1995.

Sanchez, Rene, and Serge F. Kovaleski. "Lives Apart from Their Communities," *The Washington Post*, April 26, 1995.

Senate Judiciary Committee, Subcommittee on Terrorism, Technology and Government Information, *Hearings on Militia Movement in U.S.* Written statement of John Bohlman, 104th Congress, 1st session, 1995.

Shapiro, Joseph P. "An Epidemic of Fear and Loathing," *U.S. News & World Report*, May 8, 1995.

Thomas, Jo. "Bombing Suspect's Brother Noted Building's Vulnerability in 1988, Court Papers Say," *The New York Times*, June 13, 1995.

Thomas, Pierre. "Probe Reconstructs McVeigh's Life," *The Washington Post*, May 5, 1995.

Yurman, Dan. "5/6/95 Militia Update from Idaho," Western Lands Gopher Service, May 6, 1995.

Sources for Chapter 21

ABC News Nightline #3632, "Trouble in the Heartland," April 25, 1995.

Anti-Defamation League. "Special Report: Paranoia as Patriotism—Far-Right Influences on the Militia Movement." New York, 1995.

————. "McVeigh Offered Weapons for Sale, ADL Reveals," ADL press release, April 27, 1995.

Aryan News Agency. "Clinton Orders Okla. Bombing?" Posted on the Internet in alt.politics.white-power April 19, 1995.

Associated Press. "Gadhafi Offers Clintons Refuge in Libya," May 2, 1995.

Blair, Mike. "Feds 'Fib' on Oklahoma City Bomb," *Spotlight*, May 15, 1995.

————. "Evidence Mounts That Bomb in Oklahoma Not Fertilizer," *Spotlight*, May 22, 1995.

————. "Does Your Government Want Another Jack Ruby–Oswald Scenario?" *Spotlight*, May 22, 1995.

Boswell, Mark. "Two Government Officials Confess to Oklahoma Bombing," Mark Boswell show of 4/29/95, reposted in alt.activism.

Bureau of Alcohol, Tobacco and Firearms. "ATF Refutes Rumors of Oklahoma City Evacuation," press release, May 23, 1995, reposted on Internet May 24, 1995.

Buzbee, Sally Streff. "Families Say Goodbye to Two Women whose Bodies Haven't Been Found," Associated Press, May 8, 1995.

CNN News. 8:29 A.M., May 23, 1995. Transcript in author's possession.

Coalition for Human Dignity. *Northwest Update*, May 15, 1995; August 1, 1995.

Cook, Tad. E-mail to author, June 23, 1995.

Egan, Timothy. "Terror in Oklahoma: Western Violence," *The New York Times*, April 25, 1995.

Eugene (Oregon) *Register-Guard*. "Guard 'Show and Tell' Spooks Town," May 7, 1995.

Goldberg, Jeffrey. Telephone interview with author, April 30, 1995.

————. "Mark from Michigan, Meet Tony from the Catskills," *New York*, May 8, 1995.

Good, Joshua B. "A Kinder, Gentler Militia Movement," *Salt Lake Tribune*, April 30, 1995.

Gun Owners of America. "Gun Owners of America: To Clinton," suggested editorial that "GOA Recommends for Grassroots activists everywhere to submit . . . to local papers." Posted on the Internet in alt.pol.usa.co May 12, 1995.

Janofsky, Michael. "Blast Suspect's Brother Gets Back to Basics," *The New York Times*, June 12, 1995.

Johnson, Bill. "Seismograph Shows Second Unexplained Marking After OKC Bombing," *American Reporter*. Posted on the Internet May 12, 1995.

Kennedy, Helen. "Far Right Zealots," *Boston Herald*, April 30, 1995.

Koernke, Mark. "Intelligence Report," April 19, 1995. Posted on the Internet April 21, 1995.

Leiby, Richard. "Paranoia: Fear on the Left. Fear on the Right. Whoever They Are, THEY'RE CLOSING IN," *The Washington Post*, May 8, 1995.

Mann, Martin. "Crucial Oklahoma Question: Who Profits from Blast?" *Spotlight*, May 22, 1995.

Mullins, Eustace. "J'ACCUSE!" Posted on the Internet May 1995.

National Socialist Workers Revolutionary Party. "Clinton Ordered Oklahoma Bombing," n.d. (circa April–May, 1995).

Navarro, Mireya. "At Fair for Survivalists, Fallout from Oklahoma," *The New York Times*, June 12, 1995.

The Oregonian. "Organizer of Oregon Militia Resigns and Disbands Group," April 29, 1995.

Pierce, William. "American Dissident Voices," National Vanguard Books (bookselling arm of National Alliance). Posted on the Internet April 24, 1995.

Piper, Michael Collins. "Did Self-Proclaimed 'Civil Rights' Group 'Monitor' Suspect?" *Spotlight*, May 22, 1995.

Redden, Jim. Various articles in *PDXS*, 1995.

Russakoff, Dale. "Grass Roots Rage: Below the Surface, Mid-America Simmers with Sense of Alienation," *The Washington Post*, May 5, 1995.

Santa Clara County Liberty Brigade. "Official Declaration of the Santa Clara County Liberty Brigade Regarding the Oklahoma City, Oklahoma, bomb-murder," April 25, 1995. AJC, file "Militia—Oklahoma City—Reactions."

Searchlight (London). "After the Bomb, What Next?" June 1995.

Shapiro, Joseph P. "An Epidemic of Fear and Loathing," *U.S. News & World Report*, May 8, 1995.

Skolnick, Sherman H. "Interview with Debra Von Trapp," *Conspiracy Nation*, vol. 4, no. 88. Posted on the Internet May 11, 1995. In author's possession.

Spotlight. "Mysterious 'Accident' Blanks Tape of Nichols Hearing," May 15, 1995.

Steinberg, Jeffrey. "Defeat Britain's Terror War Versus USA." Posted on the Internet in alt.conspiracy, June 23, 1995.

Thomas, Pierre, and George Lardner, Jr. "FBI Finds John Doe 2, Drops Him as Suspect," *The Washington Post*, June 15, 1995.

Washington City Paper. "Least Competent Person," July 28, 1995.

Yurman, Dan. "5/6/95 Militia Update from Idaho," Western Lands Gopher Service, May 6, 1995.

In addition, I have used various Internet postings of March 24, 1995.

Sources for Chapter 22

American Jewish Committee. Transcript of "America Under the Gun: The Militia Movement and Hate Groups in America," hearing convened by Congressman Charles Schumer, July 11, 1995. In AJC files.

Anderson, Dave. "Pat Miller Part of an Alarming Extremist Trend," *Colorado Daily*, October 26, 1994.

Anti-Defamation League. "Armed and Dangerous," 1994.

Associated Press. "NM Gov Meets with Militias," April 29, 1995; "Gadhafi Offers Clintons Refuge in Libya," May 2, 1995; "GOP Rep Denounces Waco Raid." Posted on the Internet in alt.conspiracy May 12, 1995.

Blumenthal, Sidney. "Her Own Private Idaho," *The New Yorker*, July 10, 1995.

Coalition for Human Dignity. *Northwest Imperative*, 1994.

Cohler, Lawrence. "Congressman on the Militia Hot Seat," *Jewish Week*, May 5, 1995.

Curran, Tim, and Benjamin Sheffner. "Three Members Tied to Militias," *Roll Call*, April 27, 1995.

De Lama, George. "For Militias, Invaders of the U.S. Are Everywhere," *Chicago Tribune*, October 31, 1994.

Duke, Charles R. "Column of Colorado State Senator Charles R. Duke," April 23, 1995. Posted on the Internet in co.politics April 24, 1995.

Dwyer, Jim. "Just What's Fanning These Flames," *Newsday*, April 24, 1995.

Egan, Timothy. "Terror in Oklahoma: In Congress, Trying to Explain Contacts With Paramilitary Groups," *The New York Times*, May 2, 1995.

————. "Talk by Idaho's Chenoweth Winds Up in Militia Catalog," *Oregonian* (Portland), May 2, 1995.

Gopnik, Adam. "Violence as Style: In Oklahoma City, Romantic Rhetoric Got Horribly Real," *The New Yorker*, May 8, 1995.

Harris, Dan. "Citizen-Militia Literature Distributed Among Utah Senators," *Salt Lake Tribune*, February 28, 1995.

Hawver, Martin. "Governor Was Approached About Starting a Militia," *Sun Newspapers* (Edina, Minnesota), April 26, 1995.

Hook, Janet. "Militias Have Forged Ties to Some Members of Congress," *Los Angeles Times*, April 28, 1995.

Johnson, Dirk. "Conspiracy Theories' Impact Reverberates in Legislatures," *The New York Times*, July 6, 1995.

Johnston, David. "Terror in Oklahoma: The Investigation," *The New York Times*, April 24, 1995.

Jorgensen, Leslie. "Patriots," *The Colorado Statesman*, August 5, 1994.

Kenworthy, Tom, and George Lardner, Jr. "The Militias: Guns and Bitter; Federal Push to Rein in Arms Sparked Fire of Resentment Among Owners," *The Washington Post*, May 4, 1995.

LoLordo, Ann. "Extreme-Right Views Are Finding a Place in Politics," *The Baltimore Sun*, April 29, 1995.

Mathis, Nancy. "Congresswoman's Views Mirror Those of Some Civilian Militias," *Houston Chronicle*, May 7, 1995.

Morgan, Dan. "Militias Flexing More Muscle in the Political Process," *The Washington Post*, May 1, 1995.

Nee, Sherri. "Smith Says She Has No Ties to Militia Groups," *The Columbian* (Vancouver, Washington), May 7, 1995.

Project Tocsin. Internet posting, March 17, 1995.

Reuters. "Federal Officials in West Said to Face Threats," May 9, 1995.

Rich, Frank. "The Fuse to Oklahoma City," *Sacramento Bee*, May 3, 1995.

Ridgeway, James. "The Posse Goes to Washington," *The Village Voice*, May 23, 1995.

Rodrigue, George. "U.S. House Member Proud of Intense Anti-Government Views," *Dallas Morning News*, June 14, 1995.

Russakoff, Dale. "Grass Roots Rage: Below the Surface, Mid-America Simmers with Sense of Alienation," *The Washington Post*, May 5, 1995.

Searchlight (London). "After the Bomb, What Next?" June 1995.

Shagun, Louis. "A Wave of Distrust in the West," *The Los Angeles Times*, February 3, 1995.

Shapiro, Joseph P. "An Epidemic of Fear and Loathing," *U.S. News & World Report*, May 8, 1995.

Spotlight. "Chenoweth Bill Could Slow Feds," May 22, 1995.

Stern, Kenneth S. "Politics and Bigotry." New York: American Jewish Committee, 1992.

Stockman, Steve. Letter to Janet Reno, March 22, 1995, reprinted as Appendix 94 in Kenneth Stern, "Militias: A Growing Danger." New York: American Jewish Committee, 1995.

Sullivan, Laurie. "Hansen Takes Concerns of Raid to Reno," *Salt Lake Tribune*, March 18, 1995.

Sources for Chapter 23

ABC News Nightline #3632, "Trouble in the Heartland," April 25, 1995.

Anonymous. "Topic: Flash! Militia Arrest." Posted on the Internet in alt.conspiracy at 12:16 A.M., March 4, 1995.

Anti-Defamation League. "Armed and Dangerous," 1994.

Aryan News Agency. "An Important Message from the ANA Chief Editor," forwarded on Internet April 23, 1995.

Associated Press. "German Neo-Nazis Go Online," June 26, 1995.

Carrier, Jim. "Ticking of Dangerous Time Bomb Heard Before It Exploded," *Denver Post*, April 24, 1995.

Chapman, Mike. Postings on misc.activism.militia, July 8, 1995.

Coalition for Human Dignity. *The Dignity Report*, vol. 3, no. 1 (winter 1995).

Colville (Washington) *Statesman-Examiner*, June 1992.

Constitution Society. "How to Activate the Constitutional Militia in Your Area." Posted on the Internet March 24, 1995.

————. "Military Training: Operation WitWeb." posted on Internet March 24, 1995.

————. "Militia Organizing—Advance Teams." Posted on the Internet March 24, 1995.

Dolinar, Lou. "Militias." Posted on the Internet May 24, 1995.

Eaton, Rick. "Testimony by Rick Eaton, Public Hearing on Militia Movement." Los Angeles: Simon Wiesenthal Center, July 11, 1995.

Fairness and Accuracy in Reporting. "Media Advisory: Right-Wing Talk Radio Supports Militia Movement." Posted on the Internet April 21, 1995.

Fritze, David. "Patriots Vow to Fight Off 'One-World Government'; Militias See Threat in Arizona," *Arizona Republic*, February 5, 1995.

Gopnik, Adam. "Violence as Style: In Oklahoma City, Romantic Rhetoric Got Horribly Real," *The New Yorker*, May 8, 1995.

Harrison, Michael. Telephone interview with author, September 11, 1995.

Henderson, Nell. "Another View on Talk Radio," *The Washington Post*, April 28, 1995.

Herbert, Bob. "Backing Off Bravery," *The New York Times*, April 29, 1995.

James, Meg. "Distrust Fuels Support for Pensacola Chapter," *The Palm Beach* (Florida) *Post*, April 30, 1995.

Jones, Steven T. "Arms and the Men," *Sacramento News and Review*, August 25, 1994.

Jorgensen, Leslie. "Patriots," *Colorado Statesman*, August 5, 1994.

Kenworthy, Tom, and George Lardner, Jr. "The Militias: Guns and Bitter; Federal Push to Rein in Arms Sparked Fire of Resentment Among Owners," *The Washington Post*, May 4, 1995.

Knight, Rick. Aryan News Agency, "Thule Network Frightens ZOG." Posted on the Internet June 27, 1995.

Leiby, Richard. "Paranoia: Fear on the Left. Fear on the Right. Whoever They Are, THEY'RE CLOSING IN," *The Washington Post*, May 8, 1995.

Leusner, Jim, and Jay Hamburg. "Anti-Government Militias Are Strong in Florida," *The Orlando Sentinel*, April 26, 1995.

Lind, Michael. "Understanding Oklahoma, Scofflaw Conservatism; Beyond the Hyperbole, Ideas Have Consequences," *The Washington Post*, April 30, 1995.

Martz, Ron. "Klan Marching Staunchly to Ultra-Right: 'White Power' Being Replaced by 'Sieg Heil,' " *Atlanta Journal*, March 17, 1985.

nobody@cs.utexas.edu. "Uniform Code of Military Justice for Militias." Posted on the Internet in alt.conspiracy on or before March 9, 1995.

nobody@usf.edu. "Kill, Die, or Get Out." Posted on the Internet in alt.activism, May 30, 1995.

Parfrey, Adam, and Jim Redden. "Patriot Games: Linda Thompson, a Gun-Toting Broad from Indianapolis, Wants to Know, 'Are You Ready for the Next American Revolution?'" *The Village Voice*, October 11, 1994.

Redelfs, John W. "Notice From SAMSBEST Listowner." Posted on the Internet May 4, 1995.

Richardson, Valerie. "Groups Nationwide Plan to Protest U.N. Influence," *The Washington Times*, October 22, 1994.

Rimer, Sara. "New Medium for the Far Right," *The New York Times*, April 27, 1995.

Roland, Jon. "Militia Agenda." Posted on the Internet January 23, 1995.

————. "Militia: Rumored March 25 Arrests." Posted on the Internet in talk.politics-.guns March 24, 1995.

Sahagan, Louis. "A Wave of Distrust in the West: A Protest Movement Is Rising Among People Who Resent or Fear the Government," *Los Angeles Times*, February 3, 1995.

Schneider, Keith. "Manual for Terrorists Extols 'Great Coldbloodedness': Tactics Include Bombing Federal Buildings," *The New York Times*, April 29, 1995.

Schwartz, John. "Advocates of Internet Fear Drive to Restrict Extremists' Access," *The Washington Post*, April 28, 1995.

Shapiro, Joseph P. "An Epidemic of Fear and Loathing," *U.S. News & World Report*, May 8, 1995.

Stout, David. "Terror in Oklahoma: Radio; Some Rightist Shows Pulled, and Debate Erupts," *The New York Times*, April 30, 1995.

Texas Constitutional Militia. "Texas Militia—Statement." Posted on the Internet in misc.survival, February 11, 1995.

Sources for Chapter 24

Anti-Defamation League, "The ADL Anti-Paramilitary Training Statute," 1995. Reprinted on pp. 259–60 of this volume.

Applebome, Peter. "Paramilitary Groups Are Presenting Delicate Legal Choices for States," *The New York Times*, May 10, 1995.

Associated Press. "ATF Picnic in Senate Spotlight," July 14, 1995; "Montana Militia Cries Ambush," July 19, 1995; "Tax Fugitive Wounded in Raid," July 19, 1995.

Baca, Stacy. "Secrecy the Key to Militias," *The Denver Post*, January 23, 1995.

Baucus, Max. "Montana Mean Time," *The New York Times*, May 1, 1995.

Carson, Rob. "Concern High, Facts Scare About Militias," *The News Tribune* (Tacoma, Washington), May 2, 1995.

Coalition for Human Dignity. *Northwest Update Through August 1, 1995*, August 15, 1995.

DeArmond, Paul. E-mail to author, April 13, 1995.

"Gadsen Militia Update on FBI/ATF." Posted on the Internet in alt.conspiracy July 31, 1995.

Johnson, Dirk. "Conspiracy Theories' Impact Reverberates in Legislatures," *The New York Times*, July 6, 1995.

Klausner, Andrea. "Memorandum in Support of Proposed Federal Legislation to Bar

Unauthorized Military or Paramilitary Organizations." New York: American Jewish Committee, July 19, 1995.

Rabinove, Sam. "A Federal Law to Bar Unauthorized Military or Paramilitary Organizations," American Jewish Committee, January 3, 1986.

Roland, Jon. "Attention All Law Enforcement Personnel." Posted on the Interenet in talk.politics.guns March 24, 1995.

Saul, Stephanie. "Armed, Angry: Militants in America's Heartland," *Newsday* (Nassau and Suffolk, New York, edition), April 30, 1995.

Schwartz, John. "Technology Used to Tag Explosives Gets Second Look After Bombing," *The Washington Post*, May 7, 1995.

Schneider, Keith. "Fearing a Conspiracy, Some Heed a Call to Arms," *The New York Times*, November 14, 1994.

Stanton, Sam. "On Guard," *Sacramento Bee*, January 29, 1995.

Wallace, Bill. "A Call to Arms," *San Francisco Chronicle*, March 12, 1995.

Worthington, Rogers. "Private Militias March to Beat of Deep Distrust," *Chicago Tribune*, September 25, 1994.

Sources for Chapter 25

The Australian, "Defence Staff Extremists: Arms Probe," May 4, 1995.

Brackett, Staff Sergeant. "King of the Battle," Intsum # 95-5, S-2, 1st Battalion 190th Field Artillery, Montana Army National Guard, May 5, 1995. AJC, file "Militias—Militia of Montana."

Byrne, Andrew. "Outback Militia on a War Footing," *The Sydney* (Australia) *Morning Herald*, May 5, 1995.

The Canberra (Australia) *Times*, "Police Raids on Defence Gun Cell," May 4, 1995.

Coalition for Human Dignity. *The Dignity Report*, vol. 3, no. 1, 1995.

DeArmond, Paul. "Militia of Montana Meeting at the Maltby [Washington] Community Center," February 11, 1995. AJC, file "Militias—Militia of Montana."

Farber, Bernie M. "Oklahoma's Message: Keep an Eye on the Darkness," *The Globe and Mail* (Toronto), April 27, 1995.

Garvin, Susan. Internet posting, April 24, 1995.

Germany Alert. "U.S. Extremists Linked to German Neo-Nazis," April 27, 1995.

Greason, David, and Michael Kapel. "Nexus Magazine Linked to U.S. Militias," *Australia/Israel Review* (Melbourne, Australia), May 5–18, 1995.

Hasselbach, Ingo. "Extremism: A Global Network," *The New York Times*, April 26, 1995.

Jones, Jeremy. Letter to author, May 10, 1995. In author's possession.

Militia of Montana. Letter to Governor Marc Racicot et al., May 12, 1995. AJC, file "Militias—Militia of Montana."

The Phoenix Gazette, "Abortion Clinic Fears Attacks by Militia," May 12, 1995.

Planned Parenthood of America. Video, *U.S. Taxpayers Party Wisconsin Convention*, May 27–28, 1994.

Project Tocsin. Posted on the Internet March 17, 1995.

Rich, Frank. "The Fuse to Oklahoma City," *Sacramento Bee*, May 3, 1995.

Shapiro, Joseph P. "An Epidemic of Fear and Loathing," *U.S. News & World Report*, May 8, 1995.

Tippit, Sarah. "Chilling New Link Suspected Among Anti-Abortion Activists," Reuters, January 13, 1995.

Wallace, Al. Internet message to author. May 3, 1995.

Sources for Chapter 26

McLamb, Jack. Editorial, "Police/Military Alert: United Nations Treachery Exposed!" *Aid and Abet Police Newsletter*, n.d.

Middlewood, Erin. "Racist Relations in Clark County," *The Columbian* (Vancouver, Washington), April 23, 1995.

Mullins, Eustace. "J'ACCUSE!" Posted on the Internet and forwarded to author in May 1995. In possession of author.

Reuters. "G. Gordon Liddy Blasts Efforts to Curb Militias," June 17, 1995.

Sources for Postscript

Associated Press. "Indictment in IRS Bomb Threat," September 13, 1995.

———. "Sabotage Sniffed in Derailing," October 9, 1995.

Bolan, Kim. "U.S. Dynamite Theft: B.C. Racist 'Good Friends' with Alleged Bomb Plotter," *Vancouver* (British Columbia) *Sun*, August 16, 1995.

The Coeur d'Alene Press, "Feds on Edge After Dynamite Theft," August 5, 1995.

Flatten, Mark. "Arizona Police Skeptical of 'Sons of Gestapo,'" *The Tribune*, October 10, 1995 (posted on Internet).

Harris, John F. "Clinton Lashes Out at Terrorists, Seeks Expanded Powers," *The Washington Post*, April 24, 1995.

Morlin, Bill. "Thieves Make Off with 500 Pounds of Explosives," *Spokane Spokesman-Review*, August 1, 1995.

———. "Security Up After Theft of Explosives," *Spokane Spokesman-Review*, August 5, 1995.

The New York Times. "FBI Reveals a Man's Plan to Blow Up a Courthouse," July 4, 1995.

Sparks, David. "Shooting of Militia Leader Leaves Ohio Town Edgy," *The American Reporter*, June 29, 1995 (posted on Internet).

Sullivan, Patricia. "Townsfolk Tired of Militia," *The Daily Inter Lake* (Montana), May 7, 1995.

Woods, Jim, and Jill Riepenhoff. "Plague Found in Car," *The Columbus* (Ohio) *Dispatch*, May 13, 1995.

Index

KENNETH S. STERN has been the American Jewish Committee's expert on hate and hate groups since 1989. His work in this area has ranged from writing publications to testifying before Congress. He was a full partner at the respected law firm of Rose & Stern and has argued before the United States Supreme Court. From 1985 to 1986 he was director of the National Organization Against Terrorism. He lives with his family in New York City.